Dear Mr Fridman,

please accept this ~~book~~ ~~as~~ ~~~~ wrote under the pen name, Shamot Sesju.

The book has had three prior editions, this fourth and final edition released early 2022. It is knowledge that has given me the ability to look at life through a clear lens, a lens that is joyous and burdensome at the same time

I believe it has the potential to undo much of the damage religious institutions have inflicted on minority groups and people who know they are part of a greater narrative. Listening to you interview people on your show makes me feel that you are one of these people.

Elements of the book link to current research into the phenomena commonly known as UFO/UAP. The current disclosure on this topic, by your government, has the potential to unite the world. Humanity might finally see themselves as one species.

In giving you this book my hope is that you might appreciate its importance as a bridge between science and religion.

I bow to the Divine in you.

John.

Sayings that may be of most interest:

Thomas 7: p 25
Th: 9 p 38
Th: 21 p 73
Th: 22 p 82

Thomas 44: p 160
Th 77: p 258
Th 79: p 263
Th 83: p 274
Th 96, 97: p 308
Th 113, 114: p 372

SHAMOT SESJU

77th
PEARL

THE PERPETUAL TREE

The Gospel of Thomas
interpreted and explained

To find out more about this book, visit:
www.vividpublishing.com.au/77thpearl

Copyright © 2022 Shamot Sesju (Fourth Edition)

ISBN: 978-1-922565-91-4
Published by Vivid Publishing
P.O. Box 948, Fremantle Western Australia 6959
www.vividpublishing.com.au

email: 77thpearl@protonmail.com
Facebook: www.facebook.com/ShamotSesju
Twitter: https://twitter.com/77thPearl

For those who are on the outside looking in;
for those who are seeking the truth …

about *you* He said, *"Show me the stone that the builders rejected,*
that is the keystone."

Foreword

Contemporary Christian faiths present salvation as either a firm belief in Jesus Christ and/or the completion of sacraments. Faith in the existence of Jesus (also referred to here as Yeshua) does not in itself bring us into a state of grace, nor does the completion of sacraments. These conclusions are logical. This kind of faith, and involvement in rituals, reflects the archaic needs and attributes of the primal human. They are behaviours that console, but they do not provide a *consistent connection* to the thing our soul originated from. *Understanding* the truth is crucial. Through this understanding comes inner peace.

In the middle of January 2015 Pope Francis visited the Philippines. On this visit, a twelve-year-old girl gave a speech and asked the Pope: 'why does God allow children to suffer?' This question and the girl's tears visibly moved the Pope, but he had no real answer for the child. This illustrates the problem with the current Christian orthodoxy. God has been made into a patriarchal figurehead. A majority of Christians believe that this god makes conscious decisions about the events in their everyday lives. This is evident in the numerous times we see sportspeople, musicians, and actors receive a commendation and proceed to thank *God* for their talents. God does not make one person talented above another. These talents, or attributes, are acquired through good genes, hard work, and being in the right place, at the right time. We should ask ourselves: what does this kind of rhetoric and thinking do to a young person, who does not have any of these talents or opportunities? Is the god of these talented people favouring them, just as he favours children who live in a healthy, happy environment? This kind of fictitious, patriarchal god comes to us from humanity's primal heritage, where these prehistoric groups were reliant on an alpha-male for guidance and protection. Is this the kind of *father* Yeshua spoke of? The answer is a resounding no. In response to the child's question, we would point out that our world is as it is because of the way we have evolved—from a creature that is fallible. The decisions humans made have given us a world that is overpopulated and an environment that is being eroded. Most people in our world are materialistic and make decisions favouring economic growth, rather than *ethical* approaches to community, environment, and business affairs. Believing that a supreme godhead will solve all these issues is a false perception and a very dangerous one. It is the root cause of much of the world's problems at the infancy of the twenty-first century. *77th Pearl: The Perpetual Tree* reveals a logical solution: we must understand what Yeshua truly meant in His teachings. This truth permits us to separate religion from global affairs and allows science to work with matters that relate to the material world. It means we use the logic of science to make decisions pertaining to our physical existence, which will give us a world that is free of self-imposed suffering. The world of the Spirit is completely different to the world we experience with our limited physical senses. This universe has been *inspired* by another realm/dimension, but it is not controlled by it. Ultimately, this is the answer to the child's question.

Most humans see themselves living in a dualistic existence, evident in the apparent separation of soul/mind and body. This is mirrored in the compartmentalisation of religion as an activity permeated with rituals, rather than a deep, personal understanding of the self. What people should be doing is asking the question, what is *consciousness* and how is the mind linked to the quantum field? Since around the 1950's, ufologists have been gathering evidence, which has seen links made between extra-terrestrial life and the human psyche. In June of 2021, the Pentagon released a report called, *Preliminary Assessment: Unidentified Aerial Phenomena,* which confirmed that there were indeed significant incidents of UAP incursions into military and commercial airspace. This official confirmation, together with articles about these incursions in reputable media outlets, such as the New York Times, has allowed the UFO/UAP phenomena to be taken seriously, rather than its usual relegation into the fringe, woo portion of society. It has also opened the door for a new discourse, validating the notion that current models of physics cannot explain reality as it actually stands. The Gospel of Thomas is linked to this discourse through its explanation of *what* the human is, beyond the physical body.

In 1945, at a place called Nag Hammadi, in Upper Egypt, an Arab peasant discovered fifty-two texts in an earthenware jar. Among those texts was the Gospel of Thomas. This gospel is set out in 114 sayings that are considered the *secret* sayings of Jesus. While some of these sayings appear in the New Testament Gospels, they are presented here in their unedited form. Since the time of Jesus, people have tried to comprehend the sayings, in particular, those that were omitted from the canonical gospels. In *77th Pearl: The Perpetual Tree*, all the sayings are explored in relation to each other and to pertinent New Testament Gospels. The sayings reveal truths, which lift the mystical teachings of Jesus into a logical reality, at times reflecting what scientists are discovering in the first phase of the twenty-first century.

The New Testament Gospels are referred to as the *Synoptic Gospels*, meaning that they have a *common view*. These Synoptic Gospels refer to the three New Testament Gospels of Matthew, Mark, and Luke and are considered synoptic because of their similarity. With the inclusion of the fourth Gospel of John we have the canonical gospels. In *77th Pearl: The Perpetual Tree*, the Gospel of Mark is often referred to in comparison to Thomas, as it is known to be the first of the three Synoptic Gospels written. The other Synoptic Gospels are considered elaborations on Mark. Biblical scholars have suggested that there is another source and it becomes apparent that this is indeed the Gospel of Thomas. It is the cryptic nature of significant portions of the Gospel of Thomas that categorised it as a heretical text to the early Church authorities. Christian apologists argue that the sayings, which are not in the New Testament, are words a typical rabbi, in the time of Jesus, would not have spoken. *77th Pearl: The Perpetual Tree* concurs with this point of view. Yeshua was a man that had an entirely new message, a message that was ahead of its time. In the New Testament, we see the disciples of Jesus ask Him why He speaks to them in strange riddles, yet all we find in these accounts is a narrative interwoven with fantastic feats, which are supposed to prove His divinity. In the New Testament, there is nothing about these strange riddles and mysteries that explains what we are, or our deep connection to the Father/Source. These things, which they considered strange and difficult to fathom, were omitted. The cryptic sayings were meant for the twenty-first century and beyond. In a sense, these words, revealed through *77ᵗʰ Pearl: The Perpetual Tree*, are the *second coming*.

While the Gospel of Thomas we now know was discovered in 1945, it did in fact exist at the time of the New Testament Gospels. Bishop Irenaeus of Lyon c.180. made references to the Gospel of Thomas in scathing letters, written against the Gnostic's who held it in high regard. Due to the texts being deemed heretical, orthodox believers sought to destroy them. This is why some prudent Gnostic's had the foresight to hide the documents.

The popularity of atheism and agnosticism is symptomatic of how the mainstream religions do not bridge the gap between the realities of life and the belief in a deity. A deity that is supposed to provide protection and guidance. Often we see that suffering and death can happen to any individual, group, or community. Sceptics rightly ask: why does a god, who created humans, allow them to suffer from diseases and natural disasters? The Gospel of Thomas answers these perplexing questions by revealing what we are and why we are in this *place*. If Christian readers are sceptical towards the authenticity of the Gospel of Thomas, as compared to other texts, then they should ask themselves—is the message speaking to the soul or is it speaking *from* a man?

Some scholars have labelled the Gospel of Thomas a Gnostic text but *77ᵗʰ Pearl: The Perpetual Tree* does not support this premise. The Gospel of Thomas is free of Gnostic mythology; therefore, it is not from this early Christian splinter group. The Gospel of Thomas was the springboard for Gnostic Christianity, because it challenges the reader to search for the truth. Gnostics took this to mean that they were required to find hidden messages in the sayings, to unlock the various gates leading to heaven. What we discover is that the Gnostics went too far—creating numerous complex myths, which supposedly explained our predicament in this world and how to escape from it. These myths prove to be derived from observations of human characteristics and frailties, not unlike how the Ancient Greeks attributed human weaknesses to the plethora of gods they created.

77th Pearl: The Perpetual Tree reveals knowledge hidden in cryptic sayings for millennia. It does not reconcile ancient beliefs rooted in the Old Testament with scientific fact. It also does not support Intelligent Design, which is negated in the saying of Thomas 97. What it does do is recognise what science has consistently proven—that we are flesh and bone. We exist in a world governed by physical laws of cause and effect, all of which are external layers of the source of all things—the one Jesus refers to as His *'father'*. In these sayings, the disparity between the physical world and the realm of the Spirit is an ongoing theme. Who created this world and why is not the primary concern. Its physical make-up and evolution has, for the most part, been proven by science and accepted by the Catholic Church. However, this leaves us with many questions. These questions are ones that antiquated faiths, rooted in myths and legends, are incapable of answering. Yeshua foresaw this when He warned that His teachings could not be placed into old wineskins (the context of the Old Testament). Yeshua was the new wine, which would be spoiled by this action.

The author discovered The Gospel of Thomas when he befriended a progressive young Catholic priest in the early 1990's. Inquisitive conversations often took place, which centred on the contradictions in Church teachings and the Old and New Testaments. One day, rather ironically, the young priest gave the author a book called 'The Gnostic Gospels' by Elaine Pagels. In this text, the author found references to the 'Gospel of Thomas' and these first few insights opened his eyes to a truth. For the first time he felt a deep spiritual connection, for the first time he felt whole.

A visit, in 2002, to the Vatican Basilica in Rome cemented in the author a desire to know the truth. During this visit to the Vatican he saw three altars, each presumably containing the body of a Pope. The bodies were in glass coffins, dressed in fine white robes inlaid with gold threads and jewels. The feet of the bodies were adorned with gold shoes encrusted in gems. The faces were covered in a gold mask also covered in gems. A strong smell of what seemed to be formaldehyde surrounded the coffins. As he stood in this place, which was supposed to represent the centre of Christianity, the author felt an incredible sadness and absence of Spirit. In his mind, he could see Jesus entering that space and overturning those altars in disgust at what His representatives had done in His name. This was a crucial first step toward *77th Pearl: The Perpetual Tree.*

The traditional relationship with the God of the Abraham lineage is lacking something essential. This relationship fails to answer the eternal question that humans have grappled with since, presumably, we came down from the trees—what is the meaning of life and what does it mean to *live?* The information we have had access to in the past has been tainted. The contradictions we encounter in the knowledge presented to us, through the religions sharing the Abrahamic heritage, lack logic. It is also damaging people's potential to reconcile their human condition, as a reality, *apart* from the spiritual. The Abrahamic religions of Judaism, Christianity, and Islam are the *three-sided grain,* which has entered the oyster (this realm/world) to form a *pearl.* The light that *reflects* off this pearl has made the revelations in the Gospel of Thomas shine through the fog, which are the physical barriers in this world.

Humans, who are searching for the truth, know that there is an intimate relationship shared with the source of all things—the one Jesus refers to as His *father.* This relationship is one that has been forgotten, primarily because people's physical existence steals them away from the Light they cannot see. The thing that one cannot point to when we refer to the 'self', is the thing that shares a kinship with Jesus. Within the Gospel of Thomas, there are threads that appear which link the sayings in the gospel—a prominent one is that Jesus is our brother.

The symbol on the front of this text represents the *perfect human*—one that is neither male nor female and both of these at the same time. This symbol speaks of the disparity between our knowledge of relationships, based on physical manifestations, and how Yeshua really wants us to see ourselves. This thing is *Spirit* and it cannot be defined by the parameters of this world. The vessel on top of the symbol represents the search for knowledge and truth.

The English translation of the Gospel of Thomas used here is by Stephen Patterson and Marvin Meyer: The Nag Hammadi Library. Some of the sayings have words missing due to the fragile nature of the material they were originally written upon. In such cases the scholars have indicated missing words with "[...]" or brackets with the most likely word.

Jesus [said], "One who seeks will find, and for [one who knocks]
it will be opened."

Thomas 94.

77th Pearl: The Perpetual Tree

The Gospel of Thomas (with commentary)

These are the secret sayings that the living Jesus spoke and Didymos Judas Thomas recorded.

1. And he said, "Whoever discovers the interpretation of these sayings will not taste death."

This is both an invitation and promise by the author of Thomas. There will be a reward attained by the person searching for the truth. To discover the interpretation of these sayings, a person must want to know and begin asking questions. When one knocks on this door, it is eventually opened *and the one becomes two.*

2. Jesus said, "Those who seek should not stop seeking until they find. When they find, they will be disturbed. When they are disturbed, they will marvel, and will reign over all. [And after they have reigned they will rest.]"

Yeshua cautions people on the journey to finding truth. This is not an easy quest—it requires persistence. The answers people find will disturb them, because this knowledge turns much of what they think they know on its head. The spiritual truths humans *believe* they know are based on myth and legend. What is discovered is astonishing and something wondrous. With a shift in thinking and understanding, humans will look at all things in this world through different eyes. This new way of seeing lifts this person above the souls around them and they *reign over all.* This knowledge brings the human to a point of rest – they become enlightened.

3. Jesus said, "If your leaders say to you, 'Look, the (Father's) kingdom is in the sky,' then the birds of the sky will precede you. If they say to you, 'It is in the sea,' then the fish will precede you. Rather, the (Father's) kingdom is within you and it is outside you.

When you know yourselves, then you will be known, and you will understand that you are children of the living Father. But if you do not know yourselves, then you live in poverty, and you are the poverty."

Within *77ᵗʰ Pearl: The Perpetual Tree*, this profound saying is extensively explored to reveal what is at the heart of Jesus' intention. This saying is linked to several within the Gospel of Thomas, which eventually exposes the nature of the source of all things—the one Jesus calls *father*. *77ᵗʰ Pearl* reveals that what we have referred to as *God* is at the centre of all things— like the soul. It is at the centre because of the Father's Light, which is through all things, but is hidden by *its light* (Thomas 83). Our physical realm is a layer, connected to the Father/ Source through this *Light*, which permeates *all things*. The physical realm *reflects* the inner realm of the Father, but this material realm is unstable in structure. The substances used to create it deteriorate and perish. Its nature is unlike the inner layer, which exists in another dimension. Completely different laws govern it. This understanding is necessary for us to live cohesively, in the physical/material dimension. Understanding the reality of this realm would stop people assuming divine intervention would fix whatever problems humanity causes.

This is crucial—if the soul is to have a better chance of freeing itself, then suffering must be limited. The absence of suffering means that the mind is not hindered by physical barriers and can pursue the spiritual path. However, physical barriers are not the only ones humans have created for themselves. The belief that people are not worthy of their god, because of their weaknesses, is an even greater obstacle. It is for this reason Jesus spoke of *dying for humanity's sins*—so that this ever-present obstacle could be removed, by the sacrifice of one for many. Humanity's sins stem from not understanding the *wealth* they have in their soul. Instead, people have looked to *the poverty*, which is the physical existence, as if that is permanent.

The heart of the Gospel of Thomas is found in the last two lines of Thomas 3. When people realise that their *image* is not the one they see in a mirror, but that it is hidden by the Father's Light, they open themselves to the truth. Yeshua is our brother through this realisation. He is the same as we are. If people do not accept this knowledge, they have not come to know the fullness of their potential and the intimate and powerful connection they have with the Source/Father. Moreover, if people do not come to this understanding, they live in poverty and they become the poverty.

4. Jesus said, "The person old in days won't hesitate to ask a little child seven days old about the place of life, and that person will live.

For many of the first will be last, and will become a single one."

The Gospel of Thomas requires the reader to think in metaphors and symbols. The fourth saying illustrates the cryptic nature of these sacred teachings. The last line is a warning to those who believe they have authoritative knowledge—'they will become a single one.' This means they will be resolved into the whole, the Source. Jesus tells us that if a person of great age can believe that a naïve, newborn baby knows more than themselves about 'the place of life', then they will truly *live*. Those who are arrogant or profess to have the answers do not recognise the *truth of their soul*. They do not recognise the kinship people share with Jesus—a truth that is so astonishing and powerful that it is difficult to fathom. It challenges everything humans have expected from a relationship with the divine. It is something a newly born baby can reveal when it smiles in its sleep.

To understand what Yeshua means when He says, 'and they will become a single one,' we can look at the following analogy of water, and our intuitive fascination with its properties. Consider that water is composed of two elements, hydrogen and oxygen. On their own they are not water, a liquid that can help create and sustain life in this universe. We know that without water, life as we experience it on Earth cannot exist. However, this life is not the *life* that Jesus refers to throughout the Gospel of Thomas. If a person is not joined to the Source and becomes two, they will become a single one. As all things come from the Father/Source, all things are eventually re-joined to it. Some souls will attain the stature of a Spirit, others will not. Be aware, to be alone does not mean *one* cannot be *two*. At times, it is very necessary to be alone, because in these times one can experience the connectedness of the Source, through the conduit we call the Holy Spirit (Thomas 49).

The soul draws in the Light that comes from the Father/Source, it is the thing that we seek to be joined to, to be complete, to *live*. This is why those people who do not recognise their kinship with Jesus and the Father will become a single one. They see the Father as a god, outside of themselves, which judges them on their human weaknesses. This is not the father Yeshua speaks of. Jesus' Father is in all things; *it is our Father by default connection*, not by patriarchal ownership. People are its offspring, like the salmon, which have swum far from the rivers into the oceans. We need to comprehend that without the Father/Source (the oxygen) and our accepting hearts (the hydrogen, our soul), we will remain one—separate. When we accept our true nature we *become two*—then, like water, our potential is immeasurable.

5. Jesus said, "Know what is in front of your face, and what is hidden from you will be disclosed to you.
For there is nothing hidden that will not be revealed. [And there is nothing buried that will not be raised.]"

Imagine any creature. Think about its specific characteristics and why it looks this way. Think about all the microscopic parts, such as skin and blood cells, which have come together to make this creature appear as something real. Visualise how each cell of the creature is made of smaller particles until, eventually, all we can see are atoms. Imagine how these particles joined to create this living thing. What is it that makes those cells behave in this way? This is *the Source finding expression* in the physical realm—if only for a glimpse. The Source looks for a place it can come to life, through a special creature. Currently, on this planet we call Earth, human beings are that species. This is what exists in front of people's faces, but they do not see it. When the human sees the Light in themselves, and in others, a profound awakening occurs.

In Thomas 5, Jesus asks that we see things as they truly are—this is not an easy task. In the generations preceding Jesus, religious leaders tried to describe the nature of the other realm and its mysteries, but they failed. The only point of reference they had were the natural phenomena *they could see* around them. The light from the sun became a source of good and the night a source of evil. Food that sustained people became a way to appease a jealous god. Natural disasters were signs of this god's displeasure with their sacrifices, and so it continued. In making these literal and peripheral observations people could not see past the thin veil that is this realm. Yeshua asks that we look deeper. Everything is made of atoms, even our bodies. We can, in our minds' eyes, zoom into these atoms until we find that the space between them is equivalent to the space between our sun and the planets. However, the space between the atoms is still filled with Light, Light that we cannot experience with our eyes—but we know it exists. If humans can understand that *the thing Jesus is* also exists between the fibres of wood and the spaces between atoms (Thomas 77), then people will know what is in front of their face. Then, what is hidden will be revealed and what has been buried from human understanding will be raised.

6. His disciples asked him and said to him, "Do you want us to fast? How should we pray? Should we give to charity? What diet should we observe?"

Jesus said, "Don't lie, and don't do what you hate, because all things are disclosed before heaven. After all, there is nothing hidden that will not be revealed, and there is nothing covered up that will remain undisclosed."

Sayings five and six are connected, as they both ask the seeker to look to the self for truth. The Holy Spirit guides the individual toward the right path based on their capacity and understanding. All the things that are covered up become known to the true self. This is the self that is connected to the Father/

Source, through the Holy Spirit. Similarly, when we see what is in front of our eyes (Thomas 5), all the things we do not understand are revealed to us.

The major religious groups work on the premise that the physical body determines what we are. In some cases, they use this as a rod to control their flock. People's physical desires, for sex, food, material wealth/security, and emotional satisfaction are seen as weaknesses. While these can become obstacles, they should not become reasons for failure on the journey to spiritual growth. In various cultures, ascetic masters have removed themselves from these needs, relying on isolation to be free of temptations and on community support to meet their physical needs. This practice proves to be unsustainable; if the majority of people did abstain from community life, who would be available to support their existence?

If humans take the approach that they are clothed in flesh, which the stars have created for them, if they are secure in the knowledge that they are above the body's weaknesses, then they can stop looking for absolution from an *external deity*. A parent would not stop a child playing with a toy, which can teach it much about the world; so too, the Source/Father sees no sin in the flesh. If a person of mature age takes part in physical pleasures, there is nothing unclean in these acts. When we play with this toy, we discover its true nature and failings. Then we are ready to look toward the truth. It is a process of experiential learning.

Some people find having sex with the opposite or same gender satisfying and desirable; what they are truly seeking is to feel connected. *This is the same desire of the soul to connect with the Source, the Father of all things.* It is essentially like trying to replace water with chocolate. The pseudo spiritual connection during sex is lost after the act and, like a drug, is pursued relentlessly. This is another example of how the physical world loosely mirrors the spiritual realm, but does it poorly. When people who rely on sex for this feeling of connection begin to search for the true nature of the soul, this desire is fulfilled by the satisfaction of the awakened Spirit. This catharsis is not the case for all sexual beings and certainly sex can mimic the connection to the Source—when *the one become two*. Interestingly, scans of the human brain have indicated that the same receptors are active when engaged in sex as when one is in a spiritual frame of mind.

In the context of this commentary about sin, sex is used as an example. Human sexuality has been widely exploited by religious authorities involved in dogma. The leaders of such Christian denominations have allowed their own desires and guilt about physical pleasures to taint their teachings. This is because, often, they have done the things they hate. Thus, we see dogma prevail over spiritual connectedness. Some religions try to deny physical needs, other groups use regular absolution or rituals to cleanse. All these are problematic and generally lead to failure. This failure leads to more guilt and distance from spiritual growth. In Thomas 6, Jesus warns that failure is assured under these methods of forgiveness, because they place the flesh above, or at equal measure, to the soul. If sex becomes a thing to feel guilt and hate over, it damages the heart and mind—the sentient aspects, which are linked to the metaphysical (heaven).

Jesus recognised these problems and revealed that we are above the need for physical or emotive acts of penance. He destroyed the man that clothed Him as a metaphor for this same reason. Jesus knew what was going to happen to Him and could have escaped His fate. Instead, He chose to perform the greatest act of teaching known to humanity, by giving up the *temple* He housed. After three days He rebuilt it in Spirit—the thing that cannot be destroyed.

7. Jesus said, "Lucky is the lion that the human will eat, so that the lion becomes human. And foul is the human that the lion will eat, and the lion still will become human."

Consider the metaphor of the lion, a creature of necessary violence, and its antithesis, the lamb, the traditional symbol of Jesus. Through this metaphor we may see this saying as a warning about corporally derived power. The lion also represents those people whose self-importance rules them and who seek power and control. This also extends to people who have become enamoured of this world to the point where they put their pleasure and advancement before other people. The lion often consumes politicians and business people (Thomas 64). It is important that humans project compassion towards such people, as they are on their own path and *their errors can help others* grow, through *observing* the lion at work (Thomas 42). Know too, the bear only feeds on the salmon that have chosen the exposed stream, or that are weak and dying.

The first Buddha was called Prince Siddhartha Gautama—his life ended (approximately) 483 years before the Common Era. He rejected his royal status and heritage to pursue a way out of the cycle of suffering—in his culture, reincarnation. In recognising and defining The Four Noble Truths, Buddha identified (among several issues arising from desire) the intrinsic dangers positions of leadership pose to the *individual*. In a sermon, the Buddha made the analogy of the pearl diver, who must become scratched and damaged to obtain the much-desired pearl. People should appreciate that the world may damage them at times, but these lessons should inspire us to look for the reasons why we suffer. This is the beauty and the pain of suffering. Unless these positions of authority are for the good of the whole community, they are usually imbued with desires for control and power. However, this is the way human society has evolved, and so, we must look at these devices of power through the lens of Thomas 7. In doing so, we see how the pearl diver's journey can truly be profitable.

In 77*th* Pearl: *The Perpetual Tree*, we find strong links made between Gautama Buddha and Jesus of Nazareth. They are logical links, made through the teachings in the Gospel of Thomas and the central teaching established through *Paticcasamuppada*. Here, a distinction is drawn between Buddhist teachings in the original *Pali Canon* and the popularised *Sanskrit* version of Buddhism. This distinction is similar to the difference we find between the Christian orthodoxy (denominations that only accept canonical Bible doctrine) and the teachings found in the Gospel of Thomas.

Two related topics and authors are mentioned here. They describe knowledge and understanding that is crucial in appreciating the links between Jesus of Nazareth and Gautama Buddha. The book, '*Paticcasamuppada: Practical Dependent Origination*' by Buddhadasa Bhikkhu (Bhikkhu meaning monk), will be referenced as an adjunct to the commentary for Thomas 7. Buddhadasa's text illustrates an authentic way of understanding the primary teachings of the Buddha—at the centre we find the concept of '*Paticcasamuppada*'. In addition, the views of Stephen Batchelor, a former Buddhist monk and widely published author, will be mentioned as a reflection of the dynamism Buddhist beliefs have had and he suggests should continue to have in the modern world. Batchelor's view on contemporary Buddhist communities reflects what 77*th* Pearl: *The Perpetual Tree* illustrates—the necessity for critical analysis of Christian doctrine. Such a critique would see the fundamental truths of Yeshua's teachings in the Gospel of

Thomas come to life in our everyday lives. Moreover, Batchelor shows how humans desire the structure of institutions, which are built on dogma and formalised practices. This desire in people has altered the essential meaning of *Paticcasamuppada*, due to general apathy and a lack of critical analysis. For this reason, Batchelor's views are also presented here to illustrate a parallel to the apathy we find in contemporary Christian orthodoxy. The desire for dogma and an institution that represents it demonstrates a weakness in humankind. There is a desire to *make the messenger into the message*, rather than listen to the message—perhaps because this takes more effort (we can see this in Thomas 13, 43, 52 and 88). It is this tendency that sees people worship Jesus and Buddha as deities, *their image replacing their message*.

Throughout *77ᵗʰ Pearl: The Perpetual Tree*, we see how the original teachings (sayings) of Jesus have been re-contextualised in the New Testament, through placing them within various narratives. The sayings in the Gospel of Thomas are reliable, because they are simply quotes. Indeed, this fits the scenario of an aural tradition, which would have initially been the only link to Jesus' teachings. There is strong evidence for this pattern of distortion throughout human history. We can cite such evidence in the way the Buddha's teaching of *Paticcasamuppada* was interpreted over time. This example is one that links and ratifies the words of Yeshua in Thomas 7. It also illustrates how the teachings of both men have been interpreted in different ways for various reasons.

In the commentary for Thomas 7, we see the revelation of the nature of the human—a beast, the flesh the soul inhabits. The baffling nature of this saying reflects the necessity for Jesus to conceal the true meaning of some of His teachings, as they did not fit the beliefs of His contemporaries. Indeed, Christian orthodoxy apologists argue that a typical rabbi of Jesus' time would not utter such cryptic and sometimes blasphemous rhetoric. This is true. Jesus was not typical of His time, He was the new wine. The words of Thomas 7, 'Lucky is the lion that the human will eat, so that the lion becomes human. And foul is the human that the lion will eat, and the lion still will become human,' challenge the notion of humanity as a creation separate from the animals around them. This is what the Abrahamic religions maintain. They believe Human bodies were uniquely created apart from all other creation, then the soul was created for the flesh. We see in Thomas 29 that this is incorrect. However, as in other sayings, Thomas 7 is imbued with more than just this practical and logical wisdom. Thomas 7 describes the nature we tend to fall back into, the nature of the ignorant animal, which has no altruistic feelings—it places itself at the centre of everything and becomes angered and disturbed by events that are unfavourable to its cravings and desires. How then does this relate to the primary teachings of Gautama Buddha? If we look at the profoundly insightful teaching of *Paticcasamuppada*, we can see how it is closely linked to Thomas 7.

Sitting under a bodhi tree (a *fig tree* native to India), Gautama Buddha meditated, determined to find the path out of suffering. It was at this point he attained enlightenment. In real terms, this did not mean he began to glow with light and was able to perform fantastical feats. It meant that he had a deep inner peace, acquired through a profound understanding of the reality or truth (Dharma) we encounter in this existence. The enlightenment he attained gave us *Paticcasamuppada* or *Dependent Origination*. The version given here is from the text '*Paticcasamuppada: Practical Dependent Origination*' by Buddhadasa Bhikkhu, (Published in 1992 by the Vuddhidhamma Fund, Distributed by Thammasapa)—this and other versions can be found online. The eleven conditions of *Paticcasamuppada* are given in various orders after Buddha's enlightenment, but the two presented here are *The Regular or Forward Order* and the *Extinction in the Middle*. The latter is presented as further evidence for Buddhadasa's assertion that *Paticcasamuppada* is experienced in a split second, rather than a whole lifetime.

The Regular or Forward Order:

'Ignorance gives rise to mental concocting;
Mental concocting gives rise to consciousness;
Consciousness gives rise to mentality/materiality;
Mentality/materiality gives rise to the sense bases;
The sense bases give rise to contact;
Contact gives rise to feeling;
Feeling gives rise to craving;
Craving gives rise to attachment;
Attachment gives rise to becoming;
Becoming gives rise to birth;
Birth gives rise to old age and death.'

Buddhadasa explains that this is called one turning of the chain, or wheel, of Dependent Origination, from beginning to end. He also spends significant time clarifying the conventional, and he implies misguided understanding of what this process actually involves. In some Buddhist faiths, *Paticcasamuppada* is understood as the experience of one whole lifetime, which is on a continuous loop to become endless lifetimes if craving does not cease. Therefore, it becomes an accumulative result of behaviours within a lifetime, which then determines the condition in which one is reborn—the karma effect. Buddhadasa's view is very different—it is this point of view we see linking to Thomas 7. Buddhadasa also explains that well-meaning disciples of the Buddha, who had expanded on the original Pali Canon, established some of the current, divergent, Buddhist beliefs.

Gautama Buddha chose to give his sermons in the Pali language, the native tongue of the common people. This observation is made by Buddhadasa and Stephen Batchelor, which will be explored further on. As with Christian beliefs and the Gospel of Thomas, Buddhist scholars now have access to the original Pali manuscripts, which contradict some of the beliefs within the various sects of Buddhism. Buddhadasa maintains that Gautama Buddha never spoke about the mechanism of rebirth—Batchelor also supports this. Rebirth was a mainstream ideology, the belief of the Indian culture Gautama Buddha was born into. The Buddha showed no interest in entering into a dialogue about the unknown. The questions of mind/body dualism, the mysteries of the universe, and reincarnation, were distractions to his path. He implied reincarnation's position as an accepted eventuality, but did not attempt to explain the process. The process of the soul's journey is described here, in *77th Pearl: The Perpetual Tree*, through the teachings of Yeshua in the Gospel of Thomas.

Buddhadasa asserts that *Paticcasamuppada* describes what humans go through in their everyday lives, in a split second of impassioned craving. To paraphrase Buddhadasa: the process of *Paticcasamuppada* (Dependent Origination) can be compared to a child who has a desirable toy placed within its presence. The child is symbolic of who we are when we are in a state of ignorance. In this state, we have no control over our thoughts and cravings. The toy represents any mental or material thing we might have, imagine, or desire. When the toy has been removed, or an obstacle is placed before it, our sense bases arise. This distraction makes contact with our eyes, ears, smell or touch, which then give rise to feelings of anger, loss, lust, disappointment, and so on. The attachment gives rise to the birth, which is the *illusion of self or ego*. 'Old age and death' represent the symbolic suffering within this cycle and the inevitability of this suffering arising again, due to ignorance. This process is comparable to Thomas 7. Ignorance is the rebirth of the primal animal—which is in us and is 'the human that the lion will eat' so that 'the lion still will become human'—reborn with ignorance and craving. However, as in the first part of

Thomas 7, if the lion (the physical manifestations we engage with every day) makes contact with the human (the person who consumes the lion), then the lion becomes human—the process has been profitable to the human. This human has engaged with the physical/material world and the process of *Paticcasamuppada*, becoming aware—no longer ignorant, no longer craving. The process is reversed in the *Extinction in the Middle* recitation of *Paticcasamuppada*. Here, the person is metaphorically eating the lion, because they have actively engaged with this life (Thomas 81, 110).

If we require more evidence that supports Buddhadasa's position on the interpretation of *Paticcasamuppada*, we can look at another form, the *Extinction in the Middle*.

'Ignorance gives rise to mental concocting;
Mental concocting gives rise to consciousness;
Consciousness gives rise to mentality/materiality;
Mentality/materiality gives rise to the sense bases;
The sense bases give rise to contact;
Contact gives rise to feeling;
Feeling gives rise to craving;
Because of the extinguishment of craving, attachment is extin-guished; Because of the extinguishment of attachment, becoming is extinguished; Because of the extinguishment of becoming, birth is extinguished; Because of the extinguishment of birth, old age, death, sorrow, lamentation, etc are extinguished.'

In this example of *Paticcasamuppada*, the person becomes aware of the reasons for craving and is able to rationalise the true value of the thing causing the suffering. Even though Gautama Buddha was the enlightened one, he still went through the process of his body becoming old and expiring. It is how he saw this process, and how he accepted it, which makes the difference. The recitation of *Paticcasamuppada*, with the extinction in the middle, is the one the Buddha would have become adept at using in his everyday life. It is the main reason he was the first Buddha. *Paticcasamuppada*, Extinction in the Middle, is the evidence of this process being not of a lifetime, but of a split second. The root cause of suffering is the stealthy lion under the skin, the ignorant child within, which we can extinguish, because we know where and how this rebel will attack (Thomas 103).

In *77th Pearl: The Perpetual Tree*, there are references made to several texts and writers to illustrate various points. These references should not be seen as a particular preference toward one system of beliefs over another, nor as a critique of one system over another. The point has been made in other commentaries that all faiths have aspects of truth, because the Father/Source has been seeking us out. Some have heard its voice with clarity; for others the voice has been muffled by innate human weaknesses. Here, we can make the analogy of a huge, complicated jigsaw puzzle, which has been swept off a table. Pieces have been discovered and yet other pieces have been copied through a thick fog (human weakness and this realm). They appear to fit, but do not complete the original puzzle. When we stand back and look at the picture created, it becomes obvious that certain pieces stand out as having a different tone or texture. The texts that are referred to in the commentaries make some pieces of the puzzle more defined. They have been found to have clarity and authenticity, through their harmonious fit into the picture Jesus has described in the Gospel of Thomas. Batchelor's views are used, in part, to enhance a point mentioned above. It is apparent in the lecture referenced that he had become disillusioned with the life of a monk, in both Tibetan and Zen Buddhism. This fact tends to colour his attitude toward the spiritual elements which have evolved in Buddhism. However, for the purposes of this commentary, we can see how some of his points are of relevance here.

To find the full transcript of Stephen Batchelor's lecture search for 'ABC Radio National, *Batchelor, The Secular Dharma*'.

Batchelor makes some strong points, which parallel those made for these commentaries. He points out that the Buddha's teaching, about the impermanence of all things, has been a catalyst for the many varied applications of Buddhist practice in different places.
'…if we look at this from a historical perspective, is that Buddhism has survived, and has flourished, precisely because it has the capacity to re-imagine itself, to re-think itself, to present itself in a different way, according to the needs of the particular people, the particular time, the culture, in which it finds itself at a given time. Buddhism is very fluid in this sense…each particular form of Buddhism that has come into being, has done so in its own peculiar way, which suits and is adapted to the particular situation of its historical background.'

The point Bachelor makes here is something the Christian orthodoxy needs to consider. Certainly, when we look at the history of Christian doctrine we see that it has developed in response to the context it came from. Constantine I facilitated the creation of the Nicene Creed to unify the Christian *doctrine*. At the time, various bishops had different positions on how Christianity should be established within society. Constantine wanted to have a central doctrine to stop the squabbling. One could argue that his background influenced the concept of a man seen as a living god, because of his experience with the Caesar legacy. All Caesars were responsible for ensuring the deities of their time were being worshipped appropriately. It was also not uncommon for Caesar to see himself as a god. This structure of authority, which was a pyramidal one, can be seen reflected in the Catholic and Eastern Orthodox hierarchy. It is also reflected in the Nicene Creed. The early part of the twenty-first century has seen much change; Christian Orthodoxy must change with it. What science has shown us indicates that we can no longer accept the juvenile beliefs about a Creator God. This is the legacy of Jesus' teaching, which sounds contradictory, but is what we discover through the Gospel of Thomas. It may seem like an atheist manifesto, but by definition 'atheist' means someone who does not believe in a god or gods: In *77th Pearl: The Perpetual Tree* we find that God is in all things, just as It is in Yeshua and in all of humanity. In this sense, our concept of god becomes a thing that connects all conscious beings.

To illustrate how people have desired something other or more than what the messenger is offering, we can look at some parallels in Buddhism. Batchelor makes some strong points about how people have always craved knowledge of things they cannot experience with their physical senses. They have wanted to know more than how to be happy in this life—they wanted to know what was next and what that looked like. Batchelor argues that the Buddha, according to the original Pali Canon, did not encourage this kind of thinking. He says:

'And whenever the Buddha was presented with these kinds of questions, or asked these questions, he wouldn't give an answer. All he would say was, "To explore such kinds of questions is not conducive to the path that I teach." And the point is not to pursue these kinds of questions in the hope that Buddhism will answer them for us, but actually to simply not pursue them, and to recognise that what really is important, is not having a correct description of the state of affairs in reality. But what matters is doing something that might make a real difference in the quality of your life here and now.'

Batchelor also makes an interesting point about why institutions begin to offer solutions to problems. They desire to substantiate their position as a valid system of what they purport to represent. In Christian orthodoxy, these are the sacraments of birth, marriage, and death. Similarly, Batchelor describes how contemporary Buddhist orthodoxy has claimed a kind of technology to alleviate suffering. They offer a technique that presents itself as the answer, drawing-in people wanting this relief. Batchelor states:

'...They like to present Buddhism as an effective technique for reducing suffering: "you've got a problem? OK, here's a technique, it's called meditation, and it's very effective. You do it right, you'll get rid of suffering." That I think is, again, in reducing Buddhism to a technological strategy, a kind of a self-help process that has almost claims to have a kind of quasi-scientific reliability...I think you can master all the techniques of meditation and remain just as screwed up as you were before you started.'

The attitude Batchelor describes here is also reflected in the way Buddhist monks withdraw from conventional life—but this is not a sustainable practice for the majority. In Buddhadasa's book, mentioned above, he suggests that one should avoid the enjoyment of nature and the simple pleasures of eating, because this encourages the process of craving. As Batchelor has suggested, such prescribed methods do not guarantee success. In the Gospel of Thomas, Jesus asks that we engage with the world, not withdraw from it. Moreover, through the process of 'motion and rest' (Thomas 50), at the end of this journey, we '[become] passers-by' (Thomas 42). In Thomas 7, we are asked to participate in (consume) the physical/material existence, so that we might grow and turn these experiences into *the human—the living spirit, which is the fruit Jesus loves most*. This is why, in Thomas 90, Yeshua tells us '[His] yoke... is gentle'.

In Stephen Batchelor's book *'Buddhism without Beliefs'* (published by G.P. Putnam's and Son's, 1997), he explains the way the *Four Noble Truths* should be perceived and practiced in our everyday lives. Batchelor stresses that Gautama Buddha did not intend these truths to be a kind of mantra (which become passive recitations). Rather, they should be metaphors for confronting the individual experience of suffering and for how to overcome these obstacles. They should not be used to console those who want a rebirth, which leads into wealth and prosperity. He also suggests that the Buddhist should be an *active Agnostic*—not desiring or denying the existence of a God (Ibid page 18-19). Batchelor asserts that because the Buddha Dharma has become part of a religion—imbued with dogma and discourse about the metaphysical—it has diverged from the purpose it was intended for. Here, there is a direct parallel with the way Jesus' teachings had been absorbed into a culture of fear: Fear of a creator God and His pending wrath for humanity's wickedness. Evidently, this was a wickedness that was not seeded and perpetuated by men themselves, but what became an adversary of God. This false perception sees Jesus turned into a vengeful deity in the Gospel of John (Revelations), rather than the wise avatar, all-forgiving man in the Gospel of Thomas and portions of the other gospels. This erroneous attitude reflects humanities inability to see their soul as an progeny of the Source, intimately connected to *It*.

If we consider that the soul does not die, though the flesh that houses it will, then our focus needs to be on nurturing the growth of the mind/spirit. When a person accepts the spiritual nature of all humans they consume the lion—that is, they interact with the physical world but they are not harmed or disturbed by it. The opposite is true if the person is enamoured of the physical world and denies the essence that is within. The life force that moves between all things will continue to pass through these bodies, but never truly *live*. Although the lion will manifest in human form, the essential soul becomes a victim of this world. Yeshua asks that we *interact* with the world; but first we should restrain it. Through the process of containing its impact on the mind we can benefit from what it has to offer. This enables growth from the experiences we encounter in this life, unharmed (Thomas 35 and 42).

8. And he said, "The person is like a wise fisherman who cast his net into the sea and drew it up from the sea full of little fish. Among them the wise fisherman discovered a fine large fish. He threw all the little fish back into the sea, and easily chose the large fish. Anyone here with two good ears had better listen!"

The Father/Source has found us, *the person* who is discerning, who is unlike any other creature. We are a place to inhabit and come to life *in a new way*. We have an intuitive ability to know what is right and wrong, and what is good for our growth and what is not. We are presented with many paths and ideologies. If we search within ourselves, we come to know the right choice. All non-violent beliefs/religions can be a pathway to growth; but will they sustain the soul to the end required to set oneself free? We need to be able to let go of the little fish and hold onto the large fish. The one that will give us *life* is found in the Gospel of Thomas and revealed through *77th Pearl: The Perpetual Tree*.

9. Jesus said, "Look, the sower went out, took a handful (of seeds), and scattered (them). Some fell on the road, and the birds came and gathered them. Others fell on rock, and they didn't take root in soil and didn't produce heads of grain. Others fell on thorns, and they choked the seeds and worms ate them. And others fell on good soil, and it produced a good crop: it yielded sixty per measure and one hundred twenty per measure."

Yeshua went out into the physical/material realm. He is the sower—He has scattered His words among us, through His followers. His followers are the places where the seeds fell and attempted to take root. Like the disciples, all people are the soil. The crop is the knowledge of truth grown in the good soil, which nourishes the soul on its way to becoming an enlightened Spirit.

The followers of Yeshua, who placed God outside of *the self,* scattered seeds on barren ground. However, those who recognised the soul as their identity scatter the seeds on fertile ground, which enabled them to yield without measure. *77th Pearl: The Perpetual Tree* has grown from the good soil, which is the Gospel of Thomas.

Thomas 9 is a well-known and often quoted parable. For this reason, this is an appropriate place to point out that the Gospel of Thomas sayings were a reference point for the Synoptic Gospels. The authors did not understand the *esoteric nature* of the sayings. They used what they knew from the Old Testament edicts to substantiate theories about Jesus and His teachings. This re-contextualising is what Jesus warned should not occur when He cryptically asserted not to place new wine (His teachings) into old wine skins (the myths and legends of the Old Testament) in Thomas 47. The fact that the disciples found Jesus' sayings difficult to comprehend is evident in the New Testament Gospels. The Gospel of Matthew illustrates this confusion well.

In Matthew 13, we see a plethora of sayings from the Gospel of Thomas. They are used to construct a piece of writing devised to scare and persuade the reader into believing in the salvation Matthew describes. This salvation would see the righteous taken up into heaven and the evil ones destroyed in the most agonising manner—such that there would be 'weeping and grinding of teeth'. This kind of persuasive language, devised to create frightening imagery, would have had great impact on the uneducated people of the early Christian period, and, in some Churches, right up to the twenty-first century. This fear is abundant in the Abrahamic religions and it is why *77th Pearl: The Perpetual Tree* was required for humanity to evolve.

Matthew 13 starts with the appropriation of Thomas 9. The author of the gospel uses the parable to describe the importance of faith and how the *Evil One* and daily life can sway and obstruct our faith. Just prior to the explanation of the sower parable, the disciples ask Jesus why He speaks to crowds in these parables. In reply, Matthew's Jesus says: 'Because to you is granted to understand the mysteries of the kingdom of Heaven, but to them it is not granted.' (Matthew 13:11) This is followed by a variation on Thomas 41, which suggests that those who have *the faith* (implied) will be given more; those who do not, the little they have will be taken away. This is a crafty edit of the teachings found in the Gospel of Thomas. They were not meant to sit together in this way and certainly were not to be used in such a political manner—the Son of God versus the Evil One. Moreover, suggesting that the parables were only meant to be understood by the disciples is clearly an attempt by the author to reaffirm his position and authority. At the very beginning of the Gospel of Thomas we see that this was not Jesus' intention. These teachings were for all people, but they needed to have wanted to understand them for the doors to be opened. Ironically, the statement in Matthew 13:11 confirms that there were parables that were 'mysteries' in Jesus' teachings. People found them difficult to understand; this included the disciples and the generations after Yeshua. It is only now, in the twenty-first century, that these mysteries are being revealed for the first time. In the New Testament, we generally see words about love, peace, and forgiveness, with the addition of Christology in the Gospel of John. We do not see teachings which are of an esoteric nature. Thomas understood the importance of these teachings and could not ignore them—as farmers know good, fertile soil when they see it.

In the same chapter of Matthew 13, the author uses the saying of Thomas 57, which makes reference to good and bad seed. In the synoptic text, it is used to continue the narrative of the Evil One placing obstacles in the path of Christians—obstacles that will be thrown into the furnace, where yet again: 'there will be weeping and grinding of teeth'. A brief history of the *Evil One* is discussed later. That section demonstrates how people are in fact *Satan*, which is something the synoptic writers inadvertently revealed. Following Thomas 57, the author of Matthew 13 inserts Thomas 20 (the mustard seed) and Thomas 96 (the woman who places leaven into bread). These sayings are interpreted in a peripheral, literal sense, twisted in subtle ways to suit the author's intention. Matthew 13 demonstrates how, through careful selection and juxtaposed narrative, the cryptic sayings in the Gospel of Thomas serve the synoptic authors' intentions. Matthew 13 also includes Thomas 109 (the treasure hidden in the field), Thomas 76 (the merchant and the pearl), and Thomas 8 (the large fish). The inclusion of the latter is used to persuade the reader of *'how it will be at the end of time.'* The angels will separate the wicked from the upright and there will be yet more weeping and grinding of teeth. This is not the intended meaning of Thomas 8, as we clearly see in the first line the reference is to *a person who is like a wise fisherman* – someone who is discerning and a critical thinker. This original meaning does not have purpose in a text intended to frighten and control the diaspora.

Toward the end of Matthew 13, we see a strong polemic statement in verse 52: '*Well then, every scribe who becomes a disciple of the kingdom of Heaven is like a householder who brings out from his storeroom new things as well as old.*' This infers a justification for using the Gospel of Thomas sayings in the context of knowledge derived from the Old Testament and previous gospels. It also presents an argument against Thomas 47, where Yeshua tells His followers that His teachings are *the new wine* (the new way) and should not be placed *into old wine skins*. Nor can one '*mount two horses*'—that is, two belief systems, which are not of the same essential construct. We should also note that the author describes himself as a 'disciple of the kingdom of Heaven'—not a disciple of Jesus. The author of this gospel was not the direct disciple of Jesus, nor were the authors of the other gospels.

The author ends Matthew 13 with Thomas 31. Jesus states that '…doctors don't cure those who know them', referring to a visit to His hometown, where no one was healed. Their perception of Him was that He was simply the carpenter's son. This is another device to show the reader that faith is the subject of Matthew 13. It espouses the need to believe in Jesus as *the Christ* if people are to be saved. This premise illustrates the main problem with the canonical texts. They do not tackle the *meaning* of Jesus' teachings. They instead use them to attempt to convince an audience of what Yeshua was—a definition the authors found in the Old Testament. This fundamental problem, *placing the divine outside of the self*, is what Yeshua came to this realm to correct. It is an attitude derived from humanities primal heritage, where ancient peoples looked outwardly, toward nature, for an explanation of the mysteries they could not fathom.

In the Gospel of Thomas, we are shown that we have an intimate connection with the Father—*the Source of all things*. Those who are seeking *It* are *the sons*, just as Yeshua is the *Son*, because the soul is an energy that has *come from* the Source and aggregates in humans. Thomas 9 tells us the seeds (the teachings) grow in '*good soil*'. When we read Thomas 9 out of its context, such as in Matthew 13, we see how Yeshua's lament about the rocks and thorns was realised. In Matthew, the '*seeds*' become faith, which is destroyed by external, evil forces. In Thomas 9, the '*soil*' is the focus, because it is where the roots create growth. This is what Jesus was concerned with—growth of the soul. The *fertile soil is knowledge, which allows growth.*

10. Jesus said, "I have cast fire upon the world, and look, I'm guarding it until it blazes."

Had Yeshua's contemporaries realised they could find *God* by searching within themselves, the structure of their society would have fallen apart. The Pharisees, and later the Church leaders, were aware of this potential downfall. Their inability to let go of tradition (for fear of losing their growing institution) and their failure to think in abstract terms, prevented them from knowing the truth in Jesus' teachings. When Yeshua says *He is guarding what He cast upon the earth*, He speaks about the secret teachings. When Jesus' teachings cause a 'blaze'

within the individual, He re-enters this realm through this connection. The Holy Spirit makes this *connection*, because it operates within the quantum field where singularity exists – everything is connected and operates as a whole. This relationship is non-denominational—it is the connection one has to something which escapes words, it links all beings seeking the Light of truth.

This saying has a thread which connects it to the Gospel of John (Chapter 14:16-20). Again, this shows how influential the Gospel of Thomas was on the New Testament authors. In the Gospel of John, Jesus tells His contemporaries that He will send them a *Paraclete* (a comforter or advocate). This is evidently a link to the coming of the Holy Spirit at Pentecost—as seen in the Acts of the Apostles, which was written by the same author as the Gospel of Luke. Interestingly, Muslim apologists use this verse in John's Gospel to argue that Jesus was speaking of their prophet. At Pentecost, the Holy Spirit is described as 'fire' descending from heaven, settling above the heads of the apostles. In the context of what we learn from the Gospel of Thomas, it is clear that Yeshua is referring to a *link*, which is made with the *individual*, connecting all those who are touched by it. This link is something that stimulates the fire (the Light) which is within all people. The Holy Spirit makes this link possible, because it is the thing that unifies the Source (Father) and the Son (all beings), to become the Trinity. This is ratified by what Jesus says in John 14: '…but you know him, because he is with you, he is in you.' This is a reference to both His apostles and Himself being intrinsically linked together—as one. It also confirms that all sentient beings have the capacity to tap into the quantum field – this is what researchers of extra-terrestrial contact have discovered. In the Gospel of Thomas, the Holy Spirit is lifted above all else due to this crucial function, as evident in Thomas 44. These are the *three facets* of the *one God* (the Source). Moreover, Yeshua said that whoever is near Him is *near the fire* and that whoever is far from Him is far from the kingdom—the collective consciousness (Thomas 82). Yeshua came to this realm to teach humans, thereby *linking them* to the Father/Source, so that they may truly *live*. The story surrounding Pentecost involves the element of *bridging distances between people* (who were initially unable to communicate), through the power of the Holy Spirit. The significant metaphor we draw from the story in Acts of the Apostles is the need for a link among all beings. The Holy Spirit is the catalyst, a device. The Holy Spirit touches the heart and mind of the one seeking connection with all beings of Light, throughout all the realms/dimensions. This is the 'fire' Jesus cast upon the Earth through the Gospel of Thomas, so that it might cause a 'blaze' in us.

11. Jesus said, "This heaven will pass away, and the one above it will pass away.

The dead are not alive, and the living will not die. During the days when you ate what is dead, you made it come alive. When you are in the Light, what will you do? On the day when you were one, you become two. But when you become two, what will you do?"

Thomas 11 reminds the human of their mortality and the impermanent material world. It asks us: what will we do when we realise we have become joined to the Father/Source? Jesus tells people that those who have died and have not realised the nature of the true self 'are not alive' and those who have found the spirit within are 'the living' that 'will not die'. 'During the days when you ate what was dead' meaning daily existence, giving the body food, allowing it to be in *motion, then resting*. We should appreciate it was not the physical life Yeshua was concerned with here. *'When you are one'*—when humans are born they are one, then die, they become two—joined to the Source. *'What will you do?'* when one realises the soul has joined to the *Source?* The soul is the progeny of God (the Father/ Source) just like Yeshua. If people have expected something outside of the self to bring them to *life*, they will be mistaken. Putting the hope of a new life, or afterlife, on the decision of a deity is wrong. Life in its various manifestations is a given. It exists in many forms, in this universe and other dimensions.

Science tells us the stars have a limited life—as do the planets and the life forms that rely on them. This is the nature of the physical/material universe. The lamb and the lion will never live in the same fields, unless the lion becomes herbivorous— this is not the way of this world. People who wait for this planet to become the 'kingdom of God' will never see that day. Jesus tells us the *kingdom of God is already here*—our collective souls constitute the kingdom. When we are fully *resurrected* and become a Spirit we claim our heritage.

Unless we become aware of our spiritual self, upon death the soul fades away into *the whole* (which is the Father/Source). Eventually the souls who have *tasted death* become reabsorbed into other physical forms. Some individuals, who are aware of the *soul* and are enamoured with the physical/material realm, may evolve into souls of darkness. This darkness is metaphoric. It is connected to the dynamism of the physical universe, which requires chaos to evolve and functions on survival of the fittest. The souls in darkness try to distract people who are on a journey towards liberating themselves. The distractions usually involve matters relating to everyday life—family, romantic, and other relationships; work, finances, and material posses- sions. These dark souls do not know that they are enamoured of a flawed mirror. They think the *reflection* is the truth and the ideal. In *77th Pearl: The Perpetual Tree* it is confirmed that there are indeed malevolent spirits who attempt to distract us. With reluctance, the author admits encountering these kinds of malevolent souls when writing the first draft for these commentaries. It was decided to add these experiences to the second edition of the book. The initial hesitancy to disclose these experiences stems from the desire to lift the discourse out of the paranormal (perhaps ironically), and into a *logical* reality. However, these experiences happened for a reason, so it was decided to share them. The events will be described in a later commentary.

In Thomas 11, the 'living' ones are the people aware of their true spiritual self. They also recognise the disparity between this physical realm and the dimensions *beyond* the four we experience. Unless we realise that the soul is connected to the *other*, through the Holy Spirit (the conduit), the soul fades into the Source from where it came. If we do not become *two* (Source and human) when we are alive, then this link cannot be made post-death. Jesus asks the rhetorical question: 'when you become two [when you come to the Source, at death], what will you do? [if you have not recognised *the Father* in life].'

12. The disciples said to Jesus, "We know that you are going to leave us. Who will be our leader?"

Jesus said to them, "No matter where you are, you are to go to James the Just, for whose sake heaven and earth came into being."

It is widely believed 'James the Just' was Jesus' brother or very close family relative. This is important to consider when interpreting these sayings as having symbolic references. It is significant that Jesus says, '*No matter where you are you are* to go to James the Just.' This was an impossible request—Jesus would have known the disciples would end up all over the land. Therefore, we may glean that 'James' is a metaphor. *James the Just exists in all of us*. Moreover, Yeshua makes it clear that James is symbolic of the human species, because that is *for whose sake* this universe and planet Earth came into being. If we look to our true selves and ask questions, the responses will come from the intuitive and logical self. This is the *connection* with the Holy Spirit. Jesus knew these same questions would arise in future generations, so this response is speaking to the one who comes across these pearls.

The nature of most human beings is that they need to be told how to behave, particularly in religious matters. This is evident in Thomas 6. If we consider that in the Gospel of Thomas Yeshua tells us we are like Him, we are His relatives through our soul, then we may *see ourselves* as James, for 'whose sake heaven and earth came into being'. The physical universe formed from metaphysical material transformed into physical substance. This was not something magical. It was one kind of physics changing into another, creating this universe through what we know as the Big Bang. The invisible Light, which constitutes the Source, remained in this universe after the great expansion—now sentient beings *embody this Light*. Relatively few habitable planets have evolved in which souls may dwell (Thomas 96). Knowing these truths, we can see that we are our own 'leaders' in spiritual matters. We naturally, or intuitively, know what is right when we search our heart, the link to the Holy Spirit. The Father/Source influences nature. It has provided almost all creatures with a desire to abate suffering by caring for their own. We call this survival, but this is the action of the Spirit realm influencing the material/physical universe.

History has shown the willingness of people to give up their logical and intuitive self to *beings* who have a malevolent agenda. This is of course detrimental (Thomas 7). These are not always the obvious examples (dictators, tyrants). They can be in the guise of religious leaders, whose weaknesses are transposed into their teachings. In these instances, James *the Just* is the one we go to. He is found within the *intuitive and logical self*. At all times remember: Yeshua told us we are His relatives. We are like Him, which is evident in Thomas 99.

13. Jesus said to his disciples, "Compare me to something and tell me what I am like."

Simon Peter said to him, "You are like a just messenger."

Matthew said to him, "You are like a wise philosopher."

Thomas said to him, "Teacher, my mouth is utterly unable to say what you are like."

Jesus said, "I am not your teacher. Because you have drunk, you have become intoxicated from the bubbling spring that I have tended."

And he took him, and withdrew, and spoke three sayings to him. When Thomas came back to his friends they asked him, "What did Jesus say to you?"

Thomas said to them, "If I tell you one of the sayings he spoke to me, you will pick up rocks and stone me, and fire will come from the rocks and devour you."

Thomas 13 is not the first time a religious text has a follower of Jesus claim some kind of privileged knowledge. It happens in the Gospel of Judas, The Gospel of Mary Magdalene, and in the New Testament when Peter, in Matthew 16:19, is given the keys to heaven. We now know that there are no keys, as there are no gates—the kingdom is everywhere and cannot be contained. It is what we are – a collective consciousness, the singularity. Ironically, the very next story, 'The First Prediction of the Passion' (Matthew 16:21-23), sees Jesus rebuke Peter as an obstacle, *thinking not as God does but as a man would*. People who desired power and control wrote those words, giving Peter autonomy and power. Historically, we know Mark was the first of the Synoptic Gospels, written around seventy to ninety years after Jesus' death. The other gospels are elaborated, edited, and embellished versions of Mark and Thomas – also known as the Q Source.

In Thomas 13, the author of the gospel wants to make it clear the Gospel of Thomas is like nothing else written about Jesus. This gospel is not a biographical narrative about Yeshua and who He was. *It is about His teachings—unedited.* This is what makes Thomas' response believable. Reading the sayings in the Gospel of Thomas requires meditation on the metaphors and symbols they contain. In the period Yeshua spoke these words, the Pharisees and most of His contemporaries would have considered His rhetoric blasphemous and heretical. The Gospel of Thomas essentially negates the existence of a 'creator god' outside of the self. Instead, we see that we are connected to the Father/Source—this link is through *Its remnant, which we call the soul. Like Jesus, we are Its offspring.* We could imagine the other apostles picking up stones and throwing them at Thomas if he had said such things to them. Their entire belief system would have been shaken to its core. The disciples' understanding of what Jesus was like came from their knowledge of the Torah—The Old Testament. Jesus came to us through the great Jewish tradition and culture, but He was not the Saviour they expected.

The New Testament authors, and their successors, had social and political agendas, stemming from their heritage. These people were either influenced by this heritage or opposed to its adherents, as we see in Luke's accounts. The lion we find in Thomas 7 had consumed these people, as they either desired to control a growing community or vilified those whom they blamed for Jesus' death. Consider how Mark 14:21 claims Jesus speaks of Judas: 'For the Son of Man indeed goes, as it is written of him [in the Torah], but woe to that man by whom the Son of Man is betrayed. It would be better for that man if he had never been born.' These words appear to be out of character. An enlightened being, such as Yeshua, would not utter such condemnation. Did Judas really betray Him or had he done as Jesus asked of him? The Gospel of Judas purports the latter. If Judas betrayed Jesus, then He would have seen Judas as someone consumed by the lion and taken pity on him. In this sense, we might interpret this statement as a prophetic description of how one person would be blamed for destroying Jesus, as the notion that Jesus did this to Himself would be too difficult to fathom. Thomas was different. He could see Yeshua did not fit the positions within His society the others hoped He had come to fulfil. Yeshua came to liberate the invisible— the thing we cannot comprehend without the knowledge He brought to us—*from* the realm of the Spirit.

In ultimately giving up the man that clothed Him, Yeshua showed us how we suffer because of the flesh and the materiality it dwells in. Through His sacrifice, we see that the new and everlasting covenant becomes that which is physically left behind. Jesus' words are the body, the blood He spilled for us becomes a metaphor for the Light which flows through all of us—It is the Source of all things, the Source of *life*. Through the knowledge we gain in these sayings, we awaken the Spirit and truly 'live'. This extraordinary symbolic act (seen in this didactic sacrifice) is what makes Jesus someone most people are unable to fathom.

Thomas 13 is extremely important—it is the reason why we have the Gospel of Thomas. When Jesus realised Thomas could not compare Him to anything in his past, *Jesus saw in Thomas the future*. The language Jesus' contemporaries had access to came to them from the Old Testament (the Jewish Torah). Their replies to His question (in Thomas 13), demonstrate this clearly. When Thomas claims that his mouth is utterly incapable of comparing Jesus to something, a very important thing takes place—the recognition that a new vocabulary was necessary in order to understand Jesus' teachings. It was a language that was not fully evolved until the twenty-first century. Ironically, the way Thomas replies to this question placed him in a vulnerable position and he became labelled as 'doubting Thomas'. This becomes evident in the Gospel of John 20:24-29. Here, the author(s) references Thomas in order to make his case for Jesus having been *physically resurrected*. It becomes evident the author of John was aware of the Gospel of Thomas and its inferences to a *spiritual resurrection*, rather than a physical one. The author of John found, in the saying of Thomas 13, a way to justify making Thomas a doubter. The other disciples used language from their heritage to describe what Jesus was like and, to the author of John, this was the only reference point that made sense.

The label of 'doubting Thomas' has been detrimental to the Gospel of Thomas, but when we analyse where it came from we see that the label is unfounded. Moreover, we find in Mark 16:12-14 that all the disciples were in fact doubters of Jesus' resurrection:

> 'After this, he showed himself under another form to two of them as they were on their way into the country. They went back and told the others, who did not believe them either. Lastly, he showed himself to the Eleven themselves while they were at table. He reproached them for their incredulity and obstinacy, because they had refused to believe those who had seen him after he had risen.'

Note also, the two disciples on their way into the country experienced Jesus' presence in *another form*, which tells us that

Jesus was not resurrected in flesh. After all, once *the pearl* has matured and been extracted from the oyster shell, why would one cover it up in the same shell? The author of the Gospel of John (20:24-29) changes Mark's account (16:12-14), making Thomas the singular focus of the incredulity and obstinacy. Thomas' response in Thomas 13 makes it possible for the author of John to attack his faith.

A very important and revealing statement is made by Yeshua when He says: 'Because you have drunk, you have become intoxicated from the bubbling spring that I have tended.' This is the predicament all people find themselves in when they are deep in the woods of the spiritual quest. When they find the pearl, or they catch the large fish, they become overwhelmed by its aesthetic or satisfying qualities. The satisfaction and knowledge they gain from their find makes them drunk. They start to see things that are not there or that in their intoxicated heart and mind become exaggerated. This is what happened to the teachings of both the Buddha and Jesus. These two *messengers became the message*—their *images* replaced their message. In Thomas 13, Jesus recognises this human weakness. Shamot Sesju has experienced this drunken state, which is why it has taken so long to see through the fog (that is, this existence) with clarity. The sobering process required taking steps back from the enigmatic words in the Gospel of Thomas, to enable a clear view of all its connections, complexities, and mysteries. This is what other commentaries about this gospel have struggled with. They have tended to use existing texts to decipher Thomas. These people either used Biblical references, or various Gnostic texts to analyse Thomas. This is ironic as it is equivalent to putting the cart before the horse. The Gospel of Thomas was meant to be revealed through language that was evolved enough to make the logical links revealed here. These are the threads that already exist within its intricate tapestry. These are the threads that have created *77th Pearl: The Perpetual Tree.*

14. Jesus said to them, "If you fast, you will bring sin upon your-selves, and if you pray, you will be condemned, and if you give to charity, you will harm your spirits.

When you go into any region and walk about in the country-side, when people take you in, eat what they serve you and heal the sick among them.

After all, what goes into your mouth will not defile you; rather, it's what comes out of your mouth that will defile you."

Thomas 14 extends on Thomas 6—Jesus responds directly to all three questions. In Thomas 6, He simply tells the disciples not to do the things which would lead them to guilt and failure. All things are known to the true self and they cannot be covered up. In Thomas 14, Yeshua points out that dietary laws would place a barrier between His disciples and communities which were not Jewish. Yeshua stresses it is not what they eat that would distance His followers from the realm of the Spirit. It is what they say that might become an obstacle.

Yeshua disliked dogma because it separated people into groups. Rules about ritual cleansing and what food could be consumed were a way to keep certain groups separated, if only to keep one culture distinct from another. The Good Samaritan story in Luke 10:25-37 has these undertones—the people who ignored the injured man were following cultural practices by not being 'soiled' by a bloodied man. They would have to ritually cleanse themselves (again), before entering the Temple. The Samaritan was politically opposed to the injured man, but he tended to him regardless.

The message in Thomas 14 is clear. It is the mind, tainted by what people are taught, which makes them feel like they are unworthy of God/Source. People must accept what they are and grow in Spirit, along the way helping others and having empathy and respect for all beings. It is what is in the heart and mind that can be unclean, not what is outside of it.

The leaders of the Catholic Church know that they are losing parishioners. Their reaction to this has been one of fear, so they have fallen back on the power of fear and self-condemnation to hold onto their flock. They are essentially trying to take the church back into the Dark Ages, when people believed they would go to hell if they did not adhere to church doctrine. These actions are motivated by desires for control and power; they have nothing to do with facilitating the *growth* of the soul. Yeshua warns authorities in several sayings in Thomas. He cautions leaders and the decisions they make. Often the *powerful one* (Thomas 98) makes bad decisions appear to be from good intentions. We should ask ourselves: has the lion in Thomas 7 consumed those people, so that they present as human with the heart of a beast?

In May of 2011, the Catholic Church made changes to some of the responses during their mass. Up to the 1960s the Mass was said in Latin, the decision to change to English was made by The Second Vatican Council—Vatican II. In the process of this translation, some parts of the English version were altered or left out. The changes introduced in May of 2011 were an attempt to correct these anomalies. In a positive sense, when the congregation greets the priest after he says 'The Lord be with you' they now respond with 'And with your Spirit'. Previously, the response was 'And also with you'. The recognition of the *Spirit* is a small step toward the acknowledgment and celebration of the Spirit within the congregation itself. In the negative, there have been changes that emphasise the distance some Christians assume to have from God/Source. This is the same *perceived distance* Yeshua tells us is damaging to our progression and growth, which is evident in Thomas 3. In the revised Catholic Penitential Right, the parishioners recite the following self-deprecating words, "…I have greatly sinned" and, "through my fault" (repeated three times, while beating the chest).

In Thomas 14, Yeshua asks His disciples to forget about the things that are unattainable. He asks the disciples to focus on what is important—the message *they speak* and the *actions they take*. This is what is paramount—not dogma, not rituals. The importance of Jesus' *teaching* is of primary concern. His words and wisdom are the body and blood which remains with us.

15. Jesus said, "When you see one who was not born of woman, fall on your faces and worship. That one is your Father."

Thomas 15 hints at Jesus' birth as a *human* and challenges the notion of Jesus as God. This does not diminish the fact that He was indeed the Son of the Father/Source, which He Himself affirmed. This reality is also true for us—we are Yeshua's mother, brother, and sister (Thomas 99), so we are also children of God, the Source. This truth is supported by Thomas 28, where Yeshua states that He took His place among us in flesh. If we do not understand and accept this truth, we cannot see ourselves as His kin. This is a barrier created by Church doctrine. It must be removed if souls are to have an easier path to a spiritual life. If people see themselves as unworthy (as is evident in the Catholic Penitential Right), then they will never attain what Jesus wants for them and His sacrifice will have been denigrated. When we pray, we should open ourselves to the Holy Spirit and the Father's light by saying these words:

Lord, I am worthy to receive you,
for your father's light is my soul,
I am your brother, sister, and mother,
the Holy Spirit has joined us to the Father/Source
And the one have become two

Amen

The most astonishing thing about Thomas 15 is the reference to the *Source of all things*—the one Jesus refers to as '*Father*'. In Thomas 15, Jesus does not give *It* a name, because It is beyond the capacity and limitations of a name—*It* is, and was, and forever will be. *It* is everywhere and in every thing, at the same time. *It* flows through and binds all things. We are Its offspring—'That one is your Father'—just as It is Jesus' father. Since people first started to contemplate the notion of a god, there have been many names presented as the one. However, those names reflect glimpses of what the Source is through a thick fog. Often, the characteristics of this *one true God* are taken from those of the imperfect human; who has the faults of jealousy, revenge, aggression, and violence. The comprehension of how this God functions has been taken from observations of the material/physical universe. This has been an understandable mistake, because humans, with their limited senses, only have these four dimensions to experience. In 77th *Pearl: The Perpetual Tree*, the fog has been lifted. When people allow themselves to experience what is beyond this mirror, to see this layer of existence as the external, discarded one, they are able to see the one who was not born of women. *It is beyond human language.*

16. Jesus said, "Perhaps people think that I have come to cast peace upon the world. They do not know that I have come to cast conflicts upon the earth: fire, sword, war.

For there will be five in a house: there'll be three against two and two against three, father against son and son against father, and they will stand alone."

A prophetic statement—Jesus warns of the political divisions His presence and message would bring. First, we see this happen among the Jewish followers of Jesus, who tried to exclude gentiles, then we see it in the Christian Crusades against Islam, followed by the Protestant divisions and conflicts. Their lineage is from one heritage, linked by the biblical character of Abraham, yet within their own *family* they are divided and have caused bloodshed.

Judaism, Christianity, and Islam are referred to as Abrahamic religions because of the founding position Abraham plays in their holy texts. Abraham is considered the father of the people of Israel. Jews and Christians have this lineage through Abraham's son Isaac, by his wife Sarah. For the Muslims, it is by Sarah's servant, Hagar. The biblical character of Abraham, who is based on legend, is claimed to be the tenth generation from Noah and the twentieth from the first human—Adam.

Within the Arabic community, some six hundred years after Yeshua, the opportunity arose for a very prescriptive faith. This faith was built on the premise of obedience to God. The underlying edict was derived from the story of Abraham. In Genesis 22:1-18, Abraham is willing to sacrifice his only son to demonstrate his *obedience* and faith. After showing his willingness to sacrifice his son, Abraham is promised that the generations coming from him will prosper and be in God's favour. The Islamic text took this premise and formed practices demonstrating faith and obedience.

Islam reinterpreted the Old and New Testament narratives and gave specific directions on every aspect of life. People could follow a set of guidelines, outlining how to conduct oneself within the community and how to worship God, in order to remain in God's favour. The in-house conflict in the Christian groups (and their lack of such specific directions on day-to-day life), made Islam an attractive option for other cultures. Jesus is given a peripheral role throughout the Islamic text. Interestingly, the tone when referring to the beliefs Christians had about Jesus becomes progressively negative.

The esoteric nature of the Islamic text is appealing. It attempts to bring people closer to their god, but for critical thinkers its emphasis on *fear* (of God) and obedience is an obstacle toward this objective. For this reason we have seen divisions within Islam—some factions adhere to the literal interpretation, others have a more esoteric reading of the text, such as in Sufism. The popularity of Islam comes from its promise of an intimate relationship with the God of Abraham, achieved by following strict dietary laws and daily prayer obligations. This devotion to the spiritual is admirable, as it reflects what Jesus desires for us. However, rituals and practices can become a trap, as they are prone to losing their true significance. The inherent problem with the Abrahamic religions is that they place god outside of the self. Humans simply become God's *creation*, not an *intrinsic part of what God is*. The intimate connection people should seek is in the realisation that *we are Its offspring, we are as Yeshua is*. When people place a god outside of the self they make it easy to use this God for their own purpose. This manipulation is often driven by lust for power and control over others (Thomas 7). Sadly, we have seen these fundamentalist approaches take on a barbaric face, one that echoes the Christian Crusades in the Middle Ages. We should take an approach similar to how one bows to a stranger. In this act, we recognise their soul, which is linked to ours. 'God' is not one entity, nor is 'He' *three persons yet one god*. God, the Father, is the Source of all things; the *Son* is representative of all the beings throughout the universe, who aggregate the Father's Light. The Holy Spirit joins them so that the one becomes two.

It was not long after the three Abrahamic religions formed, that conflict between Jewish, Christian, and Islamic groups occurred, resulting in bloodshed. As we see in the prophetic statement of Thomas 16, they had the same lineage, which they all recognised and accepted. Yeshua's warning, '...there will be five in a house: there'll be three against two and two against three, father against son and son against father', is truly poignant. The true *Creator* does not recognise people of hatred and division: 'they will stand alone.' After all, the nature of worldly power is that of the lion (Thomas 7), unlike the Lamb, whose nature is that of the Spirit. In this world the lion will always devour the lamb, as was shown to us by Yeshua in the *crucifixion of the flesh*, which housed the Light of God/Source. This is a metaphor for the behaviour of those who lead people into battle in the name of their God, *they stand alone*, with blood on their hands. They have given in to their desires for power and control—just as those who put Jesus' physical body to death.

Jesus came to correct perceptions stemming from the Old Testament, which harmed the potential relationship between God/Source and *Its offspring*. This is why we must remove ourselves from literal interpretations of culturally/politically-influenced texts when we are seeking the truth of our existence. These useful sources are found by engaging with our logical and intuitive self. This wisdom is revealed here in the Gospel of Thomas, supported by aspects of the Synoptic Gospels. Those aspects, which do not attempt to link Yeshua with the Old Testament, are of value to our growth and union with God/Source. The contentious statement we see in Thomas 15, followed by the warning in Thomas 16, reinforces the disparity between Jesus' teachings and what we see in the Old Testament.

Yeshua sensed that the time in which He was clothed in flesh was not one that could accept or understand His profound messages; therefore, it was necessary to be cryptic. If Jesus were truly the one who brings war (with intent), then He could have easily led His contemporaries in creating a Christian empire. Instead, Jesus showed humans His message was about the Spirit—not the body, not the piece of land or territory, and not unilateral religious control. We should ask ourselves: would someone who sacrificed Himself for all people desire war and destruction? These terrible events in our history have, at times, been brought about in God's name by those consumed by the lion we see in Thomas 7. The only war Jesus creates is one causing a separation from the belief in a god that has *human characteristics*. This is the god born of a primal heritage, when humans were creatures in need of a patriarchal figure, to protect them from natural disasters they thought were inflicted upon them.

Yeshua could see His contemporaries would not understand these contentious messages (regarding God's Kingdom being within us). He knew that charismatic individuals would take His words to justify fire, sword, and war. In 312 CE, Constantine claimed to have won the Battle at Milvian because he had a vision. He maintained Jesus instructed him to place His sign on the soldiers' shields—in doing so, Constantine would be assured victory. Yeshua would not have been concerned with worldly power and conflicts. These conflicts reflect the lion which has devoured fallible men, but the lion will continue to present as human (Thomas 7). We should ask: would Jesus suggest placing His sign on a flag, condoning killing in His name? Paradoxically, in 325, Constantine made it possible for the *Nicene Creed*, a statement of the essential beliefs of orthodox Christianity, to be written. Constantine's aim was to *unify* the Christian groups, which were under the leadership of various bishops. The disunity stemmed, in part, from theological differences regarding the belief in Jesus. They argued between Jesus being of the same substance as God or being made by God. Significant historians view Constantine's motive as political, not theological. Neglecting to understand the real meaning of the words in Thomas 16, we see how important it is not to look at something in isolation. When all the sayings in Thomas are carefully analysed, in relation to each other, we cannot read Thomas 16 in such literal, provocative and dangerous terms.

The law of an 'eye for an eye', found in the Old Testament, was designed to balance the physical injustices inflicted within the Jewish community. It extended to any part of the body and meant that if a person was physically harmed, they had the right to retaliate with the same injury. The essence of this 'law' has been justification for payback of unjust and violent acts between cultures of the Abrahamic lineage. If we look to our logical and intuitive selves, and what Yeshua has taught us, then we see this law in a very different light. If we are to take someone's eye out, in effect, what we have done is taken our own eye out. We are that person, connected in spirit. If we harm others, we harm ourselves and the spirit that flows between us. If people harm others, the lion (Thomas 7) has consumed them. This is the nature of the physical world, which has chaos, fear, and aggression at its heart. *These things are at odds with the nature of the Spirit.*

17. Jesus said, "I will give you what no eye has seen, what no ear has heard, what no hand has touched, what has not arisen in the human heart."

Humans have consistently given a god, or numerous deities, control over their lives. In this saying, Yeshua tells us that He gives people what they have never had access to in the past. He conveys the knowledge that we are more than creatures subject to the laws of this world. In this way, we come to realise we are a soul becoming a Spirit, the same as Him. History has shown us that most people find it difficult to comprehend *what* we are. People prefer to place God outside of the self, so that they can pray for intercession—they see life's hardships as inflicted upon them. This is the deception of the physical world. It is by its nature ruled by physical obstacles, where the answer to happiness is perceived, or learnt, as having material gratification. The material world is transitory—as such, so is the gratification. It does not last, hence, it is not sustainable. When we are content in our soul we are free of this desire and suffering. Yeshua presents to us a gentle way to overcome these obstacles, made clear in Thomas 90. This gentle way is through knowing the truth of *what* we are and that He has set us free from the powerful one (Thomas 98).

Realising God is in us (the soul), we have no need for idols and saints to speak for us. Religious people do not realise that praying to a thing, or performing some kind of prayerful intercession, will work if they sufficiently believe in that thing (God or deity). It also means they credit this deity wrongly. It is the Spirit within that has answered their prayers, by virtue of their faith. In the Synoptic Gospels, Yeshua often says it is the afflicted person's faith that has healed them, hinting at the conduit role He played as a link between this realm and the other. These events also tell us that, through Jesus, this connection was opened in people because they had faith. The evidence of the power of faith can be seen in the story of Jesus visiting His hometown, Nazareth (Mark 6:1-6 and Thomas 31.). In these accounts, there were only a few people healed, because they knew Him as one of their own.

If there is no omnipotent god, does this mean we should not pray? Prayer is making a connection with God/Source. We do not pray to *a god* for intercession, because *the Source* is within us—the Father's Light exists everywhere. Prayer invokes the positive and harmonious aspect that is the Source, as this is Its nature when joined by the Holy Spirit, which is the collective consciousness. It has the capacity to correct the fractures within *this mirror*. If this does not occur there is good reason, because all things are resolved into God, the Source.

What Yeshua has given us, through the Gospel of Thomas, is a profound understanding of *what* we are. It is something that has previously not been attainable, because of our limited, physical capabilities and the enticing world we exist in.

The Creed, based on the sayings in the Gospel of Thomas, gives us clarity about the mysteries we can now appreciate.

The Creed

We believe in God, the source of all that is,
the Light that is in me, and between all things.
We believe, through the mirror influence of the Spirit realm,
The Father, the Source, inspired the formation of our universe.
As the Father expanded into the abyss, It's Light was scattered
throughout our cosmos.
We believe that now, It is born in us.
It lives through this process of our motion and rest.

We believe in Jesus.
The prime example of the Son, the pure spark from God, the
Source.
As He is, so we struggle to realise the same truth in us.
We are His brother, sister, and mother.
We believe in Yeshua, sent from the realm of the Spirit.
He was clothed in flesh, only to be destroyed by the lion.
The lion that is still human.
We believe He rose above the flesh, resurrected in Spirit.
Through these actions, He showed us how, in this world,
The Lamb defeats the lion.

We believe in the Holy Spirit.
Sent to reunite us, the lost sheep in the abyss, the one most
loved.
We believe God's Light is in all of us and, through the Holy
Spirit, we are joined back to the Father, the source of all that is.
Through this action, the one becomes two.

We believe in Mary, the mother of Jesus.
Her life was as her son instructed—'be passersby'.
We believe, as she departed, untouched by this life, so too do
we. Through this motion, like Mary, we seek wealth from our
experiences.

We believe, upon our death, we will pass by all that has disturbed us, so that we may come to our rest in Spirit.

Together with those who had struggled to bring forth what was within them, we especially honor The Buddha and John The Baptist. They constituted the sword, which broke through the divide. They were the crossguard and handle grip for Jesus.
We believe in Yeshua, the hand that was sent for us.
He is the hand that guides us into the Light of truth.

We believe in the words of Jesus,
the bread that sustains me,
the Light that will bring me home,
the flame that burns within me.   Amen.

18. The disciples said to Jesus, "Tell us, how will our end come?"

Jesus said, "Have you found the beginning, then, that you are looking for the end? You see, the end will be where the beginning is.

Congratulations to the one who stands at the beginning: that one will know the end and will not taste death."

Influenced by the calamity of natural disasters and cosmological events, people continue to set a date for the end of the world. A beginning precedes an ending; this is the basis of orthodox Christianity. With this ending there is a *renewed beginning*, which includes the resurrection of the flesh, as that is *believed to be what humans are*. It should be noted that most Christians do not really believe in a bodily resurrection, although it is inferred in prayers. An example can be cited in the Catholic Mass. The last line of the Nicene Creed states: 'We look for the resurrection of the dead, and the life of the world to come.' In Thomas 18, Yeshua makes it clear that if people do not realise where they originated from, then they do not understand there is no beginning or end. They are in a state of uninterrupted sleep. The question they ask is in error, because there is no end. When one stands at the beginning, where the soul exists, one stands at the end at the same time. When this is understood, humans will not taste death and they will truly live, according to Jesus' definition of the word *live*.

Science tells us energy cannot be created or destroyed; it can only be changed from one thing to another. The soul, with the *eyes* closed, asleep, is like this. If the soul is not awake to its reality then it is unable to free itself from the physical realm. This world is peoples only reference point, existence within it becomes a cyclical process of desiring, attaining and desiring again (Thomas 7). However, we should not reject our physical reality and the experiences therein. We need to experience these things to grow, to become *wealthy*, evident in Thomas 81 and 110.

Scientific discoveries show us that we are on the threshold of finding out the true nature of the quantum universe. The same is true of other dimensions. We also cannot disregard the likelihood of other lifeforms in our universe (and others), which may be on a similar path. When we recognise we have the same struggle, and the same lifeforce, we will be better equipped to learn from each other. After all, it was for the sake of the soul that sentient bodies came into existence (Thomas 29), so that they may facilitate the growth of this *Light*. The *motion and rest* through these physical bodies (Thomas 50) is the evidence of the Source's Light in us. Through attention to the disparity between the physical and spiritual realms, the eyes are opened and *we see the end at the beginning*.

19. Jesus said, "Congratulations to the one who came into being before coming into being.

If you become my disciples and pay attention to my sayings, these stones will serve you.

For there are five trees in Paradise for you; they do not change, summer or winter, and their leaves do not fall. Whoever knows them will not taste death."

People who come into the world aware of their spiritual nature are fortunate—they are not confused by, or enamoured of, the physical world. They enter into the world without being affected by it, as an observer or passerby (Thomas 42). As we encounter various personalities in our life's journey, we realise that there are different types of individuals. People might categorise these *types* by their star sign, or genetic legacy, giving them certain characteristics accordingly. They might be defined as being pragmatic, logical, driven, or creative and spiritual, etc. Whatever the reason, it cannot be denied that there are different personality types. In the first part of Thomas 19, Yeshua congratulates those who are *born with the ability to perceive abstract concepts*. The concepts within His sayings, required a certain type of characteristic to comprehend or, at the very least, appreciate. This is why Jesus tells His disciples that if they can pay attention to His sayings and learn from them, the teachings will become stones, which will *serve them*. The knowledge we gain can be used to build a fortress around us, protecting us from this world's distractions and allowing us to become *passersby*. Moreover, *stones* can be thrown at our adversaries, in our defence.

A tree can represent food, but it can also represent knowledge— as in the Garden of Eden myth. Thomas 19 infers there are *essential truths* the disciples will learn if they pay attention to Jesus' teachings. This knowledge is something that would *perpetually sustain* all who come to Yeshua, like a tree fruiting all year round. In truth, there is no tree that does not change, unless it exists in the realm of the Spirit, just as there is no summer or winter, but an uninterrupted spring. This *spring is the knowledge gained* through the Gospel of Thomas, because it renews and *sustains the life of the Spirit*. It is *The Perpetual Tree*.

Consider the drawing by Leonardo da Vinci, 'Vitruvian Man' c.1490 (originally conceived by Vitruvius, an ancient Greek architect). The drawing indicates the proportions of the human within two essential geometric shapes. It depicts two superimposed, full body images of the same male subject. One image is outstretched in a square, the other in a circle. We can interpret this image in the context of the Divine wisdom, which is implied in Thomas 19. The square is akin to the physical realm. It represents *definitive attributes* such as the four directions and the four essential, life-sustaining elements: earth, fire, water, and air. The circle, which encompasses the square, is one unbroken whole. It is of itself and has no beginning or end, which mirrors the mysteries of the Spirit realm. In the middle is a human, which represents the soul (the Son). The hands and feet can, at different times, either be in the square or in the circle, yet the head is always in the square—this is the problem. The human mind is enveloped in the physical realm. This prevents most people from entering into the circle—the sphere of the Spirit. Yeshua's primary goal was to teach people about the disparity between the square and the circle, the physical and the spiritual. This is the kind of wisdom that sustains the growth of the soul, like a fruiting tree might sustain the body. Da Vinci's 'Vitruvian Man' illustrates that we have access to both the physical and spiritual, through our actions and decisions. Our *experiences*, represented in the feet and hands, should nourish the mind, which can then transcend the physical barriers of this realm to see into the *eternal sphere*. People who have *come into being* have access to this sphere. This wisdom is also conveyed through the sayings of Thomas 81, 85, 103, and 110.

20. The disciples said to Jesus, "Tell us what Heaven's Kingdom is like."

He said to them, "It's like a mustard seed, the smallest of all seeds, but when it falls on prepared soil, it produces a large plant and becomes a shelter for birds of the sky."

Scientific exploration has shown us that electrons, protons, and neutrons are subatomic particles that make up atoms. So far, knowledge of what is inside and between the particles and why they *behave* as they do, is only hypothetical. Scientists attempt to prove a hypothesis by finding evidence—but how can we measure forces that, for example, have a gravitational effect, but do not emit or absorb light? This is the nature of Dark Matter, which makes up eighty percent of the entire universe. It is everywhere, yet we cannot experience it—for now. This as yet undetectable material is comparable to *the Source*, the one Jesus calls *Father*. If Yeshua were in this realm now, He would use language relative to what scientists are currently discovering. This does not support the Intelligent Design premise of a God that *consciously* made all things. Nature is a reflection of subtle influences from another realm, an iteration of an expanding layer, vibrating to the sounds of the Source. This is the thing we cannot experience, but intuitively respond to. In the time of Yeshua, this kind of discourse would have been considered heretical, if not irrational. For this reason, He had to carefully construct symbols and metaphors which would survive into a period where humans could understand them—this time is here, in the twenty-first century.

This saying can easily be compared to the way science explains the birth of the universe. Everything existed in one tightly bound mass, a singularity, in the endless expanse of space. Then it expanded out, growing and forming billions of galaxies over the eons. These are the *branches* that have become places for the birds to be in motion and rest. The universe follows the logic of another realm/dimension, one that is stable. Science shows us that gravity, just as it created the planets and stars, also holds galaxies in formation. It also pushes them apart by the smallest of margins, only enough to enable separate galaxies to form. If the gravitational effect within Dark Matter did not have this function, galaxies would float around freely, potentially taking the universe back to its early post 'Big Bang' period. As time moves forward, the formation of the universe is becoming more stable and ordered. It is conceivable that the universe will reach a point of parallel *oneness* with the other realms/dimensions. This does not mean the world we live in will be a part of this oneness. By this time, the sun likely will have consumed our planet (Thomas 111). The human life force, or soul, will have evolved to *live* past this material existence—or will have moved into other lifeforms and dimensions.

Science tells us a star is created from gases being drawn into one central point. Through tremendous pressure and heat, they ignite and become a sun/star. In a similar way, physical materials gather to form spherical planets. If we use this principle (physical materials aggregating to form cosmological bodies) to think about all energies that desire structure, we can see how the Spirit dimension is mirrored in the material/ physical dimension. This is also *reflected* in the way elements come together to become another thing, such as hydrogen and oxygen becoming water. When they are separate (one), they are not a force of creativity. Just as when we are apart from the Father/Source we are one. When we are with the Source, through the Holy Spirit, we are two. We see this mystery mirrored in the phenomena of male and female, whose sex cells need to be joined to create another. When people see themselves as neither male nor female, then they enter the Father's Kingdom (Thomas 22). At this point of recognition, we have become the *other*. To get to this point, we must be *like a baby*, which is naïve to this realm's weaknesses. Then we do not carry these notions with us into the realm that does not recognise gender.

The invisible source of Light, which is the soul (what we are), varies in strength from person to person. If we take Jesus' metaphor of the mustard seed, a very small spherical seed, we can see how the soul thrives on our *awareness* of it. Through this awareness people nurture growth, so the seed 'falls on prepared soil [and] it produces a large plant'. The soil is the important aspect of Thomas 20—it is where the roots are, where *growth is promoted*. The question, 'what [is] Heaven's Kingdom like?', is about the nature of the soul—we know this because in Thomas 3, Jesus tells us *we are the kingdom*, but do not see it.

The reference to 'shelter for birds of the sky' suggests enlightened people become a haven for souls who also seek to become one with God the Source. It is human nature to pass on knowledge—this is *The Perpetual Tree*—the seed that was thrown onto good soil, growing into this bounty (Thomas 9).

21. Mary said to Jesus, "What are your disciples like?"

He said, "They are like little children living in a field that is not theirs. When the owners of the field come, they will say, 'Give us back our field.' They take off their clothes in front of them in order to give it back to them, and they return their field to them.

For this reason I say, if the owners of a house know that a thief is coming, they will be on guard before the thief arrives and will not let the thief break into their house (their domain) and steal their possessions.

As for you, then, be on guard against the world. Prepare yourselves with great strength, so the robbers can't find a way to get to you, for the trouble you expect will come.

Let there be among you a person who understands.

When the crop ripened, he came quickly carrying a sickle and harvested it. Anyone here with two good ears had better listen!"

In Thomas 21, Yeshua shows us He was aware most of His disciples were incapable of comprehending His teachings, being fearful of their god and enamoured of this world. The disciples believed the world would be restored to paradise when their god came to judge the living and the dead. Jesus saw them as having no ownership of their spiritual heritage. They waited for someone to tell them when they must give up their *physical existence: 'take off their clothes*...in order to give *it* back...and they returned *their field...'* They saw their *physical body* as their identity. This relates to the concept of Adam being created from dust—dust that belongs to a creator god. Thomas 21 redresses where we actually come from—the realm of the Spirit.

The obstacles and diversions we encounter in our daily lives: the suffering under oppressive individuals, who have been consumed by the lion (Thomas 7)—these are the distraction, *the thieves* who will invade our house (the soul). It is a fact that when our bodies are put under stress, injury, or illness, we become distracted from spiritual concerns. These things steer us away from knowing the nature of our true selves. We can no longer be '*passersby*' (Thomas 42), or observers of the world; the powerful one (Thomas 98) has consumed us, like the lion consumes its prey. This is why we must guard ourselves against the thieves. We can do this by realising we are above all these obstacles—they cannot harm what we truly are. Our clothes may be damaged or removed, but what is underneath remains whole.

The idea that other powers are at play is another obstacle. Human mortality has forced people to measure the physical self, the reference point for knowing what they are, against the immensity of nature. Nature began to take on the face of God, particularly for those who wrote biblical texts, because nature appears to be so powerful in comparison to the vulnerable body. These illusions are also a barrier to a person's growth as a spiritual being, because they have allowed the *robbers* to enter their house and steal their possessions. The 'possessions' are our understanding of what matters—we are made of the same Light, which springs from the Father/Source and was seen in its fullness in Yeshua.

Interestingly, both the Buddha (Prince Siddhartha Gautama) c. 486 BCE and Jesus (in this gospel) wanted the individual to search within to truly live in peace. In both cases, their followers reverted to creating institutions and the practices surrounding them became the focus. Religions, which have become institutions, tend to serve a peripheral purpose for people seeking spiritual growth. They comfort, but do not sustain, the soul seeking enlightenment. Christian Churches provide solace when people are in mourning, ill, or seeking absolution. The contemporary Evangelical Churches provide dynamic prayer; their pop-music and high tech light shows give followers a hit of communal ecstasy, which parishioners crave like a drug. In both cases, the only time worshippers feel truly connected to their god is when they are in the venue or Church. By themselves, they are less able to attain the same *connection*; this is what such organisations rely on. The thieves, in this instance, are the leaders of these groups, who focus on how to fill their churches with people, rather than making the pursuit of spiritual realisation the objective. Their sermons are usually about banal human concerns relating to finances, relationships, and their *perceived* distance from their God. They do not speak of the essence which makes us like Jesus. They do not teach us how to fully realise this potential. Their selective knowledge does not recognise the truth presented in the Gospel of Thomas.

Some Christian Churches use Satan as a tool to scare people into believing in the power of their Church or doctrine. The irony is that people who have aligned themselves with a negative power are worshipping something that does not have power *itself*—other than *what people have given to it*. Faith is *the Source* here. The only negative forces are individuals who have made a poor choice, because they are enamoured of these four dimensions. They want to keep other souls in this realm. This realm is how they define what it is to *live*. In the Gospel of Thomas the definition of what it is *to live* is very different.

We should appreciate that in the Jewish faith, Satan is not looked upon as a fallen angel, creating obstacles from his own will or from a malevolent nature. To a Jewish person, Satan, or rather the *satan* – meaning accuser, is doing the bidding of their God. His purpose is to improve humanity's focus on overcoming obstacles with true faith and love of God. Remembering that Jesus was Jewish, we start to see a divide between the Jewish and Christian perceptions of this character and wonder: how did this become so distorted? From this schism, we can see how the authors of the New Testament had been influenced by the Greek myths of a malevolent deity, a deity the Gnostics erroneously saw as the god of the Old Testament. Evidently, these beliefs stemmed from *Plato's Cave* allegory. The *puppet master* became the malevolent demiurge *Yaldabaoth*. In the New Testament, we see the influence of this allegory appear in Paul's letters. Paul refers to the *elemental spirits (Stoicheia)* which he suggests were responsible for creating the Law— *which Jesus made redundant*. Yeshua saw humans as the only ones capable of true evil. He explains that this happens when the lion consumes the human and then presents as human (Thomas 7). In this state, the human becomes the mythologised Satan, an obstacle to the *true self* and to others.

We should also consider the conundrum of those who claim they require the rite of exorcism, or are deemed to require this rite. These 'possessed' individuals express in their actions the antithesis of the *perfect human*. The stereotypically abusive and physically violent behaviour is symbolic of the struggle between the intelligent, spiritual human and the *primal beast* humans evolved from. An analogy would be the battle between the *nature of the lion (Thomas 7) and the nature of the lamb*. How would it benefit 'Satan' to possess people and behave in this way? Logic suggests that if such a 'fallen spirit' existed it would be subtle about the way it makes people's lives difficult. The question then arises: are these 'possessions' really manifestations of a malevolent demon, living in darkness and fear, or is it an expression of the *individual's struggle* to overcome primal urges and fears? It is likely to be a combination of these two. The Gospel of Thomas points to this ongoing struggle to find and become the perfect human—like Jesus.

Satan was initially represented as a member of an angelic group, but then in successive narratives became an accuser who suggests, and later creates, obstacles for humans and for Jesus. As mentioned previously, the Jewish community continues to see this angel in a more positive, functional position. The Jewish text refers to '*the satan*' which means *prosecutor*, who is working on behalf of Yahweh (YHWH). Nowhere in the Old Testament (Torah) is '*the satan*' a source of evil, or referred to by the proper noun, *Satan*. This characteristic is erroneously linked to the serpent in the Garden of Eden, through the New Testament. The snake/serpent was the shrewdest creature in all creation. It was the antagonist in the Garden of Eden narrative, tempting Adam and Eve to eat from the tree of knowledge. This narrative reflects the way humans wrongly perceive their predicament in this existence as punishment for sinning. It makes sense that this sin might involve people's tendency to succumb to inherent egotism, insulting their creator by wanting to be like a god. Through the Gospel of Thomas, we see this narrative in a very different way. The snake/serpent represents the same qualities we see in the lion from Thomas 7. Its inability to disconnect from the surface (the earth, or forbidden tree in this narrative) is metaphoric—it is the problem humans struggle with constantly. However, we are creatures that have taken to walking on two legs, so that our head is the furthest from the ground. *This is symbolic of our potential* to be connected to the

Spirit realm—we can think and feel beyond the parameters of day-to-day survival. It is also the reason birds are considered spiritual entities—they possess the ability to rise above this earthly plane. The serpent in the Garden of Eden offers what most people want: a quick solution to life's conundrum. If they were like God, they would want for nothing and know everything. Jesus tells us, the journey through this realm will have its difficulties, but these can be used to enrich our understanding and appreciation of the Spirit. Through this process, humans learn they are the wealth. The shell people inhabit keeps their heart and mind on the ground–this is the cause of the *poverty*. In the Christian version of the Jewish text (Old Testament) we see the proper noun of '*Satan*' replace '*the satan*'. In changing the word for this character's purpose (being *the accuser*) to a name, the name becomes imbued with negativity. This angel no longer works for Yahweh, he works for himself. Satan becomes an adversary of God and humans, working from his own volition. In the narrative of Job 1:6 we see Satan referred to as one who serves God: 'One day when the sons of God came to attend to Yahweh, among them came Satan.' Satan suggested to God that Job would not remain loyal if everything he had was taken away. The implication was that Job only loved God because he had material wealth and good health—his love of God would cease if he lost these things. God agreed to test Job and put everything Job had in Satan's control. This was the beginning of Satan's career as the source of evil—the adversary of man and God too. Here, we must recognise our definition of what is *good* is tainted by the natural world, which is not in itself evil. It is an obstacle because of its chaotic and unpredictable *nature*. As such, defining natural disasters as works of evil is incorrect—only humans and entities inhabiting other realms are capable of evil. Sometimes humans are Satan, working only for the self (Thomas 7). God does not place one person or group above another; the situation one exists in is reliant on chance. What one does with this situation is completely up to the individual. It can be a *place* of great wealth.

Eventually, this ethereal being called Satan becomes an antagonist who seeks to make people's lives miserable out of jealousy and spite. This concept also comes through the Islamic tradition—the angel who would not bow down before man, as God asked him to. In the Synoptic Gospels, Satan becomes a symbol of Jesus' destruction and a way for the gospel writers, after Mark, to vilify the Jewish people. This is evident in the way each of the gospels successively shows that the Sanhedrin, rather than the Roman Emperor (through his people) was the cause for Jesus' execution. The vilification of the Jewish community climaxes in Luke, written by a gentile who felt marginalised by the Jewish Christians. Elaine Pagels 'The Origin of Satan', First Vintage Books Edition, May 1996, develops an extensive analysis and discussion on this topic. Furthermore, we see in the Gospel of John a very disturbing statement, which some Christians have interpreted as giving Satan the position of a deity—the Antichrist. In John Chapter 14:30-31, Jesus says: 'I shall not talk to you much longer, *because the prince of this world is on his way*. He has no power over me, but the world must recognise that I love the Father and that I act just as the Father commanded.' When we look at this statement through the lens of the Gospel of Thomas, we see that it is not about Satan, the Antichrist; it describes the men who have been consumed by the lion. The context of this pronouncement would place the Emperor or Caesar of the time in the position of 'prince of this world'. The author of Revelations also made these references, calling the Emperor Nero the beast and identifying him with the numbers '666'. The early Christians used this number coding method so that the non-Christians would not know to whom they were referring. This hostile rhetoric could have gotten them killed in a most barbaric way.

In the 'Temptation of Jesus' narrative, Satan offers Jesus the kingdoms and riches of the world, mirroring a common experience of all humans. The symbol of a malevolent spirit, who claims the earth for his own, reflects the writer's struggle to explain what may have happened during Jesus' forty days and nights in the desert. The disciples would have been aware of this event, but it was apparently not passed onto the gospel authors. This is evident when we look at how this event is embellished in successive gospels. In Mark 1:12-13 (the first gospel written), Jesus is baptized by John, then goes into the desert where Satan tempts Him. This is where the story ends. In Matthew 4:9, the narrative is extended to describe how Satan said to Jesus: 'I will give you all these...' In the last Synoptic Gospel, The Gospel of Luke, the author corrects the implication that Satan is the owner and ruler of earth. In Luke 4:6 Satan says to Jesus: 'I will give you all this power and their splendour, for *it has been handed over to me*, for me to give it to anyone I choose.' The author of Luke links the way God hands over Job's wealth to Satan in the Old Testament story—enabling the elaboration on the sojourn into the desert narrative, but ignoring that *the satan* was a heavenly accuser in the original Job myth.

Jesus' temptation by Satan is *a metaphor representing this world*. Jesus was flesh and blood; like any man, He would have experienced pleasures and pain associated with this world (Thomas 28). He knew that He could have had an affluent and powerful role on this planet with the committed followers He was accumulating. Withdrawal from the world is common practice by ascetics in significant cultures. It is a pathway to knowing the true nature of self, away from the distractions of everyday life. However, as we shall see, it is not a necessary process for all to experience (Thomas 27). The *root cause of "Satan" is the world and its deceptive beauty, power, and pleasures*. It is also primal man, who is still within humanity. The fears primal man experienced is *the trouble humans may expect*. They arrive in our everyday interactions with the physical world and each other. The writers of the Synoptic Gospels only had the Satan of Job as a reference point—they would not have understood such a metaphor. This reinforces the notion that they were influenced by Greek myths. Through *77th Pearl: The Perpetual Tree*, the Gospel of Thomas opens our eyes to these truths.

In Mark 8:31 Jesus openly states: 'the Son of man was destined to suffer grievously...and to be put to death, and after three days to rise again'. Peter argues with Jesus, who rebukes him: 'Get behind me, Satan! You are thinking not as God thinks, but as human beings do.' Jesus is telling us that the nature of *Satan* is to think as one who is infatuated by this world. This person's decisions are driven by its allure. This also confirms that *people had become the adversary of the Spirit of* Yeshua. Instead of an accuser (the satan) making an individual assess their love of God, people had inadvertently become the persona, 'Satan'. The direction people take is intrinsically connected to the way they *perceive* this life; they alone can make these choices. Humans need to be on guard against the robbers, which manifest in various forms and have the same goal—to get in our way, to block our path.

When you are on your *Sabbath*, look past this world and its distractions to *The Perpetual Tree*, which is beyond the horizon. When you are not in a place of rest (Sabbath), use the soil you are in to grow and flourish.

22. Jesus saw some babies nursing. He said to his disciples, "These nursing babies are like those who enter the (Father's) kingdom."

They said to him, "Then shall we enter the (Father's) kingdom as babies?"

Jesus said to them, "When you make the two into one, and when you make the inner like the outer and the outer like the inner, and the upper like the lower, and when you make male and female into a single one, so that the male will not be male nor the female be female, when you make eyes in place of an eye, a hand in place of a hand, a foot in place of a foot, an image in place of an image, then you will enter [the kingdom]."

Aspects of Thomas 22 relate to the work of Rudolf Steiner (1861-1925), a well-published philosophical scholar. Although some of his works have been contentious, several of his theories are still worthy of our attention. Steiner saw a gap in the knowledge conventional science could attain. He practised something he called a *science of the spirit*, which drew on knowledge derived from a *psychic memory* of events long past. The gap can be identified in the following way: conventional science hypotheses that creation is a combination of chance and natural selection, but this thesis does not stand up to logic. Let us suppose that *by chance* chemicals were created and they combined to form a 'primordial soup' and, given the appropriate environment, life was created, in the form of single cell organisms. Science has not explained *where* the chemicals came from in the first instance and *what made* the chemicals combine to create an organism. Defining these events as chance would seem more remote when one considers the complexities of the human brain. What *is* thought; where does it start? Conventional science would refer to a series of complex neurological processes, involving chemicals and electrical impulses, but this does not explain *their existence* or their *motivation to do* what they do. Over the past seventy years, UFO/UAP researchers have concluded related phenomena can be both physical and non-physical – *they* can exist in the ephemeral spaces that we might define as consciousness. The spaces between the smallest particles technology can detect is the substance of the soul and consciousness. It is the influencing force on all things, It is the anatomy of God, the Source.

Steiner successfully demonstrates that there is indeed a gap in knowledge. In his book, 'Cosmic Memory: Prehistory of Earth and Man' (Steinerbooks, 1987), he describes the influences of the realm of the Father/Source (Steiner does not use the term 'Father' or 'Source') upon the creation of everything we know in this universe. Unfortunately, the Gospel of Thomas was discovered twenty years after Steiner's death; it certainly would have been of immense interest and value to his work. Thomas 22 reflects much of what Steiner established *before* the discovery of the Gospel of Thomas. This demonstrates that he truly was linked to a psychic memory, which he admitted could not always be accurate, because of the foggy nature of this information. Steiner describes the process by which the sexes came about stating: 'For only in the course of time did the forms of man and woman develop from older, basic forms in which human beings were neither the one nor the other, but rather *were both at once.*' Ibid p.84.

In Thomas 22, Yeshua tells us it is our perception of who we really are that needs to be transfigured, in order for us to enter *the kingdom*. This saying gives us the best indication of why Yeshua gave up His body to be destroyed by those people representing earthly power—the lion in Thomas 7. His sacrifice teaches us about the true nature of what we are and why our sins are negated—because we are above them. Emotions and desires driven by the physical world are the catalyst of sin.

For example, sexual desires have been an issue for many generations, particularly for those who share the Old Testament edicts. Masturbation was considered a sin because of morality narratives in the Old Testament. At the forefront is the story of Onan, a minor biblical character in Genesis 38:1-10. Onan made the decision not to impregnate his brother's widow, spilling his seed on the ground. The story asserts that Onan died prematurely because of his actions. We know that these stories were designed to encourage the growth of populations within that culture, yet religious groups continue to use this narrative to cause people to accumulate guilt and shame. This guilt hinders the individual from understanding their true nature. This is what Thomas 22 seeks to dismiss from people's minds—we are not bound by the needs and limitations of the flesh. Guilt gives the flesh power over the soul. It is a device used by the entities living in darkness, keeping souls tied to this realm. It is also the poverty blinding people from the wealth—*what* they are.

Perhaps the sin Onan brought upon his conscience was that he left his sister-in-law childless—according to the story, because the children would not be considered his. However, it is likely he did not want his children to have to split their inheritance with another half-sibling. Onan would have felt duty-bound to support this woman and child. Ironically, or perhaps predictably, people have looked to the physical act of *spilling seed on the ground* as the sin, rather than the act of pride and greed.

Thomas 22 alludes to a stripping of gender and, by association, sexuality too. In this realm, the procreation of life requires a male and female union of reproductive cells. This physical act, supposedly instigated by God, has caused significant damage to people who are born with desires for the same sex, or both. Since most of our understanding of the nature of God is dictated by what we can observe in this world, people have mistakenly come to the conclusion that it is the *intention* of God to have only heterosexual unions. All other unions must therefore be a sin or wrong. People chose to ignore that homosexual activity occurs in nature too; there are examples of animals of the same sex coupling. This is not a choice they have made.

Although a number of cultures have accepted homosexuality, at the early part of the twenty-first century, there are still places where groups actively discriminate against Lesbian, Gay, Bisexual, Transgender, Queer, and Intersex individuals. The people who vilify the LGBTQI community do not see that they damage their own potential to realise what they truly are, as is evident in Thomas 22. By hurting the soul of those whom they subordinate, they damage their own soul, for we are all connected. This is the tragedy of the generations that have been misled by people who are ruled by fear. Where there is fear, *the Satan men have created* thrives. The men who created such dogma and perpetuated it were in error. The religious leaders who continue to follow this path are, evidently, incapable of transfiguring their perceptions, away from their physical form.

The four Synoptic Gospels do not directly reference the moral question of homosexuality. However, we do see references appear in the New Testament, through the apostle Paul. The orthodoxy uses a section of Paul's letters to the Romans to argue that Jesus disapproved of homosexuality. It is not the aim of *77th Pearl: The Perpetual Tree* to erode the integrity of the Bible authors. However, it is necessary to analyse the context of the rhetoric we are presented with in these texts. Stepping back and looking at the big picture can be difficult, when we feel that it might denigrate the truth of something we want to be on a spiritual basis. This kind of objective analysis is necessary, particularly when we know that the text in question has caused harm to individuals or groups. To begin, let us look at what Romans 1:25-29 states:

'...because they exchanged God's truth for a lie and have worshipped and served the creature instead of the Creator, who is blessed forever. Amen.

That is why God abandoned them to degrading passions:

why their women have exchanged natural intercourse for unnatural practices; and the men, in a similar fashion, too, giving up normal relations with women, are consumed with passion for each other, men doing shameful things with men and receiving in themselves due reward for their perversion.

In other words, since they would not consent to acknowledge God, God abandoned them to their unacceptable thoughts and indecent behaviour.

And so now they are steeped in all sorts of injustice, rottenness, greed and malice; full of envy, murder, wrangling, treachery and spite.'

Paul was a Pharisee, initially a persecutor of those who believed in Jesus. Being a Pharisee, he would have also been a servant of the Jewish Law. Paul was not a direct apostle of Yeshua but became a champion of Jesus as the Saviour for the gentiles, *by faith*. Paul argues the stature of the gentiles through the *grace* (free, unmerited favour of God) Yeshua attained by His sacrifice. We should note that none of the New Testament was actually written by a direct apostle of Jesus. For example, Mark, an apostle of Peter, wrote the first gospel 70-90 years after Jesus' death. Much of what we see in Paul's letters is a theological struggle—how could he reconcile the Jewish Law for Jewish followers of Jesus and include the gentiles, who were outside of the Law (uncircumcised and unschooled in dietary practices and moral conduct). Galatians 2:21: 'I am not setting aside God's grace as of no value; it is merely that if saving justice comes through the Law, Christ died needlessly.' And in Galatians 5:4: 'once you seek to be reckoned as upright through the Law, then you have separated yourself from Christ, you have fallen away from grace.'

If we read Galatians 4:3, '...as long as we were still under age, we were enslaved to the elemental principles of this world', we see how Paul *deconstructs* Jewish Law as a device which was ultimately created by ethereal beings, known as Stoicheia. This is a Greek term which can be interpreted as demonic angels or beings that control elements within the physical realm. Paul concludes that the Stoicheia were to blame for creating the Jewish Law, which he surmised heightened the effectiveness of sin. Galatians 3:10: '...all those who depend on the works of the Law are under a curse, since scripture says: Accursed be he who does not make what is written in the book of the Law effective, by putting it into practice.' He comes to this conclusion by observing how the laws are associated with physical *parameters*, which are difficult to adhere to, all the while recognising the conundrum that *all* sin was forgiven through Yeshua's sacrifice. Interestingly, the reference to malevolent spirit beings reflects the Gnostic thesis. This is evidence of how the gospel authors were influenced by Greek mythology. In Galatians 4:9 Paul reiterates: 'whereas now that you have come to recognise God—or rather, be recognised by God—how can you now turn back again to those powerless and bankrupt elements whose slaves you now want to be all over again?' It would seem that Paul did indeed familiarise himself with the Greek myths, probably to argue a position using concepts the Gentiles could understand. His discourse attempted to give the Gentiles a sense of importance, by suggesting that they are the chosen ones, just as much, if not more (in Galatians), than the Jewish people.

Paul affirms the Gentiles' importance. He proposes that Sarah, Abraham's very old wife, *allegorically represents the mother of the lineage* that would have claim over the other Jerusalem, which is not of this world (Galatians 4:21-27). In this way the servant of Abraham, Hagar, gave rise to the nation who claims Jerusalem on Earth—her child's *conception was purely physical.* Since Sarah's child was conceived in her old age, *through God's help*, it follows that the Gentiles would be brought into grace *through Jesus' intervention* in this world. Galatians 3:16-17:

> 'Now the promises were addressed to Abraham and his progeny. The words were not and to his progenies in the plural, but in the singular; and to your progeny, which means Christ. What I am saying is this: once a will had been long ago ratified by God, the Law, coming four hundred and thirty years later, could not abolish it and so nullify its promise.'

Paul makes a strong case for the Gentiles being the chosen people ('and to your progeny, which means Christ'), rather than the Jews, who saw themselves as the chosen *progenies.* He suggests that the promise was made for one, not many, by pointing out the use of the singular—progeny. Of course, most contemporary scholars accept that Jesus was not the lineage of David, because He was known as *Jesus of Nazareth.* It was the author of Luke who engineered the story of a census. The story sees Jesus born in Bethlehem, fulfilling the prophecy relating to His lineage. As mentioned previously, there is no evidence of such a census happening. The question arises: would it even be feasible for a heavily pregnant woman to travel such a distance on a donkey? These facts should not denigrate the importance of the man we know as Jesus/Yeshua. However, it does show us how the gospel authors tried to place Him into the Old Testament prophecies. Indeed, it was Yeshua Himself who used the prophecies to gather a following, but His definition of the *Saviour* was very different to that of His Jewish contemporaries.

The letters to the Galatians, by Paul, were an attempt to curb the influence of the Jewish apostles of Yeshua, who preached a Jewish form of Christianity. The Jewish followers of Yeshau would have suggested that one had to become Jewish, circumcised, and follow dietary and moral laws to be saved. In Galatians, Paul constructed a strong argument against this position. In doing so, Paul put himself in a position where the Jewish Christians started to resent him. Scholars have suggested that Paul, being aware of the negative feelings toward his discourse with the Galatians, turned his attention from Jerusalem to Rome. It is generally believed that the apostle Peter was not necessarily the instigator of the Christian movement in Rome, but that it started in small independent groups. It was these groups that Paul wanted to embrace, as they were gentiles and, at that point, were free of a patriarch. At the same time, Paul needed to demonstrate that he was not antinomian; therefore, we see him attempt to retract his erroneous rhetoric about the Law (Romans 3:30-31). This was achieved by restating the importance of the Jewish moral laws in the letters to the Romans. However, this is not what we see in Romans 1:25-29. Here, we see an *opening observation* about the people in Rome, who were not believers of Christ or of one God.

The Jewish Law had much to do with moral codes of conduct. Paul was seen to be arguing the Law created a place for sin to breed. For this reason, people were suggesting Paul was implying they should give in to sinful urges. This is evident in the text Romans 3:8: '...the slanderous report...that we teach that one should do evil that good may come of it. In fact such people are justly condemned.' In the letters to the Romans, particularly after Chapter 1, Paul restates the importance of moral laws. In Romans 1:25-29, Paul *talks about the Romans*, who did not believe in *the one, true God*. Indeed, we do know the Romans of this period were involved in polytheism and experimental in their sexual practices, to say the least. What is written in Romans 1:25-29 is not an intentional condemnation of the Gay Community, but rather a warning about loose morals and *practices*, which can lead to disease and social corruptibility. Paul is saying that if one follows a hedonistic lifestyle, without *moral codes* of conduct, one will endure physical and mental anguish. This is not anything we do not know to be true in the twenty-first century. We have seen how sexually transmitted diseases can destroy lives if unhealthy behaviours are not curbed through responsible practices. This caution can be extrapolated to all activities in the physical world when we consider how overindulging in food, alcohol, or even wealth accumulation, can cause people to become physically and or mentally unwell.

Ultimately, Paul needed to *mesh together* the necessity of the Jewish Law and the concept of *grace given to all* through Jesus' sacrifice. This necessity, as shown here in a brief commentary, came from a need for diplomacy in order to maintain a tenuous position within the seminal Jewish and Gentile Christian communities. It is important to look at Paul in this light, since he is considered the reason for Christianity being what it is at the early part of the twenty-first century. Protestant reformers Calvin and Luther saw Paul's letters as evidence for why *dogma is damaging* to Jesus' message—love of God, above all else. If we take the sayings in the Gospel of Thomas as the only *real intentions of Jesus*, we can understand how Paul's letters could be damaging to the truth Jesus wanted the world to embrace. The Gospel of Thomas is free of narrative or political influences—this makes it reliable. For the seeker, it is important to examine these things personally. It is difficult to do this in the context of these commentaries, beyond what is absolutely necessary to illustrate a point. In this instance, we see that words, when put into context, suddenly have layers of new meaning, disarming *seemingly* toxic verses.

The Old Testament makes specific judgements about sexuality, directed towards men (Leviticus 18:22). This is because the men who wrote the texts were apparently heterosexual and, as with the story of Onan, concerned about the expansion of their community. They had no understanding of the damage they were incurring, because of their selective observations of the physical world, telling them their proclamation was correct. Yeshua came to show us that our reference point (this world) is a flawed and fractured mirror. This world is of its own nature, encompassing cause and effect. Humans are of their own separate nature—this is the soul. Thomas 22 reveals that people who vilify others because of their sexual orientation are without understanding. Gender is not who we are. If we are not man or woman, then whom we take as our life partner, for example, cannot be determined by gender. To do so *destroys the truth of the kingdom*, that is, we are not the flesh—*we are a soul*.

In Thomas 22, just as in other sayings in this gospel, Jesus speaks to our generation. He knew His contemporaries were not capable of understanding or perceiving the true nature of the kingdom. The disciples' perception of a kingdom was built of stones, a temple of worship, on a mount. When they heard Yeshua speak the word 'live' they thought of it as our physical life on this planet, a manifestation our senses could experience and our eyes could describe. This is what most disciples would have understood as the kingdom—something tangible. When Jesus spoke of rebuilding the temple in three days, He alluded to His resurrection in Spirit. This is the thing worthy of worship. This is the thing worthy of understanding—the truth of the kingdom, within us.

Thomas 22 has a correlation to the Buddhist text *Heart of Wisdom* by Geshe Kelsang Gyatso (Tharpa Publications 2001). Gyatso describes the way we should perceive all objects so their form becomes a construct of the mind within this realm. Since this realm is an illusion of reality, the conclusion is obvious.

In perceiving all physical matter in this way, we awaken the understanding that all things are actually only a perception of what they *truly* are. Put simply, if one breaks down any material to its smallest components (atoms) and then goes beyond this, one is left with nothing of substance. This practice is beneficial as it opens the inner eye to the truth of this realm. It reflects the wisdom of the Buddha, who extended a bridge out from this realm, to meet the one Yeshua extended from the realm of the Spirit.

Significantly, in Thomas 22, Yeshua emphasises the point about the physical body. When we recognise the flesh as something which clothes the soul, the thing that we cannot point to, then we are set free. A baby is naïve to its nature as a mortal creature of physical substance. A baby has no notion of being unworthy of a patriarchal god, due to inherent *failings*, because it has not been taught this misinformation. Only the soul on its way to becoming a Spirit is perfect. *The soul is what we really are.* As we see here, the body and the world it exists in can never be perfect, unlike the soul, which is from the *Father's Light*. As a baby grows, it becomes tainted by the world, discovers it is fallible and can suffer and incur injury, both physical and emotional. Jesus asks, what if we could maintain that naivety? How much easier would it be to know our true selves if we had not been deceived by our society and environment?

What if we could see the genders as necessary vehicles for continuing the reproduction of bodies? A manifestation of the physical world and its mechanisms of evolution. Yeshua tells us that we are not male or female. We are in fact a soul, which can be both or neither. When we replace our perception of what a hand is, or what a foot is, and what controls these, then we are open to the nature of the Spirit. When we can think of the image we see in the mirror as a manifestation of physical phenomenon and see past it to the true self, then we enter the *kingdom*, the realm of consciousness.

How do we make the outer like the inner and the inner like the outer? We can start by recognising that our bodies, and the physical world, break down to elements, which are composed of atoms. Past this, what can exist? If we had to point to ourselves, where do we point? The things we might point to are a conglomeration of cells, but they are not the conscious us—aware of this disparity.

23. Jesus said, "I shall choose you, one from a thousand and two from ten thousand, and they will stand as a single one."

Thomas 23 is linked to Thomas 4: 'many of the first will be last and will become a single one.' Thomas 23 has a similar tone of frustration. Here, we see Yeshua give His contemporaries a caution. This warning related to how the majority of His contemporaries were incapable of comprehending His teachings. At the dawn of the twenty-first century, His caution is still relevant.

To appreciate Jesus' lament, one only has to notice people who align themselves to a particular faith and see how these individuals *habitually and mindlessly* practice this faith. This is not true for all people, but a significant number do just go through the motions. This is what Jesus warns against when He asks that the Sabbath is kept sacred in Thomas 27. The Sabbath is a *space in time*, for the spiritual aspect of the self to connect with the thing we cannot point to. This saying also relates to people who are not interested in anything they cannot experience with their senses. They often refer to themselves as 'atheist' and will not believe something unless science can prove it. The difficulty with science is that it can only work with the physics of this dimension. However, there are winds of change on the horizon, with the advent of quantum physics and links to consciousness.

In Thomas 23, Yeshua makes an observation about the general population. He is troubled by how so few people desire to delve into the mysteries of existence–a difficult conundrum for most people. We know that Yeshua *wants us to knock on this door* (Thomas 94), so it is every person's choice. In making this decision Yeshua chooses us, through the spiritual *link* made in the process. For the people who do not make this choice, their soul will 'stand as a single one.' This will not be a case of damnation, fire, and brimstone, but a *fading into the whole*. They become part of the ubiquitous whole, which simply exists. They are not connected to God, the Source, through the collective consciousness we know as the Holy Spirit.

Yeshua came to show us a glimpse into the unknown through these teachings. If we meditate on the mysteries of these sayings, and begin to draw in the Source's Light then we gently come to *life*, as defined by Yeshua. Through this process, the one *becomes two* (Thomas 11).

24. His disciples said, "Show us the place where you are, for we must seek it."

He said to them, "Anyone here with two ears had better listen! There is light within a person of light, and it shines on the whole world. If it does not shine, it is dark."

Yeshua implies that there are differences in people, differences in *the Light* which represents their awareness of the kingdom—the collective consciousness. People who seek the truth have the Light within them. They have brought out what is within them, that thing will save them, as we see in Thomas 70. As they walk on this path the Light of God, the Source, aggregates into their soul and becomes a *living Spirit*. People whose Light does not shine on the world are consumed by the lion from Thomas 7. They have no knowledge of truth and will not seek it—these things are foreign to them. They have the potential to change, but it must be their decision. People seeking the connection to the Father's Light can only observe these dim souls and pity them for their suffering. They are lessons for our growth. Enlightened people can recognise the difference with their contentment compared to the constant struggle for happiness in others: a feeling they never truly attain, because they search for contentment in physical things, which ultimately perish or fade.

It is important to consider the question the disciples ask and the way Yeshua responds. They ask Him to describe the *place* where He is, so that they may strive to get to this *place*. Jesus' answer tells us that their question comes from misunderstanding. There is no *place* in the realm of the Spirit. It does not exist as this world does, It does not follow the same laws this universe does. There is no linear time, as time is a physical phenomenon. There is no up or down as the earth and the sky define these. Instead, Yeshua speaks about Light—but what does this mean? Are we literally a light that shines like a lamp? Like most of these sayings, a metaphoric rather than literal analysis is required. The Light that Yeshua makes reference to is symbolic of an immaterial thing. Notice the disciples' question refers to *a place* they think Yeshua belongs to. Spirits who are enamoured of the physical realm think of *a place*, rather than a holistic presence and connectedness. We see this in Mark 5, the story of the man possessed by many demons. The demons beg Yeshua not to cast them out of the land, but into a drove of swine. This story reflects the *desire for a place*, which in the material realm is not permanent.

Christians think of Jesus as the Light of this world, but it is not the same physical light that we obtain from our nearest star—the Sun. His teachings are a beacon guiding the soul; His aim is to shepherd humanity *through* this realm by His Light, His wisdom. This world is *the one* so beguiling to the human's physical senses that it overcomes their soul. A person's movement through this realm is difficult, but is necessary for their growth. People must remember this world is a poor reflection of the other dimensions. The physical realm attempts to mirror the realm of the Spirit, as it has evolved over time. However, by its nature this physical universe will expire as it cannot be sustained. This realm is the unstable outer layer of the Source, which has moved into the abyss to create the universe as people know it. Humans are spiritual beings, so they struggle to rationalise this existence. For this reason, those who share the Abrahamic lineage have created mythologies which look to a renewal of this world–which is the cursed paradise. Yeshua teaches us that this cannot be—a carcass will always remain a carcass. Only the soul can be resurrected to a renewed life as a spirit. The myths about an interventionist god have seen people in government deny important issues, such as climate change. This is another reason why Yeshua's revelations in the Gospel of Thomas are being revealed at this time, to foster a common-sense approach.

Our journey to growth is constant; Yeshua explains the evidence of the Source in us 'is motion and rest' (Thomas 50). The soul is in motion when it is in a body for the purposes of its growth, to *become wealthy*. The enlightened Spirit rests when it is not in a sentient body. To become reliant on one existence is damaging and limiting. Jesus reveals the truth of human-kind's predicament. In doing so, He reveals what is hidden from us—that which we cannot physically discern, because it is not of the material realm. He *reveals invisible Light* through the process of knowledge and understanding. Light is wisdom, connected to God, the Source, the Son (all beings seeking enlightenment), and the Holy Spirit (the conduit, which links the Source and Son). The Holy Spirit is of prime importance and constitutes *the source of the Light*—wisdom, knowing, the collective consciousness.

Where there is physical light we can see clearly what is around us, not unlike the child who might fear the dark sleeping with a light on. There is no fear of the unknown. In *the Light* we see and have knowledge of where we are. Physical light also allows for the growth of many things; we depend on it for our body's growth and health. This is similar to the invisible Light. The Light is created by knowledge of truth, sustaining the soul, coming to life in Spirit. This Light is also what connects us to the Source and Yeshua. When a person understands, they are no longer afraid. Their eyes are opened and they see for the first time. The human becomes two, with the Source/Father. The way physical light mirrors the *positive effects* of spiritual Light is, again, evidence of how this realm mirrors the *inner realm* of the Father's Kingdom. Physical phenomena are an *imitation*, their origin coming from the realm of the Spirit. In this sense, the Source is *the creator*, but *It* is not the conscious designer of this realm (Thomas 97). This realm follows a logic and an order that is the mirror image of the other, but it uses unstable, volatile material to create this *re-imaging*. When Yeshua states, '…it shines on the whole world. If it does not shine, it is dark', He makes it clear the Light that is truly important is the one of *wisdom*. This Light cannot be seen, but when it is felt and fostered, by prayer and/or meditation, it shines on the whole world—the world of the Father's Kingdom. This is *the place* where Yeshua exists and where human souls came from.

People who refuse to recognise the Light within can create darkness in the world. They might do this in the name of their jealous and vengeful god, or through their own ambition for power. These souls remain in darkness, returning to the physical realm. The one Yeshua calls *Father* does not recognise these souls. The lion in Thomas 7 has consumed them and they do not recognise the Father/Source. These people have been misled by their fear and love of this realm. The substance of the soul is in all things. It is light and dark, under a stone, inside a piece of wood (Thomas 77). It is also the energy that binds and flows through the universe. In a sense, we are fragments of the Source's Light clinging to a rock, fighting the current to hang onto this existence. The problem is, the soul is the *wealth* and it does not end. That is why the soul working towards becoming a Spirit is at odds with the physical. The world and body are the carcass and poverty respectively, relying on chaos and physical coupling to continue (Thomas 56 and 80).
Stars and planets were created by physical matter being drawn into one point, creating their mass and structure. Similarly, the soul aggregates its energy from the place that it origi-nated from. It is *a place of knowing*. People who are filled with

questions are hearing the soul within. Starting the journey by reading, comparing, and listening to the intuitive, logical self, one begins to learn. Eventually the Light shines brightly and *the human Spirit swims freely.*

25. Jesus said, "Love your friends like your own soul, protect them like the pupil of your eye."

It is difficult to be sure of the people Yeshua considered to be authentic friends, but Thomas was certainly close to Him. We can say this with confidence, because Thomas intuitively felt that Jesus' words were important enough to be recorded as they were spoken. The preservation of these sayings as quotes, cryptic as some are, required a great love and respect for Yeshua, because a number of them would have been interpreted as heresy and against traditional thinking and practice.

In the New Testament Gospels and some Gnostic Gospels, there are a number of examples where certain disciples are claimed to have a special relationship with Jesus. Since we know the original disciples did not write the New Testament Gospels, and significant time had passed, it is logical to see them as embellished and inaccurate. This is the beauty of the Gospel of Thomas—even though the date of the original text may be contentious, the sayings were not open to editing or embellishment, unlike a narrative text. For example, one might question why in the Gospel of John 20:29, Thomas is portrayed as someone who doubts the resurrection of Yeshua for the purpose of stating: 'Blessed are those who have not seen and yet believe.' Note that the resurrection in the New Testament is said to be a bodily one, and so Thomas had to *physically* touch the wounds of Jesus to believe. Knowing what is in the Gospel of Thomas, we can ascertain that Yeshua would not have had a physical body when 'resurrected'. If He wanted Thomas to recognise Him, Thomas would have in an instant. The author(s) of the Gospel of John were aware of the Gospel of Thomas and its inference to a *spiritual resurrection* rather than a bodily one. To the authors, who would have tried to persuade the reader of Jesus' Divine power, a physical bringing-back-to-life is much more logical and impressive.

In Thomas 13, Thomas responded to Jesus' question of '*what [He is] like*' with a statement that allowed for the author(s) of John to label him a doubter. Thomas's response was: 'my mouth is utterly unable to say what you are like.' To the authors of the New Testament texts, this would have been a very strange and naive response. They would have been sure Yeshua came to this world to fulfil the prophecies in the Old Testament. The disciples' responses to Yeshua's question is proof of the knowledge they were referencing, comparing Him to something they already understood. *Thomas did not use this reference point*, this is why the author(s) of the Gospel of John could create such a premise. Their intentions came from a desire to show faith in Yeshua's divinity, which was not an ambiguous concept—it was foretold (for them) in the Old Testament (Torah).

Thomas not having the language to describe what Jesus was like, lifted him above all the other disciples and made him worthy of *the secret teachings of the living Jesus*. Consider how in John 11:16, the story of Lazarus, the author writes: 'Then Thomas—known as the Twin—said to the other disciples, "Let us also go to die with him."' Both the names Didymos and Thomas mean 'the twin', this is the author of John definitively pointing to the author of Thomas. In John 11, Jesus raises Lazarus *from* the dead. This action contradicted the teachings in the Gospel of Thomas and the author of John, it would appear, was aware of this contradiction. The author of John suggests that Thomas would embrace death, rather than life, but the author of John did not understand what Yeshua meant by the word '*live*'. Yeshua's request to 'love your friends like your own soul, protect them like the pupil of your eye' underpins the notion that the person who is your friend is *innately a part of who you are*. This is an affirmation of our *spiritual connectedness*, and something these authors could not grasp. After all, Jesus was not concerned with creating a circle of friends. He was here to teach us about humanity's true nature—the Spirit. This is why Yeshua tells us to *love the soul and protect it from damage*. Notice the soul is referred to as a possession, which we all carry, that (like our true friend) needs protection. The Holy Spirit, the collective consciousness, wants to link with the soul—the sparks which are remnants of the Source, so *it* becomes whole, complete. Through this action, the one become two.

This need to illustrate Divine power, overriding the laws of nature, shows a lack of understanding on the part of the New Testament authors. The disparity between the authors' comprehension of who we truly are, as distinct from the physical world, is clear. In John 20:28, Thomas is said to have proclaimed, 'My Lord and my God', after he touches Jesus' wounds; this is at odds with the Thomas we know in the Gospel of Thomas. It appears as though the author of John has put words into Thomas's mouth. Thomas would not have seen Yeshua as a god, separated from who he was. This would negate the secret teachings given to him. The point of the story in John works as a polemic for Yeshua's bodily resurrection. However, as Jesus has inferred in these sayings, when *He became two (died)*, He came to life (resurrected–in Spirit). This is what the enlightened person should expect too. Yeshua could have *appeared* as flesh in the disciples' *perceived reality* if He had wanted to. This does not mean the flesh that clothed Jesus was reanimated—such a premise is what the author of John wants us to believe. Why would the flesh be resurrected if Jesus' abhorrence of it suggested it was flawed and unlike the Spirit? This is evident in this gospel (and others). After all, did not Jesus say: 'when [we are able to replace] an image in place of an image, then [we] will enter the kingdom?' (Thomas 22).

We must move away from all the politics and power plays that followed Jesus' departure from this realm. Being objective about why people may have written these things about Yeshua is necessary to attain a semblance of truth. This positions Thomas 25 in a very raw and human place because, as is evident in texts about Jesus, individuals had something to gain through personal acclamation or creation of dogma.

If we consider how Jesus' peers would have perceived Him, we see that He would have been very lonely. Most people around Yeshua wanted something from Him, something He was not going to deliver—a kingdom on earth. Yeshua alluded to this when He stated that the kingdom is here, but we do not see it. A scholar of the Bible might use John 18:36 to refute the notion that people see the kingdom as appearing on earth. Jesus replies to Pilate: 'Mine is not a kingdom of this world; if my kingdom were of this world, my men would have fought to prevent my being surrendered to the Jews. As it is, my kingdom does not belong here.' This statement identifies the author as hostile to the Jewish people, because he blames them for Jesus' death. It also identifies the author as a gentile, since the original disciples were of Jewish origin. It is also an attempt to justify why Jesus' disciples did not fight for Him—apart from the fact that they were not soldiers and were afraid for their own lives. This fear is evident in Peter's three denials of his discipleship. John 18:36 demonstrates a contradiction which can be seen throughout the narratives about Yeshua. It is a contradiction stemming from an attempt to place Yeshua in the context of the Old Testament (Torah). We see this in John 21:31 when the author states: *'these are recorded so that you may believe that Jesus is the Christ, the Son of God, and that by believing this you may have life through his name.'* Through the Gospel of Thomas, we see it is not simply a matter of claiming a belief in Jesus as *the anointed one* that sets people free. It is the knowledge of our intimate relationship with Jesus, as His kin, which brings us *to life in the Spirit.*

Christian apologists argue that Yeshua was a traditional Rabbi and teacher of the Jewish faith. Yeshua was born into the Jewish faith and used His knowledge of this faith to gather a following. However, He was unlike His contemporaries. In Yeshua's time, there were numerous men claiming to be the Messiah. They were trying to gather a following for political or personal gain. As we find through the Gospel of Thomas, Jesus was unlike any other Rabbi of His time. He was the 'young wine', which could not be poured into 'old wineskins' (Thomas 47). Jesus' cryptic teachings made Him seem very strange to His followers. Most people would not have known how to relate to Him. The experience of being surrounded by people, yet feeling completely alone, would have been a daily occurrence for Yeshua. These are common experiences of people who share the journey of the Spirit. We are alone in this world, where the lion (Thomas 7) consumes the lamb. The lamb is the nature of the Spirit. The lion is representative of all the distractions we encounter. Jesus would have experienced great sadness at times, and yet at other times, He would have felt great joy, knowing there was someone who understood Him. Thomas 25 reflects Jesus' understanding of what He had to do. The prayer for strength before He was arrested, while all His disciples wanted to do was to sleep, reflects the plea for solace we see in Thomas 25. Yeshua felt the need to be protected, or to feel that someone loved Him enough to protect Him 'like the pupil of [their] own eye'. The lesson here is that we must care for our friends, *like our soul.*

The disparity between Jesus and His contemporaries is reflected in the saying 'be passersby' (Thomas 42). This reflects Yeshua's resolve, coming to terms with the differences within Himself, which could not be reconciled with all those surrounding Him. Ultimately, Jesus could only accept the consequences of His actions—alone. Thomas 25 shows us that Yeshua was indeed flesh and blood. He had feelings and He was Human. Jesus loved unconditionally and He wanted all people to be capable of the same. Although, it is evident He understood how humans struggled to be unconditional in their love. Jesus' unconditional love was evidence of His superior spiritual status, far beyond His contemporaries. Yeshua loved humanity so much that He fulfilled the prophecies in the Old Testament (Torah), protecting humanity from the negativity of perceived sinfulness and the notion that people are unworthy of attaining complete spiritual grace.

26. Jesus said, "You see the sliver in your friend's eye, but you don't see the timber in your own eye. When you take the timber out of your own eye, then you will see well enough to remove the sliver from your friend's eye."

Shortly after Yeshua's crucifixion, there was tension between Mary Magdalene and Peter, as is evident in Thomas 114. The flow-on effect of this kind of discord saw people gravitating toward either an orthodox Christian community or various Gnostic sects. The Gnostics were labelled as heretics, because they venerated gospels outside of the Canonical New Testament.

Much has been written about this early schism in Christianity, enough to identify that Jesus' disciples were everyday people. They battled many personal and social obstacles inherent in their patriarchal society. This inevitably caused division within the early Christian groups. Unfortunately, these differences impacted upon future generations. Yeshua knew this and it is the primary reason the Gospel of Thomas is as it is—*secret* sayings. This almost politically diplomatic approach is reflected in the saying *'be as sly as snakes and as simple as doves'*, which we see in Thomas 39. In all situations we should not judge harshly. We should first realise that we have to remove the timber from our own eye, before we can remove the sliver from our friend's eye—a difficult but necessary task.

The divide between the Abrahamic religions might be closed when these groups recognise their invaluable position as *foundational elements*. These elements are combined to form *a pearl* which reflects the Father's Light. In the Jewish faith, we can celebrate the first attempt to reconcile our predicament in this realm, through the observance of the external world. This world has given people a wealth of myths and legends (Thomas 85). This reflects the desire of the Source to connect with humanity. *The world reflects what is in the Spirit realm*, so it is natural that we find early belief systems seeking truth in the material/physical elements. This world also allowed for a place where sentient bodies could form, so that the Father's Light could aggregate in them and be re-joined, through the Holy Spirit – the collective consciousness. Jesus was born into this faith and *this body*—a body He gave up in order to teach us the importance of the Spirit. Christianity attempted to decipher the selfless sacrifice of a man who called Himself a Son of God. This religion used Old Testament prophecies, which we recognise were inspired by observations of this world (Thomas 85). In the process the Son was identified and the Trinity was completed, but it was not fully understood—this became problematic. The Islamic faith, in part, grew out of this confusion toward the Trinity. It sought to create a deeper connection with the Creator God—defining Him as the one and only God. In focusing on the oneness of God, Islam sought to bring peace to the restless soul. It *restated people's relationship with God as their Creator* and made this relationship easier to understand and *submit* to.

The *three sides* of this triad, which is analogous to the Abrahamic religions, are yet another manifestation of this realm's attempt to *mirror* the realm of the Spirit. However, just as the male and female have been separated in this realm (Thomas 22), so too have the layers of the *one pearl*. Judaism, Christianity, and Islam should be seen as intrinsically connected. They have played an invaluable role in bringing us into the Light. Jesus *represents* the Holy Spirit – the collective consciousness, because He is *the link* between our soul and the Source's Light. Yeshua is the Light shining on this pearl, enabling us to see it for what it is—a precious gift. It has evolved into *this Pearl: the 77th Pearl*. When they see this truth, then they will have removed the timber from their own eye, so that they may remove the sliver from their friend's eye. Through this understanding, the Abrahamic religions could move mountains.

The most contentious obstacle for those who share Jesus as their source of faith is the way He can be defined as either man or God. Separating the spirit world from the physical world, in our minds, is helpful in solving this dichotomy. The Gospel of Thomas often speaks about this distinction and it presents the answers. If all people accepted that what we are is not flesh, but a soul, like all other sentient beings, then we might return to a common ground. We are not a unique creation by God, for his pleasure and glorification. If that were true, we would not be creatures that can cause immense suffering to other species and our own. Humans would not choose wealth accumulation over sustainable industries. People would not make their god an excuse to kill. They would not destroy the very planet they believe was created just for them. Humans have the *breath of life* in them, the creative mind that reflects our link to God, the Source. We are the *vehicles for our God to dwell in*, to become part of the collective whole, the kingdom.

Accepting that some claims of miracles may be fictional stories written by well-meaning people of faith is crucial. Theirs was a faith that so blinded them (Thomas 28), they wrote words about Jesus they confidently felt could be true, even if they were not. To them, Yeshua was the only Son of God and could do these things, if He so desired (but would He?). 'Christ' is the English version of the Greek term 'Khristós', meaning 'the anointed one', and is a translation of the Hebrew word for Messiah. Sceptics have claimed that knowledge of pagan deities may have been the inspiration for the Christ miracles found in the New Testament. Theists have made counter claims and presented research to refute these sceptics, and so it goes on. These people are missing the point—it does not matter if these events occurred, what matters is that a man called Yeshua (Jesus) brought us an important message. Teachings that have become clouded by such futile and irrelevant discourse. These issues are the 'timber in [our] eye' and people must remove these obstacles before they can move forward. Jesus being remembered and revered by so many, for so long, is testament to the fact that He was a great man. The Gospel of Thomas, devoid of narratives, is what people on a spiritual journey should look to for their progression. These words speak to the soul–what humans are; they do not speak to the flesh that clothes them. In this way, we see these two (soul and flesh) as different and separate. We must separate ourselves from what the flesh has created and embrace what we know is the truth—*we are one.*

27. "If you do not fast from the world, you will not find the (Father's) kingdom. If you do not observe the Sabbath as a Sabbath you will not see the Father."

Thomas 27 refers to the attitude of Yeshua's contemporaries, who were consumed by the business of everyday life. They began to see the Sabbath as simply a day off work. These attitudes have not changed, but people should not feel at fault. It is the nature of this world and the struggles we encounter, which make us lose sight of what is truly important. Sadly, it is when people are confronted with catastrophes that they seek solace in spiritual reflection. These are the times that we see the humanity and the soul within each person—the times people feel connected. It is because we are forced to step back from the everyday and look at what we are, in relation to our dilemma in this world, that this connection occurs. But it should not be this way.

Jesus asks us to make a conscious effort to withdraw from the world and 'be passersby' (Thomas 42). When people reflect on the absurdity that occupies most of their everyday lives, they realise how futile much of what they concern themselves with really is. Yeshua implies that this is the reason the Sabbath *evolved*. The Sabbath is a place in time to reflect. It should not be a prescribed calendar event. The teachings in the Gospel of Thomas tell us that we can find the Spirit within ourselves. To achieve this, people have to start on this journey and follow the intuitive path. It is a journey with many obstacles and Thomas 27 warns of the complacency that will be encountered. This is something a person must overcome. The reality of completely withdrawing from the world, like a monk or ascetic, is not possible or desirable for most people. Society would not function if this were the norm. Making time for reflection, meditation, or prayer, even for a moment each day, is a positive approach to unlocking the *connection with* the Father's Kingdom. When we practice meditation and reflection we will come to see the Source within us and around us, through all things.

28. Jesus said, "I took my stand in the midst of the world, and in flesh I appeared to them. I found them all drunk, and I did not find any of them thirsty. My soul aches for the children of humanity, because they are blind in their hearts and do not see, for they came into the world empty, and they also seek to depart from the world empty.

But meanwhile they are drunk. When they shake off their wine, then they will change their ways."

The first sentence of Thomas 28 is astonishing. It challenges most Christian beliefs about Jesus Christ. It would be contentious for the majority of the Christian orthodoxy, who see Jesus as something completely *unlike* what we are. They believe He is God. Jesus very clearly tells us: '[He] took [His] stand in the midst of the world, and in flesh [He] appeared [to us]'. Jesus came into the world just as we do—He took His stand in the world with a body, which grew and was eventually destroyed, because He was *human*. This is not to suggest that Yeshua was not an extraordinary being, of superior wisdom and spiritual attainment; the Gospel of Thomas supports the fact that Jesus was all of these things. It is important that we come to the realisation that Yeshua was human, the alternative is damaging to our relationship with God, the Source. If we are to become an enlightened Spirit, we must see ourselves as worthy. Humans can only do this if they reconcile with the truth of *Jesus as their brother*. In the Gospel of Thomas, we have seen that Yeshua reaches out to us, stating that we are His mother, brother, and sister, embracing us as His kin (Thomas 99). When Jesus tells us we are His siblings, He is referring to the soul becoming a spirit, because this is what we have in common. The human soul came from the Source. *It seeks* to be joined to us, through the Holy Spirit that connects us to this ubiquitous energy. The truth of Jesus' life as a human being needs to be a part of Christian doctrine; otherwise most people would see Him as inaccessible. If this does not happen, Jesus Christ will remain, in most Christians' eyes, the only Son of God—above us and unlike us. Jesus is now *as He was* before He entered this realm; this does not diminish *what* Yeshua was when He lived in this realm. On the contrary, it intensifies the sacrifice He made, revealing that His spirit was *thrust across the abyss, from the inner realm of the Spirit, to this one* (Thomas 97 and 98). This is the realm that is a *decaying* carcass, as we see in Thomas 56 and 80. Placing His flesh on the *short-lived tree of this realm*, Yeshua speaks to us of the world that is a carcass. This is in contrast to the realm of the eternal spirit, which permeates everything—time, space, and all of the dimensions. This was a conscious and essential decision, in order to break through the divide between the material and metaphysical realms.

Jesus states in Thomas 28: '[He] found them all drunk'. This speaks of the distractions His contemporaries had created *for themselves*, which stole them away from a dedicated spiritual *life*. A modern distraction has arisen with the introduction of social media, which is filled with trivial matters and people wanting to prove how happy they are, even when the truth is very different. It is the nature of most humans to want an easy life. Atheists will reject the notion of anything science cannot prove, because this is easy. Agnostics will say they do not really know if there is or is not a God to 'hedge their bets', because this is safe and easy. Theists will practice their rituals of faith and, in doing so, feel assured this will deliver them to eternal life, because these things are easy. This is the metaphor of '*being drunk*'. When people are drunk they feel free from themselves, their concerns and struggles, they feel at ease. They do not have to think about enriching their soul; they are under the impression that they are happy with their possessions, relationships, appearance, status in society, and so on. Yeshua wants these perceptions to be seen for what they are—empty pursuits. They do not fulfil the soul. Humans enter into the material world in a body, the oyster shell. As they live this life, the oyster has many irritations entering into the body, both physical and emotional. Some oyster shells are overcome by these foreign materials and do not form a pearl, others recognise how they can use these intrusions. They coat them with understanding and wisdom. These become a brilliant pearl, which shines on the world. *They do not leave empty*.

The practices of the major religions are consumed in ritual. This is because the soul seeks harmony. Ritual provides order and harmony, but it is a false God. When people say prayers and perform rituals in their temples, synagogues, and churches, they feel this satisfies a need and cleanses them of moral burdens and perceived sin. This *drunken state* of confidence makes people believe they have the answer, the right path. These people do not want to hear that they may be heading the wrong way. This is what Jesus could see in His contemporaries and it is still true for many communities of today. Ticking boxes is easier than searching for the truth within.

People seeking truth, freedom, and serenity need to take the time to stand back from the everyday. Humans need to shake off their wine and look at life as observers rather than unconscious participants. To place aspects of the spiritual life into compartments, to satisfy concerns for time or convenience, takes away from the purpose and meaning of this pursuit. To become 'passersby' (Thomas 42) it is necessary for people to step back from the picture they know as this life, so that they can see all its parts, including the frame and the wall it hangs on. This can be done any time of the day. All one needs to do is take a few seconds to see a situation for what it is. Doing this, people can put the things that disturb them into perspective. This process allows for the comparison of the soul, which is eternal, relative to this realm, which is finite. Even when people are completely overtaken by stress or issues in employment, family, or relationships, they can place the observer at the back of the mind. This observer is the perfect human—the one that is the soul and *becomes the passerby* (Thomas 42). Even while the body cries in physical or emotional pain, the *observer* sits at the back of the mind and witnesses the truth. The observer knows this *will add another layer to the pearl.*

What we know of Yeshua's life before preaching His message is very limited. It is often devised by conjecture, rooted in myth and legend. We can reasonably imagine that the Magi came to Jesus' parents to tell them they had a very special child—one that would change the world. The Magi (commonly referred to as the three wise men or kings) were from a community well known for their astrological knowledge. Reverend Don Jacobs, a Methodist preacher, used his knowledge of astronomy and computer technology to locate a celestial event which may have motivated the Magi to find this special child. Jacobs' suggests that Yeshua was born on March 1st, 7 BCE, at 1:21 a.m. in Bethlehem. We know that this is not accurate, since Jesus was born in Nazareth. The author of Luke manufactured the story of a census to have Jesus born in Bethlehem. There is no evidence of such a census having occurred in that time. The story of Jesus' birth in Luke aligns with Old Testament predictions of the Saviors lineage. According to Reverend

Don Jacobs, the birth chart for this moment in time contains a cluster of six planets in Pisces: the Sun, Moon, Jupiter, Venus, Saturn, and Uranus. In addition, Hannibal Giudice, a professional astrologer, notes that Cuneiform tablets discovered during this century (in Sippar, Babylon), reveal that astrologers were tracking movements of an extremely rare heavenly occurrence, in the year 7 BCE. This celestial event, which would only occur once in 25 thousand years, was when the two zodiacs (sidereal and tropical) met. The cosmological event correlates with Thomas 98, where we see that a special time was required for Jesus' spirit to be *thrust into* this realm. This astronomical information is *likely* to be more accurate than what we have from the New Testament. Sources that use the gospels to triangulate the actual date of Jesus' birth are referencing edited narratives, which are inaccurate and somewhat manufactured.

The Magi's exhaustive search for the child born at that time would have taken significant effort. Several years would have passed before they found the family they were looking for. When they found Yeshua's family, Mary was told of her special task. Her position as the 'Virgin Mary' is revealed later in 77th *Pearl: The Perpetual Tree*. The relevance of this information might seem extraneous. However, it demonstrates how Jesus was indeed a very special human being—to the extent that an external, gentile group of astrologers recognised His significance. After Yeshua's parents were visited by the Magi, life would have gone on as normal. As Jesus matured into an adult He would have been experiencing life the same as His brothers and sisters. This is evident in the Gospel of Thomas, when Yeshua shows His frustration toward His family, and indeed the community (Thomas 31 and 99), because they did not see Him as being extraordinary or different. Jesus was the son of a carpenter—He would have lived a relatively normal life, with all the emotions and experiences every child and adolescent encounters. What was extraordinary was that He rejected a conventional life for a turbulent and fatal path.

29. Jesus said, "If the flesh came into being because of spirit, that is a marvel, but if spirit came into being because of the body, that is a marvel of marvels.

Yet I marvel at how this great wealth has come to dwell in this poverty."

This saying strikes a blow at the Genesis myth, which saw Adam made into flesh, in a perfect paradise. From this mythical heritage, we lifted the flesh to something it is not. In Thomas 29, Yeshua makes a clear disparity between the Spirit and the flesh. He points out that to think the Spirit came into being because of the body is absurd. The breath of life existed before the body—it is the *Source of all things*. When the Source met with sentient bodies, the notion of the *Son* came into being. The Son became perfectly manifest in Jesus, the one who has opened the doors for His siblings. Those people seeking a connection with God, the Source are like Jesus—we are the offspring of the Father.

Yeshua's Divine wisdom, evident in Thomas 29, points to a hidden knowledge about the realm that precedes this one— something His contemporaries would not have been able to fathom. This saying has a cynical tone. It mocks those who romanticised the physical world as a manifestation of God's divine glory, which implied this world was created for spirits to dwell in. Yeshua was careful not to make a definitive statement, because the Pharisees were watching Him, therefore He says: '*If* the spirit came into being because of the body…' The use of 'if' clears Yeshua's statement of authoritative voice, but for us it reveals a very clever man, who speaks to the twenty-first century. This is also evident in Thomas 114, where Jesus pacifies Peter with diplomacy, all the while, revealing a prophetic metaphor about the obstacles His teachings would encounter.

In the last sentence of Thomas 29, Jesus confirms that 'this great wealth' (the soul—what humans are) has come to dwell in a place that *is not the end point and not worthy of the spirit*. Humanities' innate sinfulness did not destroy paradise—paradise never existed in this realm. People are the wealth and they are the collective paradise, *the kingdom of God*.

30. Jesus said, "Where there are three deities, they are divine. Where there are two or one, I am with that one."

In the Gospel of Thomas Yeshua constantly reminds us of our kinship with Him. This connectedness tells us that there are no *external* deities. All things are connected. Since the Father/Source flows through everything, we conclude that the soul is within a body, within the world, within the universe—these are the three *deities* referred to in the first sentence. They are divine because the Source inspired them for the growth of the soul. In the Gospel of Thomas, Jesus is telling us of the fantastic potential we have, by coming to recognise 'the kingdom.' Humans accomplish this understanding by recognising what they are through the interaction within these three deities—*body, world, and universe*. Then, like Yeshua, we become *a living Spirit*.

If we look at the canonical gospels objectively and try to ignore the biographical narratives and polemic positioning, we can see a clear distinction between the jealous, vengeful God of the Old Testament and the loving 'Father' Yeshua speaks of through most of the New Testament. We might also notice the way Jesus describes the truth of where the mythical Adam sprung from (Thomas 85). Moreover, He maintains that Adam 'was not worthy' of us. In the Gospel of Thomas, we learn that the Father is the Source, flowing through all things (Thomas 77). It is where our life force springs from and It is our kinship with Yeshua. It is not someone who made us for *his* pleasure or glorification, as is the Gnostic thesis. The *one* is the Holy Spirit and Yeshua is *with that one*. When we are joined to the Source, '[we] become two' (Thomas 11)—the *Holy Spirit is the conduit, which connects the one, making them two.* For this reason, the Holy Spirit is lifted above all things in Thomas 44. Yeshua signalled His duality as spirit-within-flesh by stating He is both at the same time, but ultimately He is *with the one—the Holy Spirit.* The *one* is the collective consciousness and it transcends space and time; it is at the beginning and at the end (Thomas 18). It is the whole. These are the reasons why we are worthy of God, the Source that is wrapped within the flesh.

The Gospel of John affirms what we see here in Thomas, but the various authors who completed this gospel could not fathom the truth of Jesus' teachings. They could only see God as a being outside of themselves. They are God's creation, not a part of Him. In John 14 we see several very clear references to how Yeshua saw Himself. In John 14:7 we read: *'If you know me, you will know my father too. From this moment you know him and have seen him.'* Prior to this, Thomas is said to have made the statement: *'Lord, we do not know where you are going, so how can we know the way?'* This statement was fabricated by the Johannine sect as an attack on the believers of the Gospel of Thomas. The statements by Yeshua in this chapter of John, which follow the naive question coming from John's *doubting*

Thomas, are meant to ratify the notion of the Father, Son, and Holy Spirit as three separate persons being one God. Christians, who believe in this definition of the Trinity, use these statements to try and prove their case. In reality, it does not prove their position at all. It in fact cements what we have discovered by connecting the threads in this gospel. When John's Jesus says, '*If you know me, you will know my father too. From this moment you know him and have seen him*', He is restating what the Gospel of Thomas has revealed. The Father is the source of all things; it is in Jesus, just as it is in sentient beings. When John's Jesus announces He will send humanity a Paraclete (referring to the Holy Spirit, the advocate), He says: '*the Spirit of truth whom the world can never accept since it neither sees nor knows him; but you know him, because he is with you, he is in you*'. This again affirms the teachings we have from the Gospel of Thomas. The last part of this statement, *he is with you, he is in you*, confirms the mechanism of this facet of the Trinity. The Holy Spirit is the thing that connects all enlightened beings – it is the collective consciousness. All these three facets are Yeshua, just as all these three facets are humanity. *We are one when we become two*, this is why Jesus states: '*Where there are two or one, I am with that one*.'

The key to Thomas 30 is found in Thomas 44, which lifts the Holy Spirit above all things. When Jesus says, 'Where there are two or one, I am with that one', He is revealing a great mystery and truth. Yeshua is referring to souls (what we are) and *our link through the Holy Spirit*. Human beings are the one and the two at the same time. Previously, the analogy of the two elements which create water was used, as a metaphor for our comparative relationship and *linking* with the Source. When we, the soul, are linked to the Father via the Holy Spirit, we are with Jesus, because *all things are connected through this conduit*. We are one when we are living in this world, because our physical world, and body, is a barrier to fully realising our true *relationship with the Source*. This recognition is only possible (for most beings) when they die—they are stripped of the flesh that clothed them, *becoming two with God, the* Source. Not understanding this mystery during the physical existence leaves people confused and unaware when they pass (Thomas 11). If this happens, the soul fades into the whole. This should not be seen as a terrible thing, because it represents the rejoining to the whole, where new possibilities are advanced.

Is it appropriate for us to invoke the 'Father, Son, and Holy Spirit'? Most Christian faiths define the *Holy Trinity* as being three different *entities*, yet 'they' are one God. In a sense this is true—these *facets* are linked. In the Gospel of Thomas, and through *77th Pearl: The Perpetual Tree*, we see what these relationships stand for in relatively simple terms. It is a relationship we see mirrored in the material universe, where elements given off from stars, combine with gravity, and dark matter to create this realm. Similarly, the *Source* is the thing that flows through everything, and aggregates in some places to eventually form *living* Spirits. The *Son* represents all sentient beings. They are the bodies formed to house souls on this planet we call Earth. The soul is the spark of Light from God, the Source, in this outer layer. The *Holy Spirit* is the binding, collective energy, not unlike dark matter. It links the Father/Source and the Son. The *Father* issues forth Its Light as an aspect of Its nature, through and over all things. The function of the *Son* is to house the Light of the Source, which is the soul on the journey to becoming a Spirit. The *Holy Spirit* is the unifying conduit connecting all enlightened beings. It is like the symbol between mathematical equations. The numbers represent the Source and the enlightened Spirit is the answer to all the equations. Invoking the three is indeed a *powerful metaphor for the formula that is our heritage and kinship with Jesus.*

Invoking the Trinity:

This can be done at any time. The actions can be visualised, rather than performed. Ideally, one would be seated on the ground or floor, cross-legged. Do not allow this to become a ritual, which may limit this profound gesture of recognition. Find your own way.

⇒ When invoking '*Father/Source*', we might touch the ground or floor with the palms of our hands, at each side of the temple (body). Here, we recognise and bless *the Source, which is over and through all things in this universe* (Thomas 77).

⇒ When invoking the '*Son*', we might lift both hands off the ground and point to the centre of the chest. Here, we *recognise and bless all human beings and interstellar beings seeking enlightenment. We are from the Source, just as Jesus is from the Father* (Thomas 49 and 50).

⇒ When invoking '*Holy Spirit*', we might extend our arms out in front of us, towards the horizon, palms facing out with fingers pointing up. As we move the hands away from each other, across the horizon, we *recognise and bless the Holy Spirit for uniting us, so that the Father and Son are no longer one, they have become two, joined as one* – the collective consciousness (Thomas 44).

⇒ Amen.

While the meaning of the word 'amen' may vary in different bible translations, it is generally considered an affirmation or an agreement towards a statement. In a collective or small group, people might say '*Namaste*' meaning, *I recognise the divine in myself and I bow to the divine in you*. A profoundly beautiful response, which has the potential to change the violent, egocentric world of the early twenty-first century.

31. Jesus said, "No prophet is welcome on his home turf; doctors don't cure those who know them."

In Mark 6:1-6 we see this saying written into a narrative. Significantly, in the last line it says: 'He was amazed at their lack of faith.' This reflects the way these sayings can be changed to suit a specific goal. The references to faith in the canonical gospels inferred that people did not have faith in Jesus' divinity. The authors wanted to impress this idea on potential followers. In Mark, the narrative tells us that the people of Yeshua's hometown, Nazareth, did not have faith in His power to *cure* them, because: '*doctors don't cure those who know them*'. The psychology behind the cure requires faith in the person or deity one goes to, in order to be healed. Therefore, the healing is from within the person and is not imposed upon the individual from outside. For the New Testament authors, healing is a matter of faith in Jesus as the Christ, the only Son of God. They did not understand what Yeshua was trying to teach people. Yeshua wanted people to have faith in the Divine wisdom He conveyed. Through this wisdom they are cured by the knowledge of the wealth they possess. After all, Yeshua brings us a gentle yoke and gives us comfort, as we see in Thomas 90.

In Mark 4:40 Jesus states, 'Why are you so frightened? Have you still no faith?', after the disciples wake Him for fear of being drowned in a storm. The inference being that the disciples, having faith in Jesus as the Son of God, would be able to quiet the storm in His name. In other chapters of the New Testament Gospels, we see Yeshua make reference to our faith as healing us, which is perceived as *faith* in Yeshua's Divine power. Such persuasion was the intention of the authors of the canonical gospels, but this is not the case in the Gospel of Thomas. Likewise, historically and in the time of these words being written, religious groups use faith *in their teaching*, rather than faith *in the true nature of the self*, in order to accumulate a following.

It is noteworthy that in Thomas 31, Jesus compares Himself to a *prophet*. This is a significant shift from the way others have defined Him after His death. Should this then mean that He is not the Son of God? Jesus tells us that He is *the son of the living one*, the Father (the Source), and that *what He is* can be found through all things (Thomas 77). This is true for all sentient beings. Yeshua also tells us that we are His brothers and sisters (Thomas 99). In this way, He is the *teacher and prophet* bearing truths that bind us to Him through the *Holy Spirit, which is the Source's Light in action*. Yeshua compares Himself to a prophet in Thomas 31, which makes His loaded question to the disciples in Thomas 13 even more revealing. When Jesus asked His disciples to compare Him to something in Thomas 13, the only disciple that *did not have the language* to describe what He was like was Thomas. This identified Thomas as *the one* who could record Jesus' most sacred teachings, without interpretation and re-contextualising. This adds another layer to Thomas 31, because in Thomas 13 we see the other disciples describe Jesus with knowledge rooted in the Old Testament (Torah). In the last line of Thomas 31 Jesus states: 'doctors don't cure those who know them'. The other disciples believed they did *know* what Jesus was like, but Thomas admitted he did not know. This is why Thomas could be *cured of the affliction, symptomatic of this realm*. This premise becomes even more apparent when we see the author of the Gospel of John make Thomas into a doubter on the basis of his response in Thomas 13. The author(s) of John believed in Yeshua as the *only Son of God*. It was the author of John who desired to disseminate this belief to others through his persuasive writing. The flip side of Thomas 31 is that when we don't know someone directly and that person has accumulated an impressive reputation, it is easier to imagine fantastical attributes this person might possess. In this context, faith can be a double edged sword. It can make people intoxicated, losing the logical, intuitive self to exaggeration and embellishment—the type of embellishment that can become harmful and erroneous to the truth. It is the *truth* Yeshua was trying to convey in His day, which was supposed to bring about *the cure*. It was never about proving He was a Spirit with Divine powers. The faith Jesus needed from His contemporaries was faith in His knowledge and wisdom. In writing *77th Pearl: The Perpetual Tree*, the author has met with the same attitude from family, friends, and peers which is reflected in Jesus' lament found in Thomas 31.

32. Jesus said, "A city built on a high hill and fortified cannot fall, nor can it be hidden."

An orthodox interpretation of this saying would be to build a Church on strong dogmatic parameters, making it unyielding to other ideologies. Such simple and peripheral interpretations have left the Abrahamic religions with splinter groups, conflict, and damaged individuals. These individuals and minority groups find it easier to ignore much of the dogma created by such institutions. This is the dogma that imbues guilt; it does not reflect the intentions of the Jesus we know through our intuitive self and the Gospel of Thomas.

Thomas 32 can be seen as a warning for institutions that take a *moral high ground*. Throughout history, there are some people who have had ill intentions and abused their positions of power. These people did a great deal of damage to the credibility and stature of such an institution, as well as to their victims. This observation ratifies what the Gospel of Thomas teaches—humans are not made perfect. Humans are a soul wrapped in flesh (Thomas 29). The flesh is the primal animal, which may carry the soul into dark places. The soul may overcome the flesh or be consumed by it (Thomas 7), but this struggle can be fruitful (Thomas 24, 103 and 110). In Thomas 32, Jesus warns humanity against building institutions to represent *the face of God*. No human can create this façade, because it would be made from the substances of this realm and body, not the realm of the Spirit.

Thomas 32 appears to be a paradox, as we know Yeshua had no interest in having an earthly kingdom, which a fortified city may represent. The word 'kingdom' was used by Yeshua to describe a *spiritual unity* and common understanding of the true nature of what we are—one. In this sense, a 'kingdom' is *a place where the Spirit exists in its awakened state*, connected by the Source, through the Holy Spirit (the collective consciousness). The tone of this saying is of *caution*; Jesus warns that while a city high on a hill and protected is safe, it *cannot be hidden*—sometimes this is necessary in order to be discreet. The need for discretion was important, because there were people all around Jesus that would take His pearls of wisdom and destroy them (Thomas 93). These people were enamoured of this realm (Thomas 7). They are the ones who would take new wine (Jesus' secret teachings), and place them into old wineskins (Old Testament myths and legends), thus making them spoil (Thomas 47). We have cited evidence of this in the Gospel of Matthew, Chapter 13.

In Mark 3:11-12 we see an example of Jesus telling *unclean souls* to stop announcing Him as the Son of God, for fear of *being disclosed* to others in the community (see also Mark 1:23-25 and 1:34). This would have seen Yeshua brought before the Pharisees, who were wary of those who might lead people astray from conventional teachings and undermine their authority. One might be curious as to the existence of these disturbed souls in Mark, and in other synoptic texts, and why, or how, they knew Yeshua. This brings into question the integrity of the authors of the canonical gospels. There is a tendency to portray Jesus as a healer and exorcist in these gospels; this was a persuasive way to convince parishioners of the early Christian Church that He was of Divine origin. These actions also drew from Greek and Roman stories of heroic figures with similar powers. To be fair, there are examples where healing and exorcism was not straightforward (Mark 9:18-29). This could point to the reality that healing, *through* faith, was lacking. It recognised that mental illness or epilepsy was not curable. Suffice to say, if Yeshua speaks of the existence of a soul here in the Gospel of Thomas, then we might accept that some may desire control over a physical body they do not own. Their fear of Yeshua came from their lack of knowledge. There are also those entities who are enamoured of the material world and who work to keep people away from the truth. This is mirrored in the conflicts caused by religious differences—these entities are adept at creating clashes, confusion, and chaos. Conflict and chaos is the nature of the world and steals humans away from the truth of their inheritance (Thomas 7). Those who cause war, or take revenge, in the name of their god, should carefully consider whom they are justifying their actions through. God, the Source does not *live* in places of conflict or chaos and therefore It should not be associated with war. The Source is everywhere and is involved in all aspects of existence, but It cannot *become realised and live* without the link to the collective consciousness we know as the Holy Spirit. The Holy Spirit functions through a willingness to accept the 'other' and connects through unspoken means. This union grows the collective consciousness like leaven in bread. Yeshua came to teach us about this *crucial union*. The spirits living in darkness lack the capacity to connect to others—theirs is an egocentric existence. They want only to connect to fear and hate, because these emotions make them feel alive.

If we accept that exorcisms happened, a revelation from these stories is that certain entities recognised Jesus as *linked to God, the Source through the collective consciousness*. This is the same place they came from, but were/are unwilling to re-join. Yeshua is a doorway, by virtue of the knowledge He brings to this realm. These entities resent this opening and work for it to be *hidden away*. This opening (knowledge) protects people from their negative persuasion. In light of Thomas 32, this appears to be a contradiction—Jesus says, 'a city on a hill and fortified cannot fall, *nor can it be hidden*', inferring that it is very visible, which presents a problem. The answer to this analogy is in the many conflicts we have seen throughout history which involve religion. These religions are the cities on the hill and the fortification is the people who align themselves to these groups, by following their doctrine. These institutions draw in people because they are visible and promise much. In reality, they offer only community, dogma, and ritual, as in Mark 7:5-8. These popular institutions can become the tools of malevolent entities. These souls have not always been ones without a heartbeat. The Gospel of Thomas is about the personal journey, awakening *our* spirit – hence the contradiction. Does this mean people should reject the Church they belong to? Not necessarily—it might mean they take what they need from it and journey on. In all religions there are truths that we know to be beneficial. This is the gentle voice of the collective consciousness directing the seeker towards the Light. It is what we must seek to continue on, but we must be wary to whom we disclose our thoughts and knowledge. Sometimes it is best to be in the valley, hidden in a quiet place, at peace.

The question of exorcism links into Thomas 32 on several levels. Exorcism is a contentious topic in the context of *77ᵗʰ Pearl: The Perpetual Tree*. On the one hand, we see that people can be the catalyst for evil. Humans can be labelled as *Satan*, because they think as men do and not as God would (Mark 8:33, see also commentary for Thomas 21). On the other hand, we acknowledge the existence of entities captivated by this world, who have embraced the darkness and seek to distract us from the pursuit of the Light. Often, they are the hands controlling corruptible institutions. It follows then, that if these malevolent souls exist, they may want to enter a body for self-indulgent reasons. The author is very reluctant to embrace the notion of exorcism. It tends to take well-meaning people down a long, narrow road, which numerous religious groups have entered. It should be acknowledged that not only Christians have taken this road. It is a road thwarted with potentially misguided actions and beliefs. However, it does relate to the idea of creating an institution fortified with dogma, which we see in Thomas 32. An apology to Catholics for using their institution as an example, but they are the *most visible*—apt link, is it not? Moreover, in recent times, the Catholic Church has been open to discussion on controversial issues and hopefully this will be added to the list.

If we take the Catholic Rite of Exorcism as an example, we see how the process can take on a polemic function. The possessed individual, or rather the demon within, is made into the adversary of Jesus (God) and all His creations. What we learn from the Gospel of Thomas is that this premise is incorrect. There are some worrying aspects to the Catholic Rite of Exorcism. Initially, we question the validity of calling upon all the saints within the Church for intercession. In Thomas 52, Jesus asks that we recognise *the living one*, which is in our presence (God, the Source that is within us), and not mention those whom *we cannot be sure are alive in spirit*. In Thomas 88, Yeshua asks us to respect messengers and prophets, but consider the question: *when will they take what belongs to them?* This suggests that while they may have an important role to play, they may not have reached the potential of a *living* spirit—connected to the Father through the collective consciousness (Holy Spirit). Calling upon all the saints in the Church for help tends to become a way to justify this particular faith's practice of canonising people. It would also seem that this is a way for the Church to show their followers that even ordinary, unworthy individuals might make it to heaven if they emulate those saints. This is a poignant segue to the question of worthiness.

In the same Catholic Rite of Exorcism, in the process of removing the demon, the priest requests Jesus' help several times, but prefaces the request with '*unworthy* servant'. The question of worthiness is addressed in several places in the Gospel of Thomas. In Thomas 94, Yeshua simply asks us to knock on the door for it to be opened. We do not have to be of a certain personage to be allowed to knock on the door, we just need to *have the desire.* In Thomas 99, we see that people who listen to and embrace Yeshua's wisdom are His brothers and sisters. In this sense, we are like Him. Moreover, the question of worthiness is addressed in the commentary for Thomas 62, where the author explains the journey he went through to get to this point—the revelations in *77th Pearl: The Perpetual Tree.* Therein, he also explains his experiences with malevolent spirits.

The question of worthiness is a device which numerous religious organisations use to gather and secure their patronage. Any such organisation needs to reassess their approach. They should question whether that line of thinking has been perpetrated because of a fact, or due to the human condition—the condition that sees a person deny their great wealth, because of *this poverty* (Thomas 29). Have these views been imposed by God or introduced by man? We might also consider if it has been profitable for these organisations to exploit the individuals' feelings of unworthiness and, by association, sinfulness? Jesus' lament in Thomas 64, that buyers and merchants will not enter the places of the Father, seems appropriate in this context.

The lengthy time the Catholic exorcism takes to complete leaves us with certain questions. Taking the accounts in the New Testament at face value, we notice that Yeshua cast out demons quickly. If a Christian Church claims to be the representative of Jesus on Earth, an exorcism in His name should be just as quick. Here, we meet with a very complex web of interrelationships, which can be called *symbiotic*. They are symbiotic because men (not women) have had everything to do with the creation of Church doctrine—men will, more often than not, *think as man does, not as God would*. It would require another book to adequately show a history of how 'man' has created two opposing and yet very *dependent sides*, but that is not necessary here. To make an analogy, to expedite this thesis, we can think of the current, popularised, idea of good versus evil as *one coin*. The Christian Church is one face of the coin and Satan is the other side. Men forged this coin with *tools made from this world*. It serves a purpose only in this world—here we might recall Thomas 100:

'They showed Jesus a gold coin and said to him, "The Roman emperor's people demand taxes from us." He said to them, "Give the emperor what belongs to the emperor, give God what belongs to God, and give me what is mine."'

The *thing* we give to Yeshua is the *ear of our hearts*. Furthermore, is what we have now, in the early part of the twenty-first century, what Yeshua envisaged? Is a faith that sees us as creations that have gone astray, punished like children, something Yeshua perpetuated in His teachings? Did Thomas' Jesus see Satan as the historical antithesis and adversary of

God? Jesus teaches us that we are from the Father's Light, lost in the abyss (the distant road—Thomas 97). Now, the Father/Source seeks us out, the *one* most loved (Thomas 107). On the question of what is evil, we should recall that Yeshua teaches in Thomas 24: 'there is light within a person of light, and it shines on the whole world. If it does not shine, it is dark'. People are both the good and the evil in the world—it is a choice. Men have created *Satan* from their desire to define things they cannot reconcile—to blame someone for the *nature of the creature humans came from* and our chaotic, material world.

In the analogy of the coin, we see that it is *one object* and cannot be separated. The coin has value in this world, which can sustain the individual's physical needs and, as in Thomas 100, the needs of the governing body. A church is a community of people believing in the same thing, living under the same doctrine. An institution, built on the premise that it represents one side or another, does not focus on the connection we share with the Source. It inevitably gets bogged-down with dogma—rules that define it and separate it from its opposition. This is what we see in the Catholic Rite of Exorcism; its protracted discourse, which encompasses so much of its mythology, works as a device to instill belief in its doctrine. The person receiving the exorcism becomes psychologically tormented by these ideas. They are convinced that they are *at the mercy of a power greater than them and outside of their dominion*. This is the coin at work. The negative entity is actually profiting from this process. Its status is being lifted from that of a human, consumed by the lion (Thomas 7), to that of the historical antithesis and *worthy adversary* of God. This notion is blasphemy. It is blasphemy because we have given this soul in darkness the prestigious position of a deity, which battles with the very thing that created it. Ironically, herein lies another truth. Humans (unknowingly) battle with the thing that *inspired* their existence constantly. It is something Jesus came to this realm to undo—so that we might understand that we are no longer the beasts we evolved from. Our soul is a spark from the Source's Light and it fights to be in communion. Perpetuating the notion of good versus evil is tantamount to *feeding* popular culture's enthusiasm for sports. The difference in religious groups is that there is no recognition of the players (people) initially coming from the same family (the Father/Source). There is also no recognition of them *making the choice* to be on one side or the other.

This brings us to the question of what an exorcism would look like under the premise of the Gospel of Thomas. We should note, a person who has embraced the teachings in the Gospel of Thomas has become aware of their link to God, the Source through the collective consciousness (Holy Spirit). They are related to Yeshua, because the Holy Spirit links us to all enlightened beings. Therefore, a person of this capacity would not become possessed, but would certainly come under attack from those who fear this Light—these antagonists are not always without a heartbeat. If a person of faith, as described in *77ᵗʰ Pearl: The Perpetual Tree*, is convinced that an individual requires an exorcism, then the following may be used as a guide. Importantly, there must be no doubt the person is not mentally ill or emotionally disturbed. This is for the protection of the afflicted and the helper, to maintain the integrity of these sacred teachings. There must be evidence of events occurring which are not normal, such as speaking unfamiliar languages or other paranormal activities. The approach that will be described is one of *education* and is not something to force onto someone. The afflicted person must want this help and is invited to continue these prayers until they feel comfortable and strong in their resolve.

The helper should have in mind Thomas 20:

'The disciples said to Jesus, "Tell us what Heaven's kingdom is like." He said to them, "It's like a mustard seed, the smallest of all seeds, but when it falls on prepared soil, it produces a large plant and becomes a shelter for birds of the sky."'

You (the helper) are seeking to plant the seed that *will become shelter* for the birds.

To start, the person who is possessed must ask for this assistance through an open, honest conversation. If the actions of the soul in darkness have been known to be physically violent, the person should be asked to restrain themselves in some way, so that they cannot harm anyone. The space should be conducive to a calm, meditative environment.

The Exorcism.
The *helper* reads:

[Name] has asked for my assistance in freeing her/him from the influences of a malevolent entity, which has entered her/his body – their temple. *[Name]* wants to stop the disruption to her/his life. My name is *[helpers* name], I am the one who has embraced the Father's Light, through the Holy Spirit. Through the Divine wisdom of Yeshua, the Holy Spirit has joined me to God, the Source and the one have become two.

Jesus said: 'The Father's kingdom is like a person who wanted to kill someone powerful. While still at home he drew his sword and thrust it into the wall to find out whether his hand would go in. Then he killed the powerful one.'

Yeshua, the pure spark of Light who came from the realm of the Spirit, the hand that broke through the divide, has symbolically destroyed the 'powerful one'. Therefore, what you have embraced is a carcass. It is this world that was *inspired by* the Spirit realm, for humanities spiritual growth, yet you desire the body that becomes this carcass. The illusions that Jesus has destroyed cannot be made real. We take pity on your lust for this body and world.

When Yeshua went into the desert for forty days, He rejected what this realm—known as the powerful one, with all its intoxicating pleasures— could offer. As children of the Father, the Source, we learn from this realm, which is the poverty, and, in due course, become wealthy. This is the wealth that the Father gives us; it is not of this world. Soul in darkness, know the truth of your poor choices.

Jesus said: 'Congratulations to those who know where the rebels are going to attack. They can get going, collect their imperial resources, and be prepared before the rebels arrive.'

I am here to give [*Name*] her/his imperial resources, so that she/he may purge you from her/his body. From this day forward, through this knowledge, [*Name*] will know you, the rebel, and will stop your advance.

Jesus said: 'Lucky is the lion that the human will eat, so that the lion becomes human. And foul is the human that the lion will eat, and the lion still will become human.'

Soul in darkness, you are the foul human who has been consumed by the lion, the physical realm that decays. Your choice is one we take pity on. If you wish to change, give yourself to the Father's Light that is through all things. Be reborn and become a source for growth and union with God, the Source, through the Holy Spirit that is the collective consciousness. If you do not take this path, at the end of this journey of motion and rest, you will be absorbed into the Source's Light, you will taste death. For the poor choices you have made we offer you forgiveness and compassion for your suffering.

Jesus said: 'If they say to you, "Where have you come from?" say to them, "We have come from the light, from the place where the light came into being by itself, established itself, and appeared in their image." If they say to you, "Is it you?" say, "We are its children, and we are the chosen of the living Father."

If they ask you, "What is the evidence of your Father in you?" say to them, "It is motion and rest."

We are all from the Father, the Source—the Light that is through all things. We are Its children, chosen above all others. [*Name*] is worthy to be called a child of the Father; as to you soul that lives in fear, we take pity on you for the choices you have made.

Jesus said: 'I am the light that is over all things. I am all: from me all came forth, and to me all attained. Split a piece of wood; I am there. Lift up the stone, and you will find me there.'

By requesting our help, [*Name*] has shown her/his desire to embrace the Light of the living God, the Source, from where all came forth and all will attain to. We are Its children and claim our right to be free of the fear and darkness that is the dwelling place of the beast, the beast from where humans evolved and evil is manifest.

Jesus said: 'Two will recline on a couch; one will die, one will live.' Salome said, 'Who are you mister? You have climbed onto my couch and eaten from my table as if you are from someone.' Jesus said to her, 'I am the one who comes from what is whole. I was granted from the things of my Father. I am your disciple. For this reason I say if one is whole, one will be filled with light, but if one is divided, one will be filled with darkness.'

Yeshua followed us into the abyss. He reclined on our couch (the world we live in), left the body that clothed Him on the cross, and went on to live in Spirit. Yeshua was from the one that is whole, just as we who embrace His teachings become whole. [*Name*] wants to embrace what is whole, to be filled with Light, but you, you have become divided and are filled with hate. You, soul in darkness, will not live, you have tasted death. Soul in darkness, for your poor choices we pity you and offer you love and compassion for your suffering.

Jesus said: 'If your leaders say to you, "Look, the Father's kingdom is in the sky," then the birds of the sky will precede you. If they say to you, "It is in the sea," then the fish will precede you. Rather, the Father's kingdom is within you and it is outside you.

When you know yourselves, then you will be known, and you will understand that you are children of the living Father. But if you do not know yourselves, then you live in poverty, and you are the poverty.'

Through the Divine wisdom of the pure spark of Light that is Yeshua, I call upon you, the rebel that disturbs [*Name*] to leave her/his body, for you are the poverty that has embraced this realm, you desire the 'powerful one' which Jesus has destroyed. Leave [*Name's*] temple, the body that is her/his vessel and do not return.

We speak these words from God, the Father that is the Source flowing through all things; the Son, of whom Yeshua is the prime example sent to us; the Holy Spirit that binds the two and links all enlightened Spirits through the collective consciousness.

Amen

Yeshua, the bringer of the Light, love and compassion, the one who has opened the door for us, His siblings, gives us the right to pray in confidence:

Lord I am worthy to receive you,
for your Father's Light is my soul,
I am your brother, sister, and mother
the Holy Spirit, the collective consciousness,
has joined us to God the Father, the source of all things
And the one have become two
Amen

The Soul's Prayer.

Our Father who is in all things,
hallowed be your presence.
Your Kingdom be recognised in each of us,
as your Light is made visible in this realm as in the other.

Give us our days of residence in this dimension and body
the recognition of its imperfections and weaknesses.
We accept our faults and the faults of others,
we see them as lessons for our growth

May we walk upon a straight path,
with open minds and open hearts,
harming no-one along our way.

Where there is knowledge of the true self,
there can be no evil.

Amen.

If the entity has not left, it is because the person seeking to be free has not fully embraced what they have been taught through this exorcism. They are encouraged to repeat the prayers. They are ultimately responsible for making the intruder leave—this cannot be imposed on them. The malevolent entity will not be able to cope with this knowledge, because it is presented with forgiveness and compassion, which these souls find foreign and abhorrent. Compassion is a powerful tool against any malevolent entity that one may encounter.

33. Jesus said, "What you will hear in your ear, in the other ear proclaim from your rooftops.

After all, no one lights a lamp and puts it under a basket, nor does one put it in a hidden place. Rather, one puts it on a lampstand so that all who come and go will see its light."

In Mark 4:21-25, the Parable of the Lamp is extended by verses 24-25, becoming a warning:

'Take notice of what you are hearing. The standard you use will be used for you—and you will receive more besides; anyone who has, will be given more; anyone who has not, will be deprived even of what he has.'

The tone of Thomas 33 is changed in the Gospel of Mark, it comes with a warning to be cautious about what one thinks one hears and how this is conveyed to others. This seems to be an attempt by the writer of Mark to prevent just anyone coming along and preaching with assumed authority. This is consolidated in the last verse. Again, the tone of this statement does not match the words we see in Thomas 33.

Thomas 33 states, 'what you hear in your ear *in the other ear proclaim from the rooftops'*, meaning that the knowledge gained should be nurtured *through the other (inner) ear* and allowed to grow. It is also significant that the last part of Thomas 33 says that one should put this knowledge 'on a lamp stand so that all who come and go will see its light.' A lamp stand is a stationary thing, but it provides light for those who come close to it. In this light they are able to see what they could not see previously. Significantly, it is *they* who are the ones that choose to *come to the light;* it is *not imposed* upon them. The lamp is inside the house (the body) and it is not on a hill for all to see (Thomas 32).

34. Jesus said, "If a blind person leads a blind person, both of them will fall into a hole."

Thomas 34 is part of a thread that links to Thomas 33. Those who have not taken what they have heard into the soul—*the other ear*—do not absorb the truth of Yeshua's teachings. People have taken His words literally and used their misguided beliefs to justify horrific acts against other cultures and religions. This is the hole they fall into, the crime of taking something at face value. Such people have claimed rights and rituals as the keys to the kingdom of God and created their fortified cities (Thomas 32). They have claimed penance will cleanse their parishioners' sins. They have convinced weak minds that paradise awaits them if they kill others and make martyrs of themselves. These are the unclean souls driven by concerns of this world

(Thomas 7). Similarly, others lust for the resurrection of their flesh (what they believe to be their image) as it was in this realm (Thomas 22).

The kingdom of God (the Source) is within those who recognise and nurture It. The flesh only has words at its disposal. The Spirit is above all things and speaks to us through the ear of the heart, intuitively, without words, without pictures. The deaf hear Its voice and the blind see Its Light. When people follow this Light they cannot fall into a hole.

35. Jesus said, "One can't enter a strong person's house and take it by force without tying his hands. Then one can loot his house."

Thomas 35 refers to the material world. The only way to unpack what this world is really about is to *bind its hands*, so that we can rummage through its contents to discover meaning. Great sages and ascetic masters have recognised this and retreated from the world, but that is not what Yeshua was suggesting. The saying takes an aggressive approach, the individual interacts with the 'strong person'—the world. It suggests that we should know what we want and be active in pursuing that goal—the 'loot'. Notice that we are the ones that have entered the strong person's house; we are the intruder, the one who *should not be there*.

In day-to-day situations, it is easy to become emotionally involved and in most instances these experiences lead us away from the pursuit of spiritual growth. Indeed, human existence engages people in concerns about emotional and physical needs. These may involve career, finances, relationships, and health. We are in the house of these 'opponents' and they will not go away, nor can we remove them. If we can bind them, stopping them from obstructing our search, we can learn what is most valuable. The lesson is the importance of their existence in relation to our true self. This is the wealth the human soul gains.

At first, the task we are given in Thomas 35 seems impossible. One can certainly see why ascetics would choose the path of seclusion to achieve this goal. Gautama Buddha spent his whole life searching for a way to extinguish the suffering associated with this existence. While aspects of his teachings are attainable, it is not possible for most people to enter a monastic life in order to avoid life's distractions – see commentary for Thomas 7 for more on the Buddha's teaching. However, escaping the reality of this world, and removing the thin veil it creates, can be done in our everyday lives. When people recognise these obstacles as impermanent and see that material wealth does not give them true happiness, the veil is lifted. Setting people free is the reality that those obstacles are like a cloud, which will fade away.

36. Jesus said, "Do not fret, from morning to evening and from evening to morning, [about your food--what you're going to eat, or about your clothing--] what you are going to wear. [You're much better than the lilies, which neither card nor spin.

As for you, when you have no garment, what will you put on? Who might add to your stature? That very one will give you your garment.]"

A parable similar to Thomas 36 appears in Matthew 6:30. The title and focus of that parable is the *dependence on God*. These verses maintain that obedience to the God of Abraham will ensure physical provisions:

'Now if that is how God clothes the wild flowers growing in the field which are there today and thrown into the furnace tomorrow, will he not much more look after you, you who have so little faith?'

This illustrates the polemical agenda the authors of the Synoptic Gospels held. It also demonstrates how they had no real understanding of what Yeshua was saying to them. The question of *who will feed us* is answered with the analogy of *who will feed the birds of the sky*. The emphasis becomes our physical needs, because these were the things that might persuade people to become followers of the newly forming Christian community. For the same reason, we see chapters and verses in the Synoptic Gospels relating to moral and social interactions. The authors of the synoptic texts provide direction to the community via the authority of Jesus. We should consider, was Jesus concerned with community affairs and our physical needs? The logical response is that Jesus was concerned primarily with teaching His definition of the word 'live', which had nothing to do with the physical body. This is supported by the secret teachings in the Gospel of Thomas.

The purpose of Thomas 36 is to question what is important. When humans answer that question, how do they move forward? When they have no garment (the flesh), what do they put on? This is a profound question, which addresses the metaphysical nature of our existence and not how our physical needs will be met. Yeshua asks: 'Who might add to [our] stature?', the answer is the Holy Spirit which is the collective consciousness—*the one* that is connected to God, the Source. 'That very one will give you your garment.' The *garment* is a symbol for the state of enlightenment, connectedness, and oneness we attain, which *makes us whole*. In this state, we come to see the Son of the *living one*. By putting on this ethereal garment humans become aware of the Divine Field, as opposed to the physical, and are no longer afraid (Thomas 37). People who are seeking the truth are *living in this garment*.

37. His disciples said, "When will you appear to us, and when will we see you?"

Jesus said, "When you strip without being ashamed, and you take your clothes and put them under your feet like little children and trample them, then [you] will see the son of the living one and you will not be afraid."

Thomas 37 makes reference to the psychology of guilt. As in previous sayings, Yeshua asks people to try and become like little children, naïve to erroneous teachings and perceptions. For His contemporaries, these discernments stemmed from their knowledge of the Garden of Eden story in Genesis. After Adam and Eve were disobedient to the god who created them, they became aware of their nakedness and were ashamed. As a side note, some Gnostics interpreted this story in a different way—the serpent became a symbol of wisdom, which set Adam and Eve free from the prison of this creation. Gnostics also described the creator god of the Old Testament as malevolent, based on his tendency to punish and cause suffering. This is at odds with God the Source, whom Yeshua calls Father and who He talks about in the New Testament and in the Gospel of Thomas.

Thomas 37 also relates to sayings where Yeshua points to the things that are important in relation to the kingdom of God. Notice, Jesus' response does not actually answer their question. It talks about an awakening, where the eyes of the disciples are opened to the truth of *what they truly are*—they would see '*the son of the living one and [they would] not be afraid.*' The reference to fear is important. When looking at light as a metaphor we see how it can relate to knowledge. If there is understanding there is nothing hidden, we can see—just as in a well-lit room. Due to this *light*, we are not afraid. When people realise that the flesh is not what they are and that it should not stunt their spiritual development through guilt and shame, they are set free. The body is an impermanent temple that houses the soul. The enlightened Spirit is above guilt and shame because that soul knows it's true heritage. These external distractions, associated with the body, stop people from understanding that they are the sons of *the living one*—they will become a Spirit.

38. Jesus said, "Often you have desired to hear these sayings that I am speaking to you, and you have no one else from whom to hear them. There will be days when you will seek me and you will not find me."

There is a tone of frustration in Thomas 38. It shows that no matter how many times Yeshua spoke to His followers about these mysteries, they had difficulty comprehending them—yet they found solace in hearing Him speak of these things. We also see this in some accounts cited in the New Testament, where the disciples are frustrated with the cryptic parables Yeshua conveyed to them. However, we find that the cryptic parables the disciples were frustrated by had been left out of the canonical texts, because they were ambiguous and suggested that God could be found within the self.

People find comfort in churches and temples. However, often when they leave, they are without that feeling of peace. This is the problem with having a god that is outside of the self. This is why Yeshua states that when He will not be with them they will not be able to find *where He is*. In reality, all anyone needs to do is to look within the self, within the soul, to find that connection. This is the same place and substance that connects all spirits of God's Kingdom. For this reason, Thomas 38 is reflected in the ritual of communion, which is particularly important to Catholic parishioners because they believe the bread and wine are transformed into Jesus' body and blood. By eating and drinking it, they believe they will be brought to everlasting life. The Gospel of Thomas shows us that this ritual is unnecessary. In light of the Gospel of Thomas, we see that the metaphor of the 'Last Supper' represents Yeshua's words as the *body* – His wisdom allows us to nourish the soul, and His *blood* represents the *Source* that is connected to all things. This connection of the *collective breath of life* is metaphoric of the Holy Spirit, the thing that joins us to God, the Source. The Holy Spirit is *the one* who is active in this union—it is the link by which we are all found and reunited with the Source.

The sense of peace people obtain from a structured religious ceremony relates to the Spirit seeking order and harmony. Religious rituals and ceremonies are ordered and predictable. In such a ceremonial space people find peace. This is because the nature of the Spirit is constant, in harmony and unity with the whole. It is calm, ordered, and in peace, It flows through all things seamlessly. The harmony of the Spirit is at odds with the chaos of this realm. It relies on disharmony to renew and determine the fittest for physical survival. Rituals make it easier for people to be still and reconnect to the soul, where they truly 'live'. The problem with ceremony and ritual is that, by their nature, they remove the emphasis from the Spirit, which is internal, to something that is external and transient. The only place humans need to worship is the place that is not visible. This is the same thing that is inside our neighbour, our friend, the stranger we walk past every day—that thing is the soul. The question of *who is my neighbour*, in the Good Samaritan parable of Luke 10:29-37, is not simply a lesson about helping others, regardless of race, or political persuasion. It speaks about the *oneness of the soul* and its importance *above dogmatic laws*. This is where we find Yeshua, in our neighbour, family, friends and all sentient beings throughout this universe.

39. Jesus said, "The Pharisees and the scholars have taken the keys of knowledge and have hidden them. They have not entered nor have they allowed those who want to enter to do so.

As for you, be as sly as snakes and as simple as doves."

To understand the significance of Thomas 39, it is important that we consider what Yeshua means by *the keys of knowledge*. The sayings of Yeshua in the Gospel of Thomas give us knowledge about the nature of this realm and what humans are. These are the *keys that were taken away*. This freedom to explore the truth was initially blocked by the Pharisees, then edited by the authors of the New Testament. This obstruction continued through organised religions following the formation of the canonical texts. The Christian institutions cite the Old and New Testament Gospels as their only source of knowledge. These institutions prevent people from seeking truth outside of what they are told to believe by the leaders of these communities. The leaders of such organisations do not understand the teachings Yeshua conveys in the Gospel of

Thomas. Evidently, it would seem as though they simply feared its power, its capacity to free souls from bondage. To let people know they could find God, the Source, within the self would have undermined their authority and made the institutionalised religion redundant. These leaders did not enter into this knowledge with an open heart and mind. Their concerns for building a Church community prevented them from entering, just as the building opens and closes its doors according to *predetermined* times. *The key* Jesus speaks of is the ability to search freely and to allow the intuitive self to explore the possibilities. It is only through this questioning and exploration that people may grow into a living Spirit.

Jesus' contemporaries, and some religious leaders of the twenty-first century, use *the physical* as a reference point for their teachings—they are wrong to do so. When a Catholic person is encouraged to state that they are not worthy of Jesus, they harm their soul. They are denying their link to God, the Source. In the Catholic Mass, the congregation replies to the priest's proclamation of the Communion Host (bread that has become the body of Christ—for Catholics), with the statement: '*Lord I am not worthy that you should enter under my roof, but only say the word and my soul shall be healed.*' This statement goes against the teachings of Jesus, who reminds us on many occasions (in the Gospel of Thomas) that we are like Him, we are His kin and intimately connected to Him. In making such a statement, these people deny this connection. This declaration comes from the belief that the flesh rules over the soul. This statement also infers that the soul is a victim of the flesh, it has been overpowered. These false perceptions stem from the notion that the God of Abraham has punished humans for Adam's transgression. This is untrue. The flesh and this realm are of their own nature and needs, and we, the soul, are of another nature. We should appreciate that this *recitation* comes to us from what a centurion said about his beloved servant. We are given a new perspective when we see it in the context of what came before and after this verse. In Matthew 8 we find:

[5] When he went into Capernaum a centurion came up and pleaded with him.
[6] 'Sir,' he said, 'my servant is lying at home paralysed and in great pain.'
[7] Jesus said to him, 'I will come myself and cure him.'
[8] The centurion replied, '*Sir, I am not worthy to have you under my roof; just give the word and my servant will be cured.*
[9] For I am under authority myself and have soldiers under me; and I say to one man, "Go," and he goes; to another, "Come here," and he comes; to my servant, "Do this," and he does it.'
[10] When Jesus heard this he was astonished and said to those following him, 'In truth I tell you, in no one in Israel have I found faith as great as this.

[Verse 8 has emphasis added to highlight its relevance to this commentary]

Verse 8 becomes contentious when one looks at the actual event. The centurion, under great threat to his position of leadership, is clearly asking for his male servant to be cured. We may glean from this that Yeshua understood there to be a special relationship between the two men. He made this assumption because the centurion was making a perilous request. Yet Jesus would eagerly go to their house and heal this man. This redresses the orthodox Christian beliefs about gay relationships. After the centurion's request Yeshua makes an observation, something that is very telling about His community. Yeshua states that nobody He had met up to that point had as much faith as that centurion. The centurion believed in Jesus' words, he did not need His physical presence. There is an inference that the gentiles were more capable of understanding Jesus' message, because His contemporaries were tainted by their belief in a stern, patriarchal god—a god that demanded sacrifices and adherence to the Law. The centurion's faith was enough to cure his beloved servant. This is what Yeshua was trying to convey throughout His ministry—faith is an intangible force that can overcome the obstacles people meet within this realm. The belief that we are not worthy is an obstacle to being free of suffering. Yeshua told the centurion *He would come to his house* and cure his servant, because love and compassion have no barriers.

Humans cannot judge themselves on the measure of this realm and its weaknesses—this would be a sin. Knowledge about God's Kingdom and what we are *based on in the physical world* is harmful to the soul. With a mind full of guilt, shame, and a sense of not being worthy, people are inclined to deny their intimate connection and kinship with Jesus. It is a principal crime, which religious leaders have inflicted on successive generations. Their antiquated attitude and beliefs must be left aside for the truth to light the way. The truth is that where there is knowledge, there is Light—no fear, only connectedness, peace, and love.

When one is allowed to enter upon oneself (explore what the human soul is) then one is *given* the keys to truth. Those who are in positions of authority and have not explored themselves lead others astray (Thomas 67). They use outdated traditions and dogma to substantiate their own position, but the reality of the *Father's Kingdom* does not support their teachings. Asking which of the major religions has caused the least amount of conflict in the world gets us closer to an idea of what is at the centre of Yeshua's message. The answer is in a system that seeks to recognise reality and abate its impact on the mind. This is Buddhism. Though there are variations within Buddhism, as there are in Christian denominations, it essentially teaches that all beings desire to end suffering and be at peace. To attain this state of contentment, we must respect each other's lives and experiences and recognise the root cause of suffering (see commentary for Thomas 7). Evidently, some Buddhist faiths have been affected by the material world. These denominations of Buddhism have delved into mystic practices and worship of deities, to ensure a fortunate afterlife or rebirth. They have moved away from Buddha's original teachings, allowing their desire to control what happens after death to change the primary canon. Desire is born of this world—the desire to survive, the desire to have physical comforts and pleasure, and so on. While adherents want to become enlightened this desire in itself becomes an obstacle. *Desire* in Buddhist teaching is seen as an obstacle to reaching the objective of enlightenment. Yeshua's teachings are a gentle yoke (Thomas 90), they show people that *they are two distinct things*. Humans are first and foremost a soul that has been blinded to the truth. Secondly, they are in a physical body that has its own requirements. When people recognise what they really are and how the soul grows, they become joined to God, the Source. This is made possible through the collective consciousness we know as the Holy Spirit.

The observations regarding Catholic dogma appear to place this Church, and its parishioners, in the one basket. However, this is not the intention, nor is it an accurate picture of reality. Within all institutions there are people who are working to shift the obstacles and, indeed, there are many nuns and priests who see the schism their leaders have created. The Church has been made into an institution concerned with wealth, power, control, and longevity. Jesus said to His disciples, as He does *to you*: 'be as sly as snakes and as simple as doves.' Entering into a discourse with those who are *lost in* dogma, ritual, and misguided tradition, is of no value; we must be able to move around undetected, to change what must be changed. In this way, you are allowed to be 'as simple as doves' and as innocent as a child, untainted by dogma and the teachings that are rooted in the material world.

40. Jesus said, "A grapevine has been planted apart from the Father. Since it is not strong, it will be pulled up by its roots and will perish."

Thomas 40 is a reference to the faith of Jesus' contemporaries, which was rooted in dogma and was based on rituals. Moreover, Thomas 40 also extends to the individuals and groups of the twenty-first century who are devoid of knowledge of their true nature. These people do not understand the reality of what they are and how they are intrinsically linked to everything through the collective consciousness (Thomas 77). Having a weak or non-existent link to the thing humanity has sprung from, these people fall back into the soil and their energy is reabsorbed into the whole—the Source—to return in another form. They will become a *single one*, as we see in Thomas 4 and 23. This truth should not be read as a warning or threat; it is a fact. This reabsorption is energy moving from one place to another—changing, not ending. The difference between the living and the dead is that the living move on with a wealth of experiences, which become manifest as wisdom and connect-edness (Thomas 3, 4, and 29). This process grows the collective consciousness as it is the joining of God, the Source, to sentient beings.

Often, Jesus refers to *the Father*; this is our father too, as we are Jesus' brother, sister, and mother (Thomas 99). We need to consider then: who is *the Father*? This description is used because of the patriarchal culture Yeshua was born into, but the title is turned on its head. Although it is unlikely Jewish people used this term to describe *their relationship to* their God, it is one Yeshua's contemporaries would have understood. The one who *inspires* life and determines lineage is the father. However, Jesus used it to describe *His relationship to God, the Source*, because this was the only way to make people of the future know what He actually meant. It is necessary for people to comprehend this relationship. In doing so, they may be *planted with* the Father/Source, so that their roots are strong; they flourish in the Light of the Source, connected through the collective consciousness (Holy Spirit).

If we take a human example of a father, we can see two ways of perceiving this one role. We can see someone who is meant to provide for his child, teach and guide them through life. Alternatively, we could see a father to whom we owe our biological make-up of genes. How does this abstract of a human father fit *the Father* Jesus speaks of? The Abrahamic faiths would see the Father (their God) as one who administers to them through the prophets and has a stern voice, very much the patriarchal leader and provider. This Father is like the first perceived role of supplier and authority figure. From what we know of the Father described in the Gospel of Thomas, Jesus was not referring to someone who played any such role. The 'Father' Jesus consistently refers to is actually symbolic. That Father is the one who has *issued us forth* as creative energy which has limitless potential. We do not need to be *told how to live* and what moral values we must uphold, because they are instilled in us through the connection of the Holy Spirit. We intuitively know what is right and wrong. Those who do wrong are either momentarily consumed by the lion (Thomas 7), have limited potential to attain an enlightened state, or have embraced a hedonistic, egocentric life, which is fixated in this material universe.

Yeshua has asked us to look upon the Father as *a source of where we come from*. If It is our Father then *we are Its offspring*—we are like *It*. This is symbolic. Put into contemporary language, we could speak of an energy that binds all things and aggregates in places where it becomes conscious of itself; otherwise, it disperses and becomes part of the whole again (Thomas 41). The soul is a spark of energy created from the initial expansion (Big Bang) of the Source into the abyss (Thomas 97). This universe has come away from the other dimensions, not unlike a spider's web that has broken away from its anchoring points and folded into itself. It has created within itself physical matter that has formed stars, planets, and countless life forms. The Father/Source, which flows through the other dimensions also flows through this one. However, Its relationship with physical matter is not constant, since It is foreign to this dimension. Material lifeforms perish and are finite; the Source does not perish. It is in motion *through* this realm. To become whole again, *this Light* seeks out places to aggregate in sentient beings. *The soul, which is this Light*, has found human bodies that have *evolved for it* (Thomas 29). The energy from the Source attracts its own substance like a magnet. It only does this while it is in a body, where it can be stored and grown. If this energy is ignored its potential remains at a level that disperses on death.

41. Jesus said, "Whoever has something in hand will be given more, and whoever has nothing will be deprived of even the little they have."

In the New Testament, Thomas 41 is linked to Thomas 33, as evident in Mark 4:24-25. The purpose of this link was to create a warning about the dissemination of knowledge. Knowledge was and still is power.

Fundamentalist and orthodox believers have generally interpreted this saying through their knowledge of the physical world, a knowledge that is at odds with spiritual wisdom. The hand is not the physical hand; it is the soul that is reaching out for knowledge of the truth. People who do not seek the truth, and accept whatever neat package is presented to them, will be deprived of even the little they have. The 'something' referred to in this saying is the 'coming into being' we see in Thomas 19. It is the ability to see reality in abstract terms, to see outside the square one lives in, to be able to experience what is in the circle, the whole.

Some preachers use biblical references to convince impressionable people that their patronage will bring them, among other human concerns, success and prowess. God, the Source does not choose one community or individual over another. We obtain the things we have through hard work, though certainly genetics and environment have an impact too. This kind of thinking can be seen in a sportsperson who makes the sign of the cross or says a prayer, thinking their god will intervene, affording them success. It is the sportsperson's skill and the factors of chance that rule this realm and these elements determine their triumph. A singer may sing well if they are genetically predisposed to having the right kind of vocal cords—God does not choose one person to be talented above another. This is not the way of the Father/Source linked to the collective consciousness (Holy Spirit). The correct physical attribute, a strong work ethic, and being in the right place at the right time, is the formula for success in these fields—God has nothing to do with it. To think otherwise is damaging to the millions of people who are striving to be successful in these fields but fail.

The physical world and the Spirit are very different. We can see this through the following analogy. In the negative of a black and white photograph, the parts that create white on photographic paper are black, no light passes through this part of the negative. The parts that create a black area are clear, light passes through this part of the negative to expose the light sensitive paper. If we look into the night sky we see the endless depths of space, with stars and planets scattered throughout. If we consider the physical world as a *mirror* of the Father's Kingdom, appearing in reverse, then the endless depths of space can be seen as the Father. In a photo negative, the night sky would appear white and the stars as black dots. This visual metaphor serves as an analogy to our perceptions of the truth, which is based on the physical world. This realm allows for a limited and distorted view of reality which we cannot fully experience with our *physical* senses.

Consider how the English language reveals a truth about the choices we might make. The word Yeshua uses to describe what it is to *truly exist*, as a perfect human, is 'live'. When we write this word in reverse (in English) it spells 'evil'. This is a symbolic way of understanding where we are in the twenty-first century. On one hand, Humans may choose to pursue a healthy planet and united world, which would also allow for spiritual growth. On the other hand, they may choose the *opposite*. On an unhealthy polluted planet filled with conflict and suffering, the souls that enter bodies are distracted and their potential to truly *live* is hampered. This is the *evil* world, but people can change this, it is a *choice*. Sadly, all too often, the way of the lamb is dominated and obscured by the way of the lion (Thomas 7), but people must believe that they have the power. If the masses desire a united, healthy world, then those in power will make it happen, if for no other reason than to satisfy their desire to remain in power. If one has knowledge of the collective consciousness in hand, the journey to endless wealth, freedom, and potential, is inevitable. This is the kingdom of the Father, the Source.

42. Jesus said, "Be passersby."

This saying speaks about the way day-to-day life can impinge on our spiritual growth. To be 'passersby' of this life is the most difficult thing people can attempt. This is why many people who seek spiritual growth choose to remove themselves from society, as we see in the first part of Thomas 27.

Often, we are either totally enamoured of this life, or upset by what we cannot have materialistically and emotionally. Ideally, we should be *passersby or observers of this realm*, so that we can see how the soul is at odds with the material world. When we have to leave this life, we should have no attachments or guilt that may hinder our union with God, the Source. Believing we are not worthy makes us unworthy, simply by these negative thoughts—unlike children who are untainted by the world, as in Thomas 22. Disseminating the notion of being unworthy is a tool of entities existing in darkness.

Ascetic masters withdraw from the world, but this is not possible for everyone, nor is it desirable. Often, denying ourselves something makes it more attractive and causes us to place greater importance on it than is necessary. This desire may also cause guilt, which is damaging to a person's growth, as seen in Thomas 14. The issue of sexual desire, mentioned previously, may become more exciting when it is made taboo. In countries where women's bodies are completely covered, we find men who may become aroused simply by the sight of a woman's leg or her hair. This ultimately leads to guilt, shame, and mistrust. In countries where both males and females wear very little, the sight of flesh is not as erotic or taboo. After all, Yeshua tells humans that when they can take off their clothes, trample them under foot, and not be ashamed, then they will see Him again. In this way, we are no longer *veiled* by this world and its falsehoods (Thomas 37). If an adult desires sex they should pursue the experience with another like-minded, consenting adult, without shame. There is no shame or sin in the flesh. We are above the flesh that clothes us, that is why we can pass by the experience and see it for what it is. It is a physical act; one that is sometimes driven by the soul's desire to connect with the Source. This kind of connection is only a pseudo one, but it reflects the compulsion of the soul to be re-joined.

As we pass through this life, we need to be aware of the disparity between the physical life and the life of the soul which *is being resurrected*. Organised religions use the human inability to see the perfection of the soul (the great wealth) to hold onto their community of followers. They achieve this by making people believe the flesh (the poverty) is somehow equivalent to the soul. In truth, we know that the flesh is just a vessel through which we experience this world. Our intellectual capacity is a double-edged sword. It is the breath of life given to us by God, the Source. It is also the reason why we have created the divide between the Spirit realm and the material realm.

The greatest example of a passerby was Mary, the mother of Jesus. As a vulnerable, innocent teenager, the physical realm tested her spiritual capacity and strength. She was victorious and, in this sense, she can claim the title of 'Virgin-Mary'. As a wife and mother to several children, Mary never lost sight of where her soul came from; this gave her the capacity to overcome the *powerful one*, which we see in Thomas 98. Human perceptions of virginity are determined by sexual contact, but this definition is not one the realm of the Spirit recognises. Sexual acts are a result of the mechanisms of the physical realm and its way of either making a connection or creating life, by mirroring *the other* (*the realm of the Spirit*). When male and female sex cells come together, the one become two and create life. This action is an attempt at *replicating the meeting of the soul with the Father/Source*, through the conduit action of the Holy Spirit. It is an unsound attempt; this body and world decays—the Spirit does not. Mary was aware of these things. Through this knowledge, she became *untouched by this realm* and was in every respect of the word, a *passerby* (*ever-virgin*).

43. His disciples said to him, "Who are you to say these things to us?"

"You don't understand who I am from what I say to you.

Rather, you have become like the Judeans, for they love the tree but hate its fruit, or they love the fruit but hate the tree."

Yeshua could see that His disciples had a polarised attitude, because of their limited view of reality. This attitude came from their culture, which was in waiting for the *Messiah*—one who would liberate them from oppression. The Jewish people of His time wanted a soldier-king who would bring them order, stability, and prosperity. There were numerous individuals claiming to be this Messiah, but Yeshua was different. Yeshua was not concerned about this world in the way His contemporaries hoped He would be. We see in the Synoptic Gospels that the authors had woven Jesus' life into the prophecies of the Old Testament (Torah). Through this process, Jesus essentially becomes the King of Heaven and of Earth—seated at the right hand of the Father (God). Jesus would come back to judge the living and the dead. This conflicts with the teachings in the Gospel of Thomas. Moreover, it is seen with more clarity as each of the gospels is produced, climaxing in the Gospel of John. The author(s) of John cement the god-like persona of Jesus through Christology, but they did not accept the Gospel of Thomas as part of this definition. The first statement in Thomas 43, by the disciples, is also reflected in the synoptic gospels – there too we find that they were confused by His teachings. Yet, in the synoptic texts we do not see these cryptic teachings, because they were left out for this very reason. Yeshua's statement, *'you don't understand who I am from what I say to you'* demonstrates His frustration with His followers. Their desire to compartmentalise Yeshua's purpose, based on their subjective aspirations, is symbolically explained through the analogy of a tree and its fruit.

The *contentious* nature of Jesus' secret teachings made it necessary to keep these messages ambiguous and cryptic. This was essential because the sayings were in conflict with contemporary knowledge. Their understanding about the nature of God and what their relationship with *Him* should be like was different to Jesus' primary teaching. Through those cryptic parables, Yeshua's contemporaries would not have been able to accuse Him of heresy. More importantly, only those who intuitively felt that their knowledge was incomplete would bother attempting to decipher the Gospel of Thomas. Sadly, most of Yeshua's contemporaries, and the generations following His death, were not seeking this kind of truth. These people liked the idea of an earthly king, with powers ordained from a patriarchal God—this is *the tree* they liked, a tree that has its roots in this realm, not the other. This is why the Old Testament was so appealing to the authors of the canonical texts. The authors of the New Testament circumvented sayings that were too difficult to comprehend, or that suggested one could find God by searching within. They used only those sayings that fitted what people already understood. If the parables (sayings) were too difficult, they were ignored, this is at the heart of Thomas . *The fruit* the disciples rejected was the reality of Yeshua's messages—the transitory nature of the material world and the *wealth* that exists inside the flesh. Instead, these people desired a divinely ordained king who would one day come back to reclaim what is his. For this reason, in the early part of the twenty-first century, we still have religious institutions, which have grandiose, aesthetically pleasing buildings to represent this tree. They are equivalent to *the tree*, because they are the things people can physically *relate to*. To His contemporaries, Yeshua was a man who was going to liberate them from the oppression they lived under—to them He was a holy warrior. Jesus' messages did not reflect the words of a soldier sent by their god. To His contemporaries, Jesus' messages did not come from *this kind of tree*. For this reason, Yeshua makes the observation that they only liked what they preferred from a tree, either its aesthetic or its fruit, not the whole package. His contemporaries did not appreciate what this *tree of life* was actually giving them—a crucial message. If people only appreciate *the image*, or the fruit of the tree, they cannot understand how the whole thing exists as an entirety. This is the soil (the Father/Source), the tree (the Son), the fruits, (the wisdom, wherein exists the seed, the genetic lineage that is the Holy Spirit, the DNA chain of the collective consciousness). This is *The Perpetual Tree*.

44. Jesus said, "Whoever blasphemes against the Father will be forgiven, and whoever blasphemes against the Son will be forgiven, but whoever blasphemes against the Holy Spirit will not be forgiven, either on earth or in heaven."

Pneumatology is a branch of Christian theology which refers to the study of the Holy Spirit. Delving into this area demonstrates how allusive a definition can become, particularly when it has a history stemming from the Jewish Torah to the New Testament. This kind of archaeology illustrates how various authors had made nuanced references, such that it made the definition of what the Holy Spirit embodied (pun intended)

very broad and difficult to encapsulate. The confusion becomes more obvious when we see the schism it has caused among various denominations of the Christian faith.

The definition of the Holy Spirit from the perspective of the Gospel of Thomas is, at first glance, controversial. Through *77th Pearl: The Perpetual Tree*, we see that the Father, Son and Holy Spirit are *one*. The two anthropomorphised characteristics (father and son) describe *attributes of this one*. The Source is like the human father who combines his genes with the mothers. In this analogy, *the mother* is the sentient bodies, planet Earth and universe. The seed of the Father is the soul – this becomes the Son when it matures into a *living Spirit*. It is no surprise that the ethereal nature of the Holy Spirit has been attributed to elemental forces, such as wind, fire and water. This is evidence of the human drawing on what they experience in the material realm to describe what is in the realm of the Spirit. Evidence of these three (Father, Son and Holy Spirit) being attributes of the one thing can be seen in Thomas 30, where Yeshua affirms He is *with the one*. The *one* is the Source (Father), joined to the Son (sentient beings), *through* the collective consciousness (Holy Spirit). In this triad, the Holy Spirit connects the Father and Son through consciousness – the mind of God, the Source. After all, if *the mind* is disconnected from the body then the body cannot function. If we look at the broad, visual symbology of the Holy Spirit then this notion of connection becomes even more apparent. In the Old Testament (Torah), God (the Spirit) is described as the breath of life, also understood as wind, to create life and give people prophetic vision. In Hebrew, the word 'ruach' (meaning wind or breath) can be used in both masculine and feminine form. In the New Testament, the Holy Spirit is symbolised as water, which becomes a dove during Jesus' baptism. In Acts of the Apostles, it is described as fire coming down upon the disciples, allowing them to be understood by the diverse cultural groups who were present. Notice, these descriptions have a common characteristic, that is *connection*. The air flows all around us, we could not survive without it. The air we breathe is shared by all and it shifts from one corner of the globe to the other, via the wind. The human Spirit, in its enlightened state, is neither male nor female, rather, it is both of these at the same time. Water is composed of two elements that are *connected* to form this life giving, and sustaining, liquid. The properties of fire have been used by humanity for aeons – it can act as light, protection and warmth that all humans may benefit from. These observations allow us to see what *the Comforter*, mentioned by Jesus in the Gospel of John, has always been – it is consciousness. This is God, the Father, the Source. At the beginning of the twenty-first century, the importance of consciousness was recognised by scientists and researchers studying UAP (Unidentified Aerial Phenomena) and associated paranormal incidents. This is *the Comforter* being disclosed to many.

People are now becoming aware of the dynamics of quantum physics, how particles on a subatomic level may behave in this universe. These theories allow us to consider the human body as a conglomeration of atoms, which combine and are held together by an unknown force. We can relate this force to the teachings about the Holy Spirit, referenced previously. Consciousness is awareness, thought; but where does it come from? It can only be a collective whole – joined in a singularity humans have called God. *It* is a form of light that has expanded into this realm. *It* has inspired the creation of physical forms to house *Its* Light. In this way, the fractured Source is reunited to the whole (Thomas 107). This is what beings from other worlds/dimensions know and have been trying to teach humanity. Evidence of this triad is not unlike human intuition. We can find this truth in the Gospel of Mark, Chapter 13: 11, where we see Jesus state,

And when you are taken to be handed over, do not worry before-hand about what to say; no, say whatever is given to you when the time comes, because it is not you who will be speaking; it is the Holy Spirit.

Here we see Yeshua assure His disciples that they will know what to say, because they are connected to the collective consciousness. This is God the Father (the Source) communicating through the *conduit*, the Holy Spirit.

In Thomas 44, we see Yeshua warn people that if they deny their heritage this is blaspheme against the Holy Spirit, because they are negating *its action of unification*. This is evident in the last part of the saying: *'either on earth or in heaven'*. We have seen that the way humans have perceived heaven is not correct (Thomas 3, 11, 18, 20, 22, 24), so these words have another, more cryptic meaning. In referring to both *heaven and earth*, Yeshua gives people a clue as to what the Holy Spirit does—it is the thing that is the link between the physical and metaphysical, the intangible. The *Son* (sentient bodies) exist in this material realm. They are the life forms where the light of the Source, which went out onto the distant road (the abyss), may dwell. The *Trinity* is describing a relationship between what humans have called God and humanity, which is something profoundly intimate and sacred. Denying this *intimacy* and this link is to blaspheme. The Earth represents the material manifestation and *heaven* represents the metaphysical—*the Soul*. Heaven and Earth become one through the presence of consciousness – what people have called the Holy Spirit.

People whose faith denies the existence of the Holy Spirit are not being condemned here. Their deep love and commitment for their God is the Holy Spirit in action–it is their soul seeking *connection* with God, the Source. When Yeshua states that blasphemy against the Holy Spirit cannot be forgiven on earth or in heaven, He means that this is not a way of thinking that can be made whole. All other perceptions are something people can redeem themselves from, but this is different. This blasphemy is about denying the logic of the heart; the sin here is to not understand the reality, the truth. Forgiveness cannot make someone accept *the truth*. To not accept consciousness as an integral part of the *God anatomy* is to deny the existence of the human heart, without which, the human tastes death, becoming the lion (Thomas 7).

In Thomas 44, Yeshua reveals to us the importance of the Holy Spirit (consciousness), confirming that it is the thing that connects all spiritual beings. God, the Source is the invisible Light that is through all things (Thomas 77) and *It* is the thing our soul is made of. In this realm (this universe) the Sons are male, female, those people identifying as transgender, and intersex. In 'heaven' (the other realms/dimensions) the Son is the genderless Spirit. It is for the recognition of this link that Yeshua's spirit was thrust through the divide, into this dimension, so that the powerful one (this realm's allure) could be metaphorically destroyed (Thomas 98). Through the actions of the collective consciousness, humans could recognise the poverty and, instead, embrace the wealth—which they truly are (Thomas 3 and 29).

45. Jesus said, "Grapes are not harvested from thorn trees, nor are figs gathered from thistles, for they yield no fruit.

Good persons produce good from what they've stored up; bad persons produce evil from the wickedness they've stored up in their hearts, and say evil things. For from the overflow of the heart they produce evil."

Throughout human history, there have been individuals who have been identified as the manifestation of evil. In Thomas 45, Yeshua tells us that it is the human heart that has the potential to create good or evil in this world. It depends on *what humans store up in their hearts*. In Thomas 44, we see that the heart is the place linked to the Holy Spirit, because it is intrinsically linked to the mind, the collective consciousness. If people deny this link then the lion may consume them, and the lion will still appear as human (Thomas 7). The nature of the Spirit is to have harmony, balance, and peace; the nature of evil is the opposite. Chaos is an intrinsic element of the material universe. Through this contrast we see the divide between the soul and the flesh. Any person, from any faith background can make this link. Naming this phenomenon as the Father, Son, and Holy Spirit is not important, but knowing that God is one, and humanity is connected to this one, is crucial. Jesus uses the word 'live' to describe *the coming to life of the enlightened Spirit*; when we create obstacles toward this process, we create evil. These obstacles are stored up in the human heart—these are the thoughts and emotions which are based on physical responses, rather than spiritual mindfulness.

The evil people may create is broad. It can be seen in the vilification of minority groups or other cultures, based on their sexuality, beliefs, or appearance. It can also be seen in apathetic attitudes towards the environment, such as polluting and so on. Physical suffering is an obstacle to the *awakening* of the Spirit. If the body is in pain it overrides our ability to focus on the nature of the soul, in effect, making the body a prison. This is why it is imperative that we find a solution to the growing pollution and population crisis. It is faith that 'God will provide' which sees people in economically disadvantaged countries have more children than they can afford to support. This is due to a lack of education, primarily for women. Would it not be wise to have two children and allow them to have all the essentials of life, rather than struggle to feed six children? Certainly, a lack of education can be harmful, but it is the Church authorities who see this suffering and continue to position doctrine against contraception. Their desire for control, through dogma, is evidence of the *lion*, which has *consumed them* (Thomas 7). *In their heart*, a greater population of members creates a larger, stronger institution. What they have *stored up in their heart* is the notion that their institution must override all other religious communities; otherwise, the other will take over, simply through greater numbers. The same attitude can be seen in production companies that grow their business at the cost of the environment. This way of thinking is completely devoid of spiritual pursuits, which is what Yeshua was concerned about. Souls that are devoid of the Light have carefully created situations where their primary concern is wealth accumulation. This attitude needs to change if the human species is to survive. A solution for these people might be to focus on building their wealth through sustainable production. In this way, the lion may indeed create a place for the lamb to exist, while still satisfying its lust for power and control.

Yeshua rejected the world and all of its riches, offered to Him *by* Satan (Matthew 4:8-10). In doing this, Yeshua was saying that the only *one* deserving of attention and desire is the Spirit, which dwells in the realm of the collective consciousness. The kingdom is *not of this realm*, yet it is in front of us and most people refuse to recognise it. Its *seed* is in each one of us (Thomas 20). As mentioned previously, in the commentary for Thomas 21, the story of the temptation of Jesus is one that resembles humanity's plight. *The satan* is historically an angel working for God. However, in this context *it is people's weakness* for this world and their decision not to think as the Spirit does—*as God would*. Denial of the world does not mean people should walk off into the desert and become ascetics. What it does mean is that humans need to set aside time to recognise the truth of what they are as conscious beings, in control of their limitless potential. In this sense, what people need to store up in their hearts is that they are worthy of God, the Source, because they are made of *It*, just as Jesus is made of *the Source*—He is our kin, we are His brothers and sisters (Thomas 99).

46. Jesus said, "From Adam to John the Baptist, among those born of women, no one is so much greater than John the Baptist that his eyes should not be averted.

But I have said that whoever among you becomes a child will recognize the (Father's) Kingdom and will become greater than John."

John the Baptist represents someone who is closest to the thing Jesus wants people to be. John rejected the religious doctrine of the pious Pharisees for the simplest of lives, stripped of all earthly influences and desires. He became a messenger—heralding the coming of Jesus, the Light in this realm, which was *veiled in darkness*. Yeshua was the great white owl who saw through the darkness in all directions.

Yeshua describes John as one whose eyes should not be averted, because he was worthy. He knew who Yeshua was and who He was akin to. This is also a reference to the question Yeshua asks His disciples in Thomas 13 and, interestingly, in the Gospel of Judas. In the Gospel of Judas *'The Disciples Become Angry'* Jesus asks:

"'[Let] any one of you who is [strong enough] among human beings bring out the perfect human and stand before my face" They all said "We have the strength" But their Spirits did not dare to stand before [him], except for Judas Iscariot. He was able to stand before him, but he could not look him in the eyes, and he turned his face away. Judas said to him, "I

know who you are and where you have come from. You are
from the immortal realm of Barbelo. And I am not worthy to
utter the name of the one who has sent you.'"
(Extract from The Gospel of Judas, Edited by Rodolphe
Kasser, Marvin Meyer and Gregor Wurst, p.22-23, National
Geographic Society 2006).

What is of most relevance to the saying in Thomas 46 is that
Judas knows where Jesus is from, but even he, regarded as the
one who stood above the other disciples in this text, had to
avert his eyes. We can conclude the Gnostic author of Judas
recognised that, like the other disciples, Judas was still tainted
by this realm, unlike John the Baptist. According to the Gospel
of Judas, he did what the other disciples could not do for
Jesus—destroy the flesh that clothed His Spirit. Through this,
Yeshua created the ultimate allegory, showing us the disparity
between the lamb and the lion (Thomas 7)—the Spirit and the
flesh. Although reference has been made here to the Gospel
of Judas, it should be recognised that this text does not have
the merit the Gospel of Thomas has. It is evident that an individual or group who was being marginalised by the orthodox
Christians of the time has tainted the Gospel of Judas with
vindictiveness. The Gospel of Judas is very much a Gnostic
text, as it uses myths which are known to be of Gnostic origin.
There is also homophobic vilification used against orthodox
Christian leaders and a polemic undercurrent, which brings
into question most of its contents. The difference with the
Gospel of Thomas is that it is purely focused on Jesus' message
and teaching. It does not attempt to turn *the messenger into the
message* or use His words to vilify and condemn others. The
message (gospel) was the reason and purpose Jesus entered
into this layer (world).

In Thomas 46, Yeshua points to John's recognition of this world's
inadequacies. It is not the kingdom of God, the Father, the
Source; it is the realm of the elemental forces, ruled by natural,

chaotic cycles. John recognised the importance of the Spirit above the corporeal life and tried to find a way to separate the two. He did this by the ritual of Baptism, which was designed to make a person feel one with God and to wash away the sin of self-condemnation. In the process, the individual is reborn in Spirit. John used the concept of ritual washing, which was mandatory before entering the Temple, as a way to switch on the recognition of our connection to God, opening our eyes to *our connection* to God. Baptism was a ritual designed to *wash away* the things that taint our true nature and become permeated by the Divine mind. Through this process, people would reject their ties to this realm, accepting and recognising the Spirit (God). However, in light of Thomas 46, we might ask: did John really understand these things and did this work in the long-term for most people?

In the time of John the Baptist, the ritual action of washing before entering the place of God (the Temple) was necessary because people understood the function of ritual. It gave a sense of righteousness. Yeshua wanted His contemporaries to be free from ritual, because in reality, they were always worthy of God, the Father, the Source. Yeshua tells people that if they become innocent and naïve like a child, unaffected by this realm, they will recognise the kingdom and will become greater than John the Baptist. As difficult as this may sound, it is possible. If people can become 'passersby' (Thomas 42), observers of this life, if they can interact with it, if they can appreciate and enjoy their temples (planet and body), and walk away untouched—like Jesus' mother, Mary—then humans are on their way. In these sayings, Yeshua has shown us how, through recognising our true nature and our kinship with Him, we are set free from all sin. The human soul is above all of these obstacles. Jesus has shown us the path and it is found in our logical, *intuitive self.*

47. Jesus said, "A person cannot mount two horses or bend two bows.

And a slave cannot serve two masters, otherwise that slave will honour the one and offend the other.

Nobody drinks aged wine and immediately wants to drink young wine. Young wine is not poured into old wine skins, or they might break, and aged wine is not poured into a new wineskin, or it might spoil.

An old patch is not sewn onto a new garment since it would create a tear."

In the Gospel of Mark 2:18-22 'The Question about Fasting', we see this saying adopted in a puzzling way, combined with the saying of Thomas 104. In the Gospel of Mark, we see the writer combine the metaphor of Jesus as the bridegroom and His followers as the guests. The disciples celebrate His presence, aware of His impending departure from them, when they will mourn losing Yeshua with fasting—with the last three sentences in Thomas 47. This, again, indicates how the authors of the Synoptic Gospels have used Thomas, a text they could not comprehend, as a reference point. It also indicates the way Jesus' words had been interpreted by people who felt they were knowledgeable enough about Jesus' purpose and intentions to make such arbitrary links. The Gospel of Thomas does not have such pretence; these are the statements left as they were. The sayings in Thomas 47 and 104 are not intended to sit together, they are addressing two different issues. The disciples would have understood the metaphor of Jesus as the bridegroom, who will eventually leave them, because He told them He would (Matthew 16:21-23). What they could not comprehend was the disparity between the old and the new, because the new was not fully formed in that time. The new was a comprehension of what it means to *live* and what the *kingdom* was. (Thomas 113).

The reference point the Synoptic Gospel writers had for grasping who Yeshua was and what His teachings meant was the Torah (Old Testament). As mentioned previously, the Gospel of Mark is known to be the first Synoptic Gospel, written seventy to ninety years after Jesus' death. We see in Mark, and in the other canonical gospels, a development of the narrative, in which they describe why Yeshua came to this world and the reasons He was crucified. Yeshua becomes the perfect sacrifice, replacing the burnt offerings made in the Temple—atoning for the sins of humanity. Apart from this sacrifice, the Synoptic Gospels illustrate a battle between good and evil. Ironically, the face of evil becomes the very community Jesus came from. This can be seen through the climatic vilification of the Jewish society in Luke, rather than the few insecure Pharisees and the Roman leader who bear the blame in the previous gospels. Luke presents the Jewish community as a source of darkness through subtle changes in the narrative descriptions. Luke was a gentile, he would have been marginalised by the Jewish Christians, hence this author's antagonistic feelings toward this community.

The Synoptic Gospels are driven by polemic discourse. They are meant to persuade the reader of the links between the prophecies in the Torah and the meaning and purpose of Jesus' teachings. While Jesus may have *used* these prophecies to establish His ministry, did He want an *old patch (Old Testament edicts) sewn onto a new garment (His teachings)?* The Source flows through all things and, via the collective consciousness (Holy Spirit), works in stunningly complex ways. It would have been near impossible for someone like Jesus to establish a significant following without the Old Testament prophecies (like those seen in Psalm 69:22, a reference to His crucifixion; and in Psalm 16:10-11, a reference to resurrection; and other references to a saviour in Isaiah 52:1-15). Jesus could have been dismissed as an eccentric, if He was not born into the Jewish community. This was (is) a society searching for a saviour. How much the canonical gospel authors had edited and embellished what was known about Jesus' teachings might continue to be a point of contention. If we look to the Gospel of Thomas, we see an important truth. Yeshua came to our realm (the material layer) to give us keys, which can unlock something we were not capable of comprehending until the twenty-first century. This is the time when people may comprehend His messages, untainted by old wine, because Yeshua's wisdom is the new and everlasting garment. This should in no way denigrate or subvert the importance of the Old Testament, which has played an integral part in establishing the concept of *the saviour*. It is the definition and perception of *saviour* that must be reassessed through these revelations.

The beauty of the Gospel of Thomas is that it is what it is— sayings that *the living Jesus* gave to us. They are as direct and pure as they could be, given that they needed to be cryptic for their protection. The fact that they remained in this cryptic form is evidence of their importance and relevance. The Gospel of Thomas holds truth, because the words are not presented in persuasive narratives. This gospel invites the reader to search for the truth, just as the Father has been searching for us (Thomas 107). As we have seen, similar words can be found in the parables and verses of the New Testament, but they are put into a didactic framework, based on Old Testament prophecies of a saviour king. This is the problem and warning Yeshua presents to us in Thomas 47. Yeshua is the saviour of our soul—that is, the energy issued forth from God, the Source, whose Light has been *dispersed along a distant road* (Thomas 97). He came into this realm to guide this energy back to the realm of the Spirit, a dimension most humans cannot experience in this life. This is how we should know *Jesus as the saviour*.

When we look at Thomas 47 we see Yeshua ask us—the generation that is at a threshold of a new enlightened period—not to put His *new teachings* into an *old framework*, because they will not fit. His messages are unlike anything from the past, they herald a new beginning. Placing His teachings into *old wineskins* would make them *spoil*, as we have seen happen in the faiths built entirely upon the New Testament. These narratives predominantly focus on a battle between good and evil. In the secret teachings of Thomas, we see that people, through their own mind, create evil. The same mind that should, instead, be linked by the Holy Spirit to the Father (Source). The covenant, in the Gospel of Thomas, is one that tells people they are exceptional beings, capable of reaching a potential they cannot imagine until they *let go of the old*.

Scientists exploring the quantum universe will begin to give us a glimpse into other dimensions. These other dimensions are *reflected in* this unbalanced and chaotic realm, which is the outer layer of the Source (it is the father, the one who seeds). The *life force* is within and the outer layer has been discarded, like the shell around the pearl—this was the hypothesised 'Big Bang'. There is a school of thought among the scientific community suggesting there is a kind of greater *consciousness* which has placed vital parameters into action, creating this richly diverse universe. The parameters are so finely tuned the possibility of them being accidental is negligible. Without these natural forces the laws of physics in this material world would not exist. This is *the mirror influence of the Spirit realm* described here, in *77th Pearl: The Perpetual Tree*.

The analogies Yeshua presents in this saying show us that we must move forward into a new way of thinking. Humans cannot mount two horses—they cannot believe in a patriarchal god, which created them for *his* pleasure and then punished them for wanting knowledge. This is not the god Yeshua refers to in the Gospel of Thomas, nor in most of the New Testament. We are very much connected to God, the Source through our soul, like Jesus. People cannot serve two masters or schools of thought, since these are at odds in their essential nature. The institution of the Christian church benefits from teachings which use fear to maintain patronage. This is not the way Jesus wanted us to feel. The days where people require spiritual comfort through sacraments and other such rights and rituals are passing. We are looking to a new truth, one that has been hidden from us and is now being revealed in *77th Pearl: The Perpetual Tree*. The new garment is Jesus' teaching through the Gospel of Thomas. To pollute His message and teachings with an old patch, derived from myths and legends, weakens the fabric of this garment. It is the garment the Father (Source) is offering to humanity (Thomas 36), the Holy Spirit is the thread holding it together, *connecting all the pieces into one.*

48. Jesus said, "If two make peace with each other in a single house, they will say to the mountain, 'Move from here!' and it will move."

In Thomas 48, there is a direct link to Thomas 47. Jesus struggled with the knowledge that the *old belief* system would sully His teachings, evident in Thomas 47. The desire of the Father (the source) to reunite with the soul that came from It, can be found in the Jewish faith through Kabbalah, through Islam in Sufism, and through Christianity in esoteric groups. Kabbalah sources the Torah, as a code, which became a way to unlock secret teachings about the universe and the nature of God and man. These revelations came through a process of intense prayer or meditation—the resulting text being the Zohar. Sufism, universal in nature, is the mystical *internalisation* of Islam and its essential philosophy concerning our spiritual link to God. The objective of Sufism is to focus one's heart and mind on God. In Christian mysticism, William Inge and Oswald Chambers were involved in seeking out the divine through metaphoric interpretations of biblical narratives. This is one of many examples of Christian groups that used the New Testament as a vehicle for a *deeper relationship* with God. The sub-groups derived from the three Abrahamic religions demonstrate the struggle of those who have the Light within them. They feel the pull of the Source. This shows how inadequate the primary texts have been in providing a convincing, holistic truth.

Thomas 48 references the limiting nature of the patriarchal belief system that preceded Jesus; this system diminished our connection to the Source. Consider how fundamentalist Christians position themselves when contemplating the difference between the God Jesus speaks of in the Synoptic Gospels, as compared to the jealous and wrathful God of the Old Testament. They have argued that God (like a father) punishes His children for going astray, because He loves them. This punishment ultimately brings His wayward children back to the right path. They also argue that the jealousy God feels for us is like the jealousy a husband feels for his wife, because she *belongs* to him. They would argue this kind of jealousy is justified. Jesus tells us that to be children of the *Father* we must be like babies (Thomas 22)—naïve to the world and naïve to the way of the lion, which consumes vulnerable souls (Thomas 7). A God who is perfect does not have human imperfections. Imperfections are endemic in this realm and people are tainted by these. The Father of all things is not wrathful or jealous—these are the ways of men, not of God. The Father is Light, which flows through everything. It cannot be jealous of anything since *It* exists everywhere at the same time (Thomas 77). The archaic, patriarchal view of God places *It* outside of the self. This is not what Jesus wanted. For this reason, Thomas 52 highlights the disparity between the prophecies and who Yeshua really was.

To argue that the Old Testament God is the same as the God Jesus speaks of is not healthy. We know that these texts were produced by a particular group of people, for the purposes of unifying that community. Israel Finkelstein (Professor of Archaeology at Tel Aviv University) and Neil Silberman (Director of Ename Centre for Public Archaeology and Heritage Presentation) produced a book, 'The Bible Unearthed', which compares archaeological facts with the stories in the Old Testament. In the book and a documentary television series, the archaeologists uncover evidence which shows that people fled the lands around Egypt after the ruling classes fell out of favour with the working classes. The deities of the elite class were rejected, the same deities of the soon to be dispossessed people. This led to the story of Exodus as an epic tale of deliverance, told many generations after the event. As the working class Egyptians headed into the land of Canaan, avoiding the fortifications, they came across communities that helped them along the way. Some of these communities worshipped a god which ended up sharing a phonetic relationship (similar name) with the Old Testament God—Yahweh. The trials and tribulations of this great culture of the Jewish nation became interwoven with myths and legends. One of these legends is of a god and his heroes leading the community to a land of plenty. This is the same land that was promised to the other descendants of Abraham, the people of Islam. Thomas 48 is given a pragmatic sense of importance when we consider what could be if all conflicts were set aside. How much more productive would it be if these factions of the Abrahamic religions focused on the development of new sciences and technologies? This would benefit the souls that enter this realm, but the lineages from Abraham continue to be consumed by the lion (Thomas 7). If they were to recognise each other as *three facets of the one thing*, then the Jewish, Christian, and Islamic communities would be able to move mountains. The Gospel of Thomas is the key. It seeks to *free us from a literal interpretation*, to see that all of these communities *have desired to answer the call of God, the Source*. Humans may have to admit that a *tabula rasa* needs to be the approach. *77th Pearl: The Perpetual Tree* is the new garment by which this species can travel forward—both physically and spiritually.

Thomas 48 shows how this realm/dimension attempts to reflect aspects of *the place* of the spirit, with the outcome being less than ideal. The conflict between religious groups mirrors how humans grapple with the duality of soul and flesh. Moreover, the dogma created by the major religious groups is also comparable to the struggle humans go through in their physical form. Just as a human mind should, religious groups must focus on spiritual matters. However, all too often we see these groups become involved in matters of the flesh. These matters may encompass cultural differences, borders between states, and subverting the rights of minority groups. Humans may make peace with this physical existence. Realising the body is a vehicle for the soul and the universe is the body's mother, they come to understand the purpose of physical existence. In understanding this, people may see how *the two making peace with each other, in a single house, can move mountains.* A mountain may be an obstacle, but it can also lift us high above our surroundings, enabling us to *see the place for the first time.* If we see where humans are on this speck of dust humans call Earth, we might appreciate that *we are one.*

49. Jesus said, "Congratulations to those who are alone and chosen, for you will find the kingdom. For you have come from it, and you will return there again."

Thomas 49 demonstrates a human realisation of the personal journey people experience when searching for meaning and truth. In a sense, it is accepting the sad disparity in Thomas 25, where we also see Yeshua being very human, by commenting on the precious nature of a true friend. It is clear that this kind of connection was difficult for Yeshua, because He was like no other human being. We have seen that even His disciples could not stand before Him and look into His eyes—as only a true friend could. In Thomas 49, we see Jesus give solace to those on the journey He made possible. This saying is one that brings great joy and comfort; people who are touched by it know the loneliness being on the periphery of society can bring. In this saying, people on this journey can see that their difference and feeling of isolation is due to their strong connection to the Source. These people are often the only voice of reason. A person may at times feel alone, but they are not because the collective consciousness (Holy Spirit) recognises the Light in them. A person is *chosen* when they recognise that what they see in this realm is a reflection of the truth that exists within.

People who experience this isolation are often conflicted, because they want happiness and contentment. They find these difficult to find in a normal life. The normality of life becomes banal and trivial. We see things through the lens of wisdom acquired through Yeshua's teaching. People who are on this journey feel a sense of grace through their link to the Source, connected by the collective consciousness. However, all around them, they see people involved in matters relating to physical and emotional satisfaction. Society tells them this is what they should be striving for too. This is a conflict Jesus would have felt, which, as mentioned previously, is linked to the temptation in the desert (Thomas 21). He could have had an earthly kingdom, but this was not what Jesus came here for. His decision to fulfil the prophecies in the Torah was the greatest selfless act known to humanity. This action stands as a metaphor for the importance of the Spirit over the flesh. Only we can take our first breath and our last breath—we do this alone.

If you are standing alone in a group of friends, know that you are chosen, because you will find the answers. If you ask the questions, you should know that those questions come from a longing. It is a desire to come back to a place where a part of you once *lived* (Thomas 50). Consider also that being alone allows you to be with God, the Father (Source), through the

Holy Spirit. By yourself, you are not alone, you are connected, *the one has become two.*

50. Jesus said, "If they say to you, 'Where have you come from?' say to them, 'We have come from the light, from the place where the light came into being by itself, established [itself], and appeared in their image.'

If they say to you, 'Is it you?' Say, 'We are its children, and we are the chosen of the living Father.'

If they ask you, 'What is the evidence of your Father in you?' say to them, 'It is motion and rest.'"

Thomas 50 is a profound saying because it gives us an *insight into the mysteries behind what we are.* Since Yeshua knew that giving His contemporaries such responses would make the disciples appear to be speaking heresy, the questions are presented as if from a foreigner, pre-empting the apostles' journeys into other regions. In this way, the responses are benign because of their cryptic nature. Through this ambiguity they have been delivered to the future, where now they can be understood. In this saying, Yeshua tells us how we should respond to questions we might ask ourselves on our journey to enlightenment—the union with the Source.

A person reading this with scepticism is right to do so. It is this questioning and examining that makes you worthy – *chosen.* A sceptic will interrogate everything, which is a healthy thing to do. However, it is prudent to consider that science is only beginning to understand where our cosmos came from and how many dimensions there are. When one considers the infinite expanse of space, which lies beyond our insignificant galaxy, we can see endless possibilities. If we take the romantic, medieval notion of heaven out of the equation and think about other forms of life, we begin to accept that there are things we are not aware of. The possibility that we are more than flesh and bone has already been shown to us by what one man did over two thousand years ago. The sin that has been eradicated is the one that sees us limit our potential to evolve. For the sceptic, consider the context of where and when Jesus came into this world. The concepts He speaks of were impossible for His contemporaries to comprehend, much less accept. This is partly why Jesus emphasised the notion of faith. He wanted His disciples to have faith in what He was telling them, even if they had no clue as to what it meant. Unfortunately, this faith became a double-edged sword; church groups *made the messenger into the message*, maintaining that all one needs is to believe in Jesus Christ. We know that this is not true. Yeshua hoped that His crucial teachings might make it to our time, if at least one of the disciples had enough faith in His words— this was Thomas. The evidence of the disciples' lack of understanding is in the New Testament. The Gospel of Thomas includes all of Yeshua's teachings, even the ones the disciples did not understand. In the twenty-first century, people have the language. If Yeshua were living in this world today, He would be using similar language to scientists involved in various forms of physics.

Generally, when people think of light they think of the physical effects of the light spectrum. The same light given off by stars and other light sources. This is not the way we should think about the Light Yeshua refers to in Thomas 50. Physical light, the one we can see and feel, has created life in the material universe. This dimension *mirrors* what the other does. It *creates* through the actions derived from chemicals and elements, which are combined with gravity, bringing mass together. The slight anomalies in the mass of different materials mean that the smaller particles are drawn toward the larger ones, eventually creating stars and planets. Science has proven that the countless individual galaxies are moving away from each other, which suggests that at some point, before the 'big bang', they were all in one central place. Why the big bang occurred in the first place is unknown. Furthermore, what existed around this *singularity*, which contained everything known in the physical universe, is a conundrum in itself. Visible light, in this realm, creates life and allows us to see what is hidden. Likewise, the Light Yeshua speaks of has the same quality, but it is invisible to us, because it is not of this realm. The physical phenomenon of light is a metaphor for what happens through the Spirit realm. In this realm, where there is light there is no darkness. Likewise, where there is knowledge tempered by wisdom, there is the *invisible Light*; resulting in no fear—no evil. This place of the invisible Light allows the soul to come to life. Linked to this concept of the Light is Thomas 83, wherein Jesus tells us the Father's image is hidden by His Light. This knowledge ratifies our understanding of *the nature* (phenomena) of this invisible Light.

If we look to the history of man's preoccupation with sun worship, we get a clue as to the need for reconnecting to *the Light*. Many great civilisations, such as the Aztecs and the Ancient Egyptians, placed significance on the sun, giving it the status of a god. This is an example of how people have been struggling with the knowledge deep within the psyche, a knowledge that has been scattered. Since *the breath of life* entered human kind, their souls have been evolving towards this point. It is as though their eyes have been shut and are now opening, particularly in the past couple of millennia. Just as people associate the sun to a creator god, through the suppressed psyche, we see this appear in human mythologies. Consider how humans who believe in an afterlife might describe what hell is like. It is usually either a frozen wasteland or a burning landscape of molten rock and flames. This is, again, a memory we have deep within our physical makeup (DNA), which becomes linked to the notion of the metaphysical. We intuitively know what happens when a habitable planet dies. A planet is either consumed in flames as its sun expands before collapsing on itself, or the atmosphere is damaged in some way, so that it becomes too cold or hot for a human-like species to exist. Humans have this knowledge because they are connected to the Source. This information is within us; it also exists because some may have experienced it in previous life forms. This knowledge has presented itself as myths about the worst-case scenario after death—some people call it hell. Yeshua came to this realm to give humans the knowledge that would open their third eye, so that they can see (comprehend) the invisible Light. In this way, humans would not *taste death*— their Spirit would be in another realm when this one expires. People should also understand that it is beneficial for church groups to preserve the idea of hell; this ensures that their venues will be filled with people wanting to be saved from perdition. It is also beneficial to the dark spirits who have embraced the material realm. They have created hell and purgatory from this mythology. The leaders of the institutions, who have come to realise their teachings are false, use the guilt people die with to misguide souls into this place of darkness. This is the only *place* they have control, because people have given it to them. Guilt is one of the main substances that constitute the coin forged in this world (see commentary for Thomas 32).

The Light is essentially what we are as a life force. How else does one describe a consciousness? A consciousness, in this sense, is an awareness and knowledge of self, *without* the world's physiological and psychological parameters. This would allow us to be like a naïve newly born baby (Thomas 22). This knowledge is calm, harmonious, and at peace; at the same time it is dynamic and creative. This is the key to the response Yeshua tells us to give to the question: '*What is the evidence of your Father in you?*' '*It is motion and rest.*' In this way, we see another mystery relating to the nature of the soul—it is on a series of journeys. The soul inhabits different states of being. Each time it is in *motion* through a *place*, experiencing new things. This is a logical conclusion when we consider the endless possibilities within the numerous galaxies and dimensions. Compare how people, at the early stages of the Industrial Revolution, dreamt of flying around the world and then, even to the moon. All these things eventuated because people made them happen, it is our creative nature. Sadly, what humans find difficult is to not listen to the nature of the beast, which is part of their *physical* DNA. *This is the lion* that consumes them, but the lion still presents as human (Thomas 7). These people become characteristic of the narcissistic lion, rather than of the perfect human. In doing so they put their creative energy, which is from the Source, into negative actions. It is at this point they become the egotistical Satan, as described in the New Testament. Too often, people think like creatures born of this world and not as the offspring of the one Yeshua refers to as His father (the Source).

When Yeshua says the Light '*established [itself], and appeared in their image*', He reveals how this source of energy and consciousness came into existence, through its own awakening. This energy is something humans cannot comprehend, because it is difficult to fathom how something can appear from nothing—but this is its nature. It is nothing and everything at the same time. It is analogous to the voids in space, which are only apparent because of the billions of galaxies highlighting the empty space. When Yeshua states it '*appeared in their image*', He is referring to the prophets and Himself. Jesus took on the image of the human to communicate His messages, as we see in Thomas 28. The prophets, and all humans, are weaker manifestations of this Light. These prophets were the collective sword, which tested this realm and the capacity of humans to accept *the hand of God* (the Father/Source), through the physical image of Jesus (Thomas 98). This was the Source in search of Its most beloved sheep, Its sparks of Light scattered into the abyss (Thomas 107).

The evidence of the Father/Source, in us, is *'motion and rest'*. We can identify this as creativity and it can be seen throughout the cosmos. Activity (motion) can be seen in the formation of a star and its planets, as much as it can be seen in a baby exploring the new world. Rest, in the physical universe, can be seen in the slow evolution of an organism and in people's ability to dream, linking to the subconscious mind. The mind is an aspect of the soul. The soul is at rest between bodies, during death. The Light (energy) of most souls is reabsorbed into the omnipresent Source – the two become one. The physical realm mirrors the other dimension because it is parallel, a layer next to it and through it.

51. His disciples said to him, "When will the rest for the dead take place, and when will the new world come?"

He said to them, "What you are looking forward to has come, but you don't know it."

Jesus tells His disciples the knowledge of truth (*new world*) has come through His teaching and presence in this realm. In opening humanity's eyes to the Light that is within them, they are awakened to the reality of what they really are. Humans are a life force (soul); in this knowledge we take steps towards nurturing this Light, *resurrecting it from the death born in flesh.* Yeshua's contemporaries, and successive generations, took life as they experience it in the material world as the reference point for what the ideal existence is like. The problem with life is that humans grow old, get sick, and eventually die. So the perfect 'new world', where this cycle would end, was seen as one that would come down from heaven, stopping this natural cycle. Hence the question: *'when will the new world come?'* This would see the (mythical) Garden of Eden re-established, as it was before Adam and Eve's sin. We see in Thomas 51 that our perceptions and concepts must change. The physical has its own nature, as does the realm of the Spirit. The energy animating human bodies as a conscious, creative entity is the soul (the essence of the Source—the father). This is what we are; it is the thing that we cannot point to when we describe *the self.*

'What [people look] forward to has come'—this is something humans find near impossible to comprehend, because it is difficult to see beyond the physical *veil* that is this realm. The *energy* from the other realm/dimension can be felt when the mind is in a still place and in a calm environment. It is something that is very soothing; it feels like the comfort of home. It is here and it is what we are, the collective kingdom of souls. We are one, connected to all.

52. His disciples said to him, "Twenty-four prophets have spoken in Israel, and they all spoke of you."

He said to them, "You have disregarded the living one who is in your presence, and have spoken of the dead."

It cannot be disputed that the prophets referred to a great liberator of people. They sensed the coming of this great man, Jesus. However, what they could not comprehend is that He was not a liberator of an oppressed people or nation. Yeshua was to serve a greater purpose. He came to liberate all humans from the veil that keeps them blind to the truth. Yeshua refers to the prophets that foresaw His light, as *speaking 'of the dead'*, this is a significant statement. Yet, Yeshua refers to Himself as representative of *'the living one'* (God, the Source). In various sayings, He also tells those who embrace His teachings they are *the living that will not taste death*. This difference demonstrates the barrier those of the past had to accessing the truth. Jesus warns people not to be complacent when He asks, what they will do when the *one becomes two* in Thomas 11. He refers to the union that has not been realised in this life, and which cannot be made in death. As well intended as they may have been, those prophets saw themselves as flesh and bone, which would one day be brought back from death. They lived in hope that they might be *resurrected* to this life by the power of their God. In the early part of the twenty-first century, some faiths still espouse this canon. In this misguided hope, most prophets would have indeed tasted death. Their soul, like their flesh, was reabsorbed into this world and became manifest as other energies. This should not be looked upon as a bad thing; this process is one of rejuvenation and growth. Death, on several levels, is the ending of one thing and the beginning of another. It is a significant part of the 'motion and rest' mentioned in Thomas 50.

Thomas 52 has another layer of meaning, which refers back to Thomas 43, where Jesus points out that the disciples liked only one aspect of what He represented—they liked the tree or they liked the fruit, but not both. In a similar way, Thomas 52 describes how the disciples tried to define Jesus by knowledge found in their contemporary faith. They *liked the idea* of the Messiah as defined by their prophets and religious leaders. While Yeshua needed to use these prophecies, which were indeed about Him, He also knew that the prophets' definition of the Messiah was not what the realm of the Spirit intended. This is how man has been *influenced by the beast* he evolved from. This *creature* (in Thomas 7) saw the Messiah as a soldier or warrior sent by God, to mercilessly destroy their enemies and *restore paradise* on Earth. Yeshua was a different kind of soldier, one who used *knowledge tempered by wisdom as His sword* (Thomas 16). This is why Yeshua tells the disciples they are looking to the dead to explain what is in their presence— the *living one*. This is the Source, brought into an instance of motion through us, so that we may become wealthy through our conscious experiences. People who are alive with the Father/Source are joined through the collective consciousness (Holy Spirit), becoming one.

53. His disciples said to him, "Is circumcision useful or not?"

He said to them, "If it were useful, their father would produce children already circumcised from their mother. Rather, the true circumcision in spirit has become profitable in every respect."

Jesus was a Jew; therefore, He would have been circumcised. This fact makes Thomas 53 even more powerful. Yeshua tells His contemporaries what He has repeated in other sayings—the importance of the Spirit, above all things. The practice of circumcision was introduced to define the Jewish believers apart from other faiths, reminding them of their connection to their God. Yeshua recognised the practice as another ritual, which had no real relevance to the spiritual awakening of the individual. To this end, Yeshua adds that the only useful circumcision is the one *in spirit*. This analogy is a physical one. In this existence, if we remove what is around the soul, we remove the flesh—this is the useful circumcision. In a significant proportion of the sayings in the Gospel of Thomas, we see Yeshua asking us to respond to the soul, to escape the day-to-day and the flesh that contains the Light. This is what a symbolic circumcision means, a circumcision that makes us aware of the true nature of what we are, unhindered by the physical obstacles of the flesh and this world. It means that people should make a conscious effort to withdraw from the everyday routine; it does not mean we cut into the flesh which houses the soul. When Yeshua had His flesh put onto the crucifix, it was to *remove it* from His living Spirit. This symbolic action resonates in Thomas 53, for it was profitable for all human beings that this brutal event took place.

54. Jesus said, "Congratulations to the poor, for to you belongs Heaven's kingdom."

Thomas 54 has a dual meaning, depending on where one stands regarding the concept of *wealth*. In the first instance, this saying refers to a reward that is described as 'Heaven's Kingdom'. Since Yeshua tells us that the kingdom is not a place but *a state of being*, we know it is a realm unified through the Holy Spirit, which is the collective consciousness. This suggests that those who are *poor in spiritual wealth* await a reward that is of a kingdom portrayed in traditional, human terms. This portrayal is a kind of cautioning; the kingdom is already here, but most people cannot experience it (Thomas 51). The definition of Heaven's Kingdom as a place that is *not physically experienced* brings us to the other aspect of the dichotomy within Thomas 54.

Thomas 54 reinforces other sayings where the focus is on the distractions in this life. This saying gives solace to the poor, who *may* see the disparity between those who have great wealth and their own, less than adequate, financial state. According to Yeshua, this unfortunate situation *may serve as a position that is better than being wealthy*. The reason for this is that it is easy to become infatuated with worldly possessions. Having attachments to material things creates an illusion of contentment and denies the transitory nature of this world. Consider how

people on a spiritual quest discard all their worldly possessions, so as to have as little distractions as possible. Should all
people need to get rid of their possessions and find a cave in
the wilderness? Certainly not, though all humans should be
aware of the emptiness material wealth brings. People need to
see possessions for what they are—finite—and they must stop
wanting for the sake of having. If not for their spiritual growth,
then for the sake of the environment, which is suffering at
the hand of this consumerist society. Our concept of wealth
and poverty needs to be based on spiritual attainment and
growth; only then can we belong to the kingdom. For those
of us who are the average person (in societies' eyes), a holiday
can become a time of reflection and meditation. After all, the
word 'holiday' is derived from the notion of a *holy day*. At this
time we are more prone to *removing ourselves from the physical
layer*—a profitable circumcision (Thomas 53).

55. Jesus said, "Whoever does not hate father and mother cannot
be my disciple, and whoever does not hate brothers and sisters,
and carry the cross as I do, will not be worthy of me."

Parents and siblings represent genetic links, which humans
traditionally hold above all others. In Thomas 55, Yeshua tells
people they need to let go of these attachments, to pursue
the journey toward the kingdom within. We are not asked to
literally reject filial love, but people must realise the journey
they are on is an individual one, which is encumbered by all the
distractions in this world. Family lineage can sometimes make
the search for truth difficult. The expectations of behaviour,

beliefs, traditions, and customs make this journey difficult. A human's biological parents created a body belonging to an individual, within it they journey through this world. If the soul is not awakened to its nature—drawing in this Light, growing—it becomes reabsorbed into this realm. In this respect, it has tasted death. The soul, which we might think of as light or energy, re-enters a body and has a new biological or adopted family. Thomas 55 supports the notion that we are caught up in a frustrating cycle, since rarely do we hear Yeshua use such strong language. In Yeshua asking people to *hate* we realise there is a disparity between what humans think happens and what actually happens. If people only had one life, with one family, then this should be cherished—not despised, as one might a familiar prison cell. Consider that in the realm of the Spirit all things are connected, so that we are all part of the same energy. Placing one individual above all others (mother, father, brother, sister) denies the truth of this connection. The collective consciousness we know as the Holy Spirit is the thing connecting all beings of the Light. To deny its importance as the conduit is perilous (Thomas 44). In this realm, it is physically manifest as the feeling of love and connectedness humans may have for family, children, or spouses. It is love, before the chemicals that come with this feeling have been released in the body. Yeshua tries to free us from the earthly ideas of family by presenting us with a controversial and seemingly impossible request.

Yeshua would have seen crucifixions, so He used the analogy of *carrying the cross* to illustrate a point. This metaphor makes sense when we consider that those being crucified would have been looked upon as *dead men walking*. This is the way Yeshua saw Himself and the symbol He wanted us to consider for ourselves. Yeshua knew that His teachings would eventually get Him into trouble, because His views were far from what the religious leaders believed and indoctrinated. Yeshua speaks of His impending death in the Synoptic Gospels, such as in

Matthew 16:21-23, and Thomas 55 reflects the same prophetic vision. What is poignant in Thomas 55 is that Jesus speaks to us about a tenacity and single-minded vision of where we should be headed. Understanding that death is as certain as our first breath, we need to prepare our minds for that experience. If people see their biological family as the same one they will have after their death, they are mistaken. Such an attachment is an illusion, created within the context of this realm and its *physical actions*.

56. Jesus said, "Whoever has come to know the world has discovered a carcass, and whoever has discovered a carcass, of that person the world is not worthy."

In Thomas 56, Yeshua shows His feelings towards this world through the metaphor of a dead body. This imagery shows that the world is in a state of decay. Yeshua adds that a person who recognises this fact is outside of this realm and has become a passerby (Thomas 42). To be such a person, one sees the world as transitory and impermanent, unlike the Spirit and the kingdom that it comprises. The kingdom is not a place, as we might imagine—it is an existence in another form. It is not above or below us, it is here, but we cannot experience it. It is another dimension, which our senses cannot detect. It is mirrored in the natural world, but this material world cannot sustain its reflection of the other. Chaos rules over this dimension and the materials constituting its physicality will decay.

That Yeshua calls the world both a body, in Thomas 80, and a carcass, in Thomas 56, is significant. It tells people that the world has been created from *the Source of all things* (Father) and has attempted to reflect what the realm of the Spirit is like. It also makes people think about their own body, which they mistakenly see as their identity. However, we know that no part of the body can be called 'I'. The body perishes, just like all physical matter. If we can imagine the universe as discarded material, such as the shell surrounding a pearl, or a seed with its husk, then we come close to understanding the mystery of this existence (Thomas 97). All biological life forms have layers, from the external to the internal. Every organ and cell that makes up a complete creature has layers. At the centre is a driving force like the brain, heart, and the nucleus of a cell with its DNA. Another analogy would be if we were to start in space and zoom in to the individual cells inside the brain, listing all the elements that are visible along the way. When our limitations of seeing can take us no further, we know there is more—this is the Source (Father). We may conclude that this realm has *elements of the divine within it*. We see these *divine reflections* in the wonders of nature and in phenomena experienced through sight, sound, touch, smell, and taste. For this reason, some artists of the Romantic period painted nature as a glorification of the power of God. Understanding the truth is a path to recognising that this realm is a creation *from* the Source (Father). This dimension is not of a permanent nature. A body becomes a carcass, which is an empty shell. In this way, the universe is the discarded shell of the Father/Source—it is the *outer layer* discarded into the abyss. At the centre of everything are Its remnants, as we see in Thomas 77. The soul is the only viable remnant of the Father/Source in the physical universe. It seeks to be re-joined to the original spring—*the living one*. Souls are like the cells in a body—they all have functions that *form the whole*. As enlightened Spirits we become the body of the Father/Source, connected through the Holy Spirit—*this is the body and blood, carrying its DNA.*

57. Jesus said, "The Father's Kingdom is like a person who has [good] seed. His enemy came during the night and sowed weeds among the good seed. The person did not let the workers pull up the weeds, but said to them, 'No, otherwise you might go to pull up the weeds and pull up the wheat along with them.' For on the day of the harvest the weeds will be conspicuous, and will be pulled up and burned."

When Yeshua describes what the Father's Kingdom is like He does not speak about a place, as would be the expectation from His contemporaries. Rather, He speaks of the mysteries relating to the nature of the Spirit and the journey toward the realm in which it exists.

In Thomas 57, Yeshua tells us to ignore those who lack the ability to comprehend the true nature of who they are. People have to live among antagonists and learn from their suffering, which is driven by worldly desires. They are the ones who are resolved back into this realm, because it is all they know. People seeking the truth, the Light, are the good seed, which benefits the kingdom's growth.

Thomas 57 describes the reality of existence within this realm. In the traditional view of the *ideal world*, one that is derived from myths, all people are God's creation. Therefore, they are worthy of eternal life—if they follow the rules. The truth is that a person's path to *eternal life* is not dependent on an external entity or deity and that god's *judgement* of their life. It is dependent on a person's ability to connect with the Father and *become an offspring of the Source*. In Thomas 57, we see that there are people who attempt to stop this connection; they consume the space around us and obstruct our path. Individuals and groups along this path may hinder those who seek the Light of truth. This is why Yeshua uses the analogy of a weed, which takes the light away from the wheat and competes for space in the soil. These people should not be offered the pearls we have, because they would destroy their capacity to inspire growth (Thomas 93). These *weeds* will be resolved into the ubiquitous whole. Like weeds that rot back into the soil or whose ashes are scattered onto it, they become nutrients for other life forms. The reference to weeds also infers that, in this realm, there are human beings that are *of darkness* (Thomas 24). They are human souls, and entities from other realms, who have embraced this world and its allure. This is 'the powerful one' we see in Thomas 98. It is the material/physical realm hindering those people wanting to nurture the soul. These antagonists exist as manifestations of the lion we see in Thomas 7. Power and control is the fertiliser for those weeds; they do not know the nutrients they seek out are transitory and fleeting. The Light of *the kingdom* is eternal and it yields an endless crop.

58. Jesus said, "Congratulations to the person who has toiled and has found life."

In Thomas 58, we see that to toil is to search for the truth—to bring one's soul to *life*. In this sense 'toil' is not so much physical work as it is mental and emotional focus. However, physical work can be a form of meditation.

The journey to knowing the truth can be lonely and difficult. This existence is filled with obstacles that are challenging to navigate or remove from our lives. The obstacles may be in the form of a job, expectations from family, or cultural traditions, which *appear* to block our path. It can be painful and emotionally draining for an individual to overcome these obstacles. Yeshua regularly experienced a sense of sadness and frustration, because the majority of people whom He encountered were incapable of understanding His teachings. Yeshua's contemporaries were unwilling to work towards that understanding. This frustration becomes increasingly evident in the Gospel of Thomas.

As seen in Thomas 57, we have weeds amongst us, which will obstruct our growth, but the good seed *must toil* to have its place in the field. When we overcome these obstacles, there is a great reward—the union with the Father/Source. Horticulturists know that the fig tree will fruit better when it grows in rocky soil and its roots are stressed. The contemporaries of Jesus may not have known this fact, but gardeners in the twenty-first century are aware of it. When Yeshua cursed the fig (Mark 11:13-14) for not giving fruit, He metaphorically called for humankind to become aware of the suffering that is around us, and *grow from this knowledge.* This is the fruit that Yeshua desires most, because when people bear fruit from this truth they join with Him. In this way, the process of toil may become the very thing making people bear fruit. Moreover, the weeds strangling our roots (Thomas 57) become a positive experience *for our spiritual growth.*

59. Jesus said, "Look to the living one as long as you live, otherwise you might die and then try to see the living one, and you will be unable to see."

Thomas 59 speaks to the assumption some people have, that to be a member of a religion is all one needs to secure a life after death. Performing rituals and observing dietary laws will not guarantee life after death. These practices are tied to existence within this realm. They make the stomach go hungry, but is that hunger for food or for the Spirit? (Thomas 69). It is the knowledge we gain from meditating on the true nature of what we are, and finding that link before death, which is of benefit. Rituals, that are habitual and have become devoid of meaning, are of no use.

The living one is the energy (invisible Light) flowing through all things. On this planet, it finds its preferred vehicle in humans. If people do not find that connection in this mortal existence, they cannot do it after death. Remember, in humans, the evidence of the Father is described as 'motion and rest' (Thomas 50). It is while people are in motion, *through a body,* that they are able to create this link. The disparity between the physical and metaphysical allows people to learn about this difference and *opens their inner eye*. The physical is motion and the metaphysical is rest. We know this to be true when Yeshua tells us *there is no rest for humans* in Thomas 86. *The rest* has two states of being. It can be *a step forward for those who are alive in Spirit* or, for those who have not looked to *the living one*, a period of dissolving into a new existence. Here, we see again how the physical mirrors aspects of the Spirit realm, through the dissolving of the flesh into the earth. The myth of Yeshua's physical resurrection comes from the fear of the New Testament authors. They did not understand the dynamism of the soul or its need for growth. For them, the soul was the end point and the body was inexorably joined to it—the body was who they were. Their religion taught them that God made a body from the dust and *breathed life into it*. Thus, a physical resurrection was the only thing that made sense. Yeshua clearly tells us this is not so. The soul is what we are, not the body. *The soul must be brought to life, resurrected*, through nurturing its growth. It is resurrected to become part of the collective consciousness, the kingdom from where it came, before the expansion separated it.

The language Yeshua uses to describe what His contemporaries would have called God is symbolic. He needed to be very careful about the way He described the Father (Source). Even the words He uses in Thomas were on the edge of heresy. When God, the Source, was described as '*the living one*', Yeshua's contemporaries thought of their god. However, He was speaking to our generation, one that has evolved enough to understand the broader implications and symbolism. The history and failings of the established faiths has opened our eyes to the truth. People have seen religious institutions become consumed by the lion (Thomas 7). In this regard, we see that the separation of the canonical and Gnostic texts was a necessary event in Christian history, inspired by the wisdom that sprouts from the collective consciousness (Holy Spirit)—the link between all spirit-beings. This action protected the Gospel of Thomas from being manipulated through editing and polemic interpretations. Due to the marginalisation and exclusion of this gospel, it remained protected from people who were incapable of seeing beyond this world. It is this world the orthodox Christians used as their reference point in understanding the nature of the *other* realm. In this context, orthodox refers to those who accepted only the canonical texts as truth. The generations inheriting the twenty-first century will be capable of perceiving a realm (dimension) which is completely different to this one. *77th Pearl: The Perpetual Tree* has been conceived for the generations who will experience significant changes in the environment and global community. If souls are to attain to the Spirit, this world must become a conducive and healthy place for them to journey through. In this way, people are able to look to the living one for as long as they live—throughout their motion in this life and into their rest in the next.

60. He saw a Samaritan carrying a lamb and going to Judea. He said to his disciples, "that person ... around the lamb." They said to him, "So that he may kill it and eat it." He said to them, "He will not eat it while it is alive, but only after he has killed it and it has become a carcass."

They said, "Otherwise he can't do it."

He said to them, "So also with you, seek for yourselves a place for rest, or you might become a carcass and be eaten."

Thomas 60 describes how humans become a carcass if they allow this existence to bind them. When people are completely encumbered by day-to-day living they are not allowed the time to contemplate the nature of what they are. If people do not find rest from the world they are at risk of becoming a carcass. A carcass is *absorbed* by this world. It is the soul that is the ultimate victim (Thomas 7).

Yeshua describes the evidence of the Father in us as *'motion and rest'*. This is a thread linking Thomas 50 and 60—evident in the reality of this life, because humans have no rest (Thomas 86). Every waking moment is filled with an expectation of some kind—to eat, work, look after family, participate in amicable relationships, and so on. All these day-to-day aspects of human life consume our time and our minds. Yeshua asks, through Thomas 60, that we understand the dilemma and disparity between what it is to live in Spirit and what it means to live in this realm. If we do not seek a place to stop and be at peace (rest) in this life, then we become a carcass, consumed by this realm (Thomas 7). This is why Yeshua says it is imperative people treat the Sabbath as a time to contemplate our relationship with God, the Source (Thomas 27). It should not just be a break from work. In our era, this means we set aside time to focus on what we are, in relation to the universe and all other things. One avenue might be through meditation. This mediation can be in various forms, such as walking, swimming, or even just sitting and observing others. Becoming aware of other life forms in this universe (and others) by sky watching at night has become popular. Indeed, various phenomena make themselves visible to those seeking the truth, because they want the human species to rise above their current level of awareness. Every individual can find their own way, but it is important to make that time for the soul—what we are.

Seeking a place of rest asks more of us than a holiday from work. A place of rest is an intellectual space where we ask the questions pertaining to the Soul. In this space, a human is able to exclude all other distractions and consider the answers, which will come to them in time. Without this repose the questions will not be asked, nor will the answers be heard. By avoiding a place of rest, people are at danger of becoming a carcass—the lion consumes the human and will still present as a human, regardless of its external truth (Thomas 7).

77ᵗʰ Pearl: the Perpetual Tree contains important revelations, but some of its most significant discoveries are the prayers, which are directly linked to the words of the *living Jesus in the Gospel of Thomas*. At any time of the day or night, people are invited to say the following prayer, while being mindful of what each line is saying *to the soul*. This is your time of growth and connection through the collective consciousness (Holy Spirit). *The Soul's Prayer* brings comfort to those pursuing the truth, seeking rest. They are the words Yeshua gives us *through this gospel*.

The Soul's Prayer:

Our Father, who is in all things,
hallowed be your presence.
Your Kingdom be recognised in each of us,
as your Light is made visible in this realm, as in the other.

Give us our days of residence in this dimension and body,
the recognition of its imperfections and weaknesses.
We accept our faults and the faults of others,
We see them as lessons for our growth.

May we walk upon a straight path,
with open minds and open hearts,
harming no-one along our way.

Where there is knowledge of the true self,
there can be no evil.
Amen.

61. Jesus said, "Two will recline on a couch; one will die, one will live."

Salome said, "Who are you mister? You have climbed onto my couch and eaten from my table as if you are from someone."

Jesus said to her, "I am the one who comes from what is whole. I was granted from the things of my Father."

"I am your disciple."

"For this reason I say, if one is whole, one will be filled with light, but if one is divided, one will be filled with darkness."

Yeshua makes a contentious statement about Himself; we conclude from Salome's statement that He is the only one on the couch—'You have climbed onto my couch.' This is significant as it symbolically refers to the separate nature of Jesus as human (flesh) and as Spirit. By stating, 'Two will recline on a couch; one will die, one will live', Yeshua draws our attention to *the difference between the flesh and the soul*. Yeshua understood His body was destined for destruction, while the Spirit would be brought to life through this action. So it is for all humans, if they become aware and nurture the connection they have to the Father—the Source of all things.

Jesus responds to Salome's question with several mysteries which would have baffled His contemporaries. First, Yeshua states that He comes 'from what is whole'. This is important;

He speaks not of one entity, but of a thing that is everywhere and beyond a name or label. It is perfect. It flows through all things. It is the *Father*, because all things are derived *from It*. Words are incapable of defining It—It is the whole. Yeshua goes on to say He is from another dimension; stating He was: 'granted from the things of my Father, I am your disciple.' This tells us the Source is the thing that positioned Jesus in this realm, for our benefit. In saying He is *our disciple*, Yeshua is indicating that we are filled with the same Light that constitutes what He is. It also means that He *followed* us to this realm, *to bring back this Light* (Thomas 107). Yeshua then describes how humans struggle with the disparity between this world and the realm of the Spirit. When people are whole, they are aware of their true nature; their soul shines brightly, as an enlightened Spirit (Thomas 24). When humans are distracted and consumed by this world, they are in darkness (Thomas 7). The darkness and the light are figurative expressions. If a human is filled with *Light* they are content, at peace, and connected to God, the Source, through the collective consciousness (Holy Spirit). If they are in darkness they are angry, jealous, envious, worried, and hateful. These are emotions driven by this world and by the body. People need to remember that they can rise above these negative emotions. In recognising what we really are, people set themselves free from the notion of sin. Sin is a construct derived from the flesh and this realm. It damages a person's potential to connect with God, the Source. To be *whole* is to be in a state of perpetual peace and acceptance—to recognise the collective consciousness (Thomas 44), which links all enlightened beings.

We see in the Gospel of Thomas what is at the heart of Yeshua's message and purpose for coming to our realm. In St Paul's letters to the Romans we see a completely different view—one that has caused a schism between humans and God, the Father. Paul writes in Romans 5:19: *Just as by one man's disobedience many were made sinners, so by one man's obedience are many to be made upright.* This refers to the disobedience of Adam and Eve in Genesis and suggests that Jesus died to correct this 'original sin'. Interestingly, Catholics and most Christians of today know and accept that the Genesis story is just a myth and has no real basis of truth. It is a reflection of human evolution, from animal to *somewhat* intelligent and occasionally wise beings. In the animal kingdom, apes look to an alpha male to lead and look after their group. This male creates order in the group and protects them from predators. To go against this patriarch would be foolish, if not fatal. This instinct has been buried deep within the human psyche; even as the breath of life entered into them, people still held onto these primal needs to have protection and guidance. As humans began to try and understand the nature of their world and who made it, they transposed these ideals onto an omnipotent godhead, who created everything for them. To explain why humans suffered in this life it made sense that they must have done something to anger *him*. From this conclusion, we obtain the story of the Garden of Eden. This begs the question: did Yeshua really die to correct something that never happened? This is a question the orthodoxy needs to ask themselves. In the Gospel of Thomas, people are presented with mysteries that require them to consider what they really are, beyond the flesh and bones they see and feel. The Gospel of Thomas tells us we are a Soul, connected to something that is *the Source*. Humans are not aware of this until they seek it out. The necessity for this quest is what Yeshua came to show humans. His willingness to give up His mortal life was a symbolic gesture, which speaks to the disparity between flesh and Spirit. Yeshua's selfless act showed people that they were (are) overwhelmed by the powerful one—representing this realm and its enticing pleasures and promises.

62. Jesus said, "I disclose my mysteries to those [who are worthy] of [my] mysteries."

Thomas 62 may sound contradictory to other sayings in this gospel, but this is not the case. Humans need to consider what it means to be *worthy*; in Thomas 2 and 94 people are invited to seek out the truths behind these mysteries, in doing so, they are disclosed to them. It follows that those who are worthy are the ones who are touched by these words. The teachings resonate a truth deep within the one seeking this disclosure. People on this journey have a spirit evolved enough to know what these sayings mean in a profound sense. Moreover, in Thomas 108 we see Yeshua tell us if we drink from His mouth (take in His teachings), we become like Him and He becomes like us—the mysteries of the inner realm are revealed.

People to whom *77ᵗʰ Pearl: The Perpetual Tree* has been revealed might be asking why this author is worthy. Shamot Sesju's life could not be compared to any great sages, ascetic masters, or saints—quite the opposite. The author was born to Croatian parents in Grasse, a picturesque town in the south of France. In 1968, when he was two, his family migrated to Australia. His father took the family to a small opal-mining town in central South Australia, called Andamooka. It is here, while attending regular Sunday school meetings, run by a local Evangelical Christian family, that he first remembers thinking about the nature of God. His strongest memory of this place is the red desert sands against the blue sky and the massive expanse of space, clearly visible at night. The arid landscape, sparsely dotted with tortured vegetation, juxtaposed against the miraculous burst of desert flowers and plants after the rainy season. His memories of playing with the local Aboriginal children, finding amazing reptiles and bugs surviving in the searing heat of summer, was a formative period.

After five years of hard labour, manually winching buckets of soil up a mineshaft in the burning desert sun, his mother reached the end of her tether. She demanded they move to Port Kembla, a town on the New South Wales coast, eighty kilometres south of Sydney. She wanted her two sons to have better education and job prospects. Shamot's mother could not see this happening in the small opal-mining town. Port Kembla had a steelworks company where his father could obtain unskilled labouring jobs. His mother received a position in a factory, machine-sewing garments.

The change in climate, from dry desert to humid coast, is what doctors surmise gave him an almost fatal case of pneumonia. It left him with damaged lungs, which made him very conscious of his health. Most of his school life was not pleasant. Due to his illness, he could not play the sports boys were expected to play in Australian culture. He had a passion for the Visual Arts, even in South Australia where he would draw the bulldozers and other machinery with pen and notepad. This interest developed further at a tertiary level. His interest in the arts and the fact that most of his friends were female made him a target of bullies, who saw him as weak and different from the other 'normal' boys. This made early school life miserable and he spent much of his time at home, using his poor health as a convenient escape.

Shamot was a child that needed the love and support of both parents. His father's alcoholism, and his jealousy towards his wife, distanced him from both son's. Shamot's brother was a strong, self-sufficient person and was not influenced by this absence of care. The author of *77ᵗʰ Pearl: The Perpetual Tree* reflected on his life experiences in relation to *the Soul*. This is why he was *made worthy*. Your experiences have led you here and you have had your own revelations. You are worthy because you have knocked on the door.

Shamot was inspired to write the following prayer one night, shortly after he had been taken to hospital suffering an anxiety attack. The stress was brought on by his marriage breakdown and the resulting legal proceedings. This prayer is the connection he made with God, the Source, at one of the lowest points in his life. *It* was speaking to him through the collective consciousness (Holy Spirit). He reflects on this as something that was meant to happen, because it will help others. They were *the scratches* he experienced as he swam down for *this pearl*.

A Meditation on Seeing:

You take your first breath in this dream.

People rush from place to place.
Everybody seeks more of everything,
always rushing, never enough time.

Occasionally you bump into a kind man, a gentle man,
He asks you to wake, you don't hear,
you are too busy.
Sometimes He is an old woman in a grocery store
smelling the sweet perfume of a new season mango
Sometimes He is the friend that comes to your home
when you have been unwell,
Sometimes He is the child you observe on a swing,
giggling at the birds as they fly by,
Sometimes He is the baby you watch in its bed
that smiles for no apparent reason,
Sometimes He is the colleague who gives you a warm hug when you
need one the most.

Imagine......this world.

Imagine being born into this dream.

People starve while others destroy excess food crops, because it is not profitable to give them away.

People commit acts of extreme violence because they want pieces of ephemeral land.

Imagine.......this world.

Imagine the gentle man who so often asks you to wake up, but you ignore Him because you are too busy, too tired, too obsessed with whatever it is you need to do, have, achieve, get to, complete on time.

Imagine that one day the dream you walk around in becomes too much for you.

You stop.

He asks you—'What do you want?'
You say—'I want to know, I want to stop, I want to see'

You open your eyes...for the first time.

In Thomas 7, Yeshua says: '*Lucky is the lion that the human will eat, so that the lion becomes human. And foul is the human that the lion will eat, and the lion still will become human.*' Shamot Sesju was the one that consumed the lion (the experiences we are exposed to in this realm). He was able to look at these experiences as lessons and impetus to search for truth. This is the difference between the lion that becomes human and the human that is *consumed* by the lion, but presents as human (Thomas 7).

Shamot was married at the age of twenty-one, primarily to escape his parents' toxic relationship. His marriage was initially healthy and positive. However, due to family differences and the realisation that they were very different people, they drifted apart after five years. The final decision to divorce took eighteen years and was painful for both parties. His wife's concern over their separation stemmed from what other people would think, his desire was to not live an inauthentic life.

Shamot's post-married life was filled with all night outings at nightclubs. This eventually became monotonous. He quickly discovered that the friends one meets in these places rarely become true friends, just acquaintances. He found himself searching for something, but he did not know what it was. Shamot became deeply depressed. His place to escape was Byron Bay, about two hours south of the Queensland border, the most *easterly point* of Australia. Perhaps this is an appropriate metaphor for the first draft of this book, since Byron Bay is the place in Australia where the sun's *light* reaches first. *77th Pearl: The Perpetual Tree*, was to be the book's final iteration. One experience, among several at Byron Bay, became a turning point. Standing alone on a rocky hilltop lookout at the southern end of a long white sandy beach, Shamot asked himself: What now? What will be of my life? As he was contemplating these questions, a lone dolphin appeared, riding the waves towards the beach. When he saw this inspiring spectacle of nature below him, he felt a correlation between that lone dolphin and himself. It was then that he knew everything was going toward a certain destination. Shamot knew he would find the purpose of his life. He intuitively knew that his life, to this point, had been a sojourn into the desert for forty days.

Shortly after this Shamot began to read the sayings in the Gospel of Thomas. He found them baffling and yet uplifting; Shamot struggled to understand them. When he would go for a walk or run he would quietly say to himself—*Yeshua, the bringer of spiritual wisdom to this realm, open the doors for me, so I can understand the words you spoke.* This mantra went on sporadically for several months. It was on another holiday to Byron Bay that Shamot decided to take a diary and begin to formally hand write a commentary for each of the sayings in the Gospel of Thomas. Quite often, what he wrote astonished him, because it seemed to come from a collective conscious- ness. When Shamot would read over the words, he could not imagine that he had discovered these truths. Thus began the physical manifestation of *77th Pearl: The Perpetual Tree*. It took many more digital drafts, after the initial handwritten version, to arrive in this final form. The final edition was written in the eleventh month of 2021.

Throughout this life's journey, Shamot Sesju had much self-doubt. He questioned the validity and the possible repercus- sions of scrutinising a long lineage of religious tradition. Yet he felt driven, knowing this was absolutely necessary. One day he had what might be called a revelation. When Shamot was going through this period of self-doubt and questioning he found himself asking: *am I on the right path?* A few days later Shamot brought home some of his students' biographies for marking. He took the students' biographies out of his bag to place them on the table. Before Shamot placed them on the table he flicked through them and noticed one had a picture of Mother Teresa on the front. He noticed it because students were asked not to include images in the biographies, he also noticed it was around the middle of the pile. Shamot left the biography in the pile and put the bundle on the dining table. He walked into the kitchen to make a cup of motivating coffee, so he could start grading the scripts. When he came back he was astonished to see the biography with the image of Mother Teresa on top of the pile. Shamot picked it up and read a quote the student had placed at the top of her biography. The quote read: *'If I ever become a saint I will surely be one of 'darkness'. I will continually be absent from heaven to light the light for those in darkness on earth.'* (Mother Teresa of Calcutta). The student's surname was 'Hope'. These *apparent signs* could be seen as serendipitous, but they assured Shamot that he was on the right path and that what he was doing would help others.

Paranormal experiences were never something Shamot desired to have, or had ever encountered in his past. However, in the process of writing the commentaries for the Gospel of Thomas certain paranormal phenomena did occur. The decision to include them came from a realisation that they happened to him for a reason. They were integral to the journey of writing *77ᵗʰ Pearl: The Perpetual Tree*. It occurred to Shamot that even though the aim was to lift the discourse to a logical, perhaps even scientific level, he could not ignore the fact that the Gospel of Thomas is about the intangible, *the Spirit*.

The encounters occurred around the time Shamot was handwriting the first draft of the book, in the diary mentioned previously. The process of writing was both physically and intellectually taxing. He felt as if he was a vehicle, driven with an adamant and focused intent. Shamot would often feel his heart pounding in his ears, as the words poured out onto the page. After about two hours of writing, he would feel the need to rest. Shamot would leave the diary closed on the kitchen table, which was directly below the bedroom, in the open plan, split-level loft apartment. It was during one of these breaks that he was woken to the sound of pages being turned at an urgent, purposeful pace. He listened for about thirty seconds, until he became concerned it might be a robber. Shamot carefully walked to the balcony that looked down onto the combined living and dining space. As he looked over the railing, a dark shadow shot across the living area and out between the blinds, which scraped and bent as the blurred figure flew out between them. The apartment was on the second floor; the outside balcony was only a meter deep and five meters wide. The shadowy figure seemed to have disappeared into the light of day. When he checked the dining table, the diary was there, as he had left it. While this incident intrigued Shamot, it did not concern him a great deal. He tried to convince himself that he did not really experience what he knew he had.

The second incident was very similar to the first—only Shamot did not get up to see who was downstairs. He waited, listening to the pages turning. They were being turned as one would when browsing a magazine, scanning the articles. There were several pages that seemed to be of particular interest, as they were not turned as quickly as the others. When Shamot sat up in bed the pages stopped turning. He went down stairs to see if anything had been moved—everything was in its original place. In both cases he did not wake-up as if from a dream. Shamot knew he was awake during and after these events.

The third incident was more confronting than the previous two. As was the case in the previous experiences, it was a clear and sunny day. It was about midmorning when Shamot decided to take a break from writing. This time he did fall asleep. He was unsure for how long he was sleeping, but he recalled being tormented by something. It was as if Shamot was being verbally abused, being made to feel weak and unworthy. In the dream, he was angry at the thing that was making him feel this way. It was like meeting an old adversary who had come back to reclaim what was slipping through its fingers. When Shamot woke up, he was on his left side, facing the ensuite. The sliding door was open. As he opened his eyes, repeating the mantra, *you don't scare me; you have no power over me*, he saw in the bathroom doorway the silhouette of a man wearing a stiff, broad brimmed hat. The figure was like a pitch-black cut out of a man with a very slim, harshly defined nose, mouth, and chin. He appeared to be crouching down and leaning forward, so that he was only visible from the lower chest up. The back half of the head and body were behind the door frame. There were no three dimensional features that were visible, the entity was flat, black. Shamot stared directly at the figure as he repeated the mantra. The silhouette slowly withdrew behind the door frame, until it was out of sight. He cautiously got out of bed to look in the bathroom. Nothing was there. At this point, Shamot was beginning to question how far these experiences would go. Perhaps a reason for the antagonism was that he was writing about the malevolent entities. Sceptics might then suggest that these experiences were dreams, resulting from the writing process. However, Shamot is certain he was awake when the things he saw and heard were present.

The fourth incident was physical. Shamot had been writing about the Holy Spirit and its active role of *connectivity* within the Trinity. This time, it was early evening when he decided to go to bed. He was lying on his right side, thinking about the revelations experienced in that session of writing. Suddenly, Shamot felt a presence quickly come from behind him, onto his body, trying to take control of his mouth. It was trying to profane the Holy Spirit through his mouth. However, this thing felt as though it had been repelled off his body, unable to grip onto him. It was as if it had jumped onto him from behind, but slid off a kind of force field.

Fundamentalists might consider the events described here as the work of Satan. This is a simplistic and treacherous approach to take. We have seen in *77ᵗʰ Pearl: The Perpetual Tree* that the explanation is rather more complicated. We see in Mark 8:31-33, Yeshua accuses all humans (through Peter) of being Satan, when they think *not as God would, but as men do*. In Thomas 70, we also see that if we bring out what is within us, that thing will save us. If we do not have that thing within us, then that thing will destroy us. These are references to self-awareness of the soul, in the first part, and knowledge of the truth in the second part of this saying. It follows then, if we do not have a logical understanding of what has actually happened in the events described here, they could become a catalyst for something damaging. Undeniably, these paranormal experiences were not pleasant—they seemed to have been antagonistic. To suggest it is the work of a dark angel and his minions allows us to fall into the trap that some churches have entered. The battle between Jesus Christ and Satan should be looked upon as an internal battle—to be a good person who pursues light, not darkness (see commentary for Thomas 21). This realm captivates certain entities, they wanted to see what Shamot was writing and tried to discourage him. They see this world as something they can take pleasure from, through gaining influence and power. Churches that buy into the notion of a prince of darkness give these souls/entities what they desire—fear and notoriety. We must accept that what we have previously called a demon is actually a remnant of the primal animal humans came from. These *demons* want control and power, which is achieved through fear and aggression (Thomas 7). They *evolved* from the myth and infamy of Satan, as described in the New Testament, and have taken on *his* role. In reality, some of these entities are human souls lusting after the material world. The New Testament authors used the character of *the satan*, from the Torah, to create God's enemy, because it made sense of the tragic events surrounding Jesus. They did not understand what Thomas knew. When the specters in the events above sensed the Light of *77th Pearl: The Perpetual Tree*, they felt fearful of what it would do to their power and control. After all, knowledge is power, it is our *imperial garment.*

There was a final experience, which was the antithesis of those described previously. After the four *negative* experiences, Shamot was beginning to wonder if there were *angelic* beings, from the Light. Would they be aware of his work and perhaps even be encouraging its progression? Apart from the *connection* he felt while writing *77th Pearl: The Perpetual Tree*, he was beginning to think that the beings from the Light were just a sense of hope. Shortly after the fourth experience, Shamot was lying on his bed, around midday, pondering the contents of the book. Above his bed was a skylight, which was clear glass. He had his eyes closed, but could hear a scratching noise on the glass. He opened his eyes to see three white cockatoos standing on the skylight, all of them with their heads turned, looking down at him. Their three white heads, with dark eyes and long yellow crests, were striking against the blue sky. Shamot's initial reaction was fear, which was unusual because he does not fear birds or any other creature. He knew instantly that this was *a sign*. There is a fine line between making claims of a divine presence and dismissing something as coincidence. Experiences like this need to be analyzed in the context of what has happened previously. The possible implications also need to be considered. It is for this reason that these events were edited out of the first edition of this text. Shamot chose to look at the *visitation of the birds* as the collective consciousness (Holy Spirit), answering an important question. The birds were probably interested in seeing what was through the skylight. That there were three, and that he happened to be asking those questions at that time, may have been a set of events influenced by the collective consciousness. Shamot believes it was necessary for him to experience all the events described here. It ratified what he was discovering through the secret teachings found in the Gospel of Thomas.

63. Jesus said, "There was a rich person who had a great deal of money. He said, 'I shall invest my money so that I may sow, reap, plant, and fill my storehouses with produce, that I may lack nothing.' These were the things he was thinking in his heart, but that very night he died. Anyone here with two ears had better listen!"

Yeshua would have had followers from all walks of life but many would have been poor. They would have sought solace from poverty through listening to His sermons. In this context, Jesus provides these people with comfort, while also presenting a warning to people occupied with accumulating wealth. Focus on building wealth steals people away from thinking about the soul—what they are. Yeshua's intention is not that people should retreat from life as they know it; they need to think of themselves as '*passersby*' (Thomas 42)—*as observers of this life*. This is difficult when we are distracted by the things that affect our mortal existence. Often in the Gospel of Thomas, Yeshua asks people to consider what is overlooked due to these distractions—the realm of the collective consciousness (Holy Spirit). At times, this task would seem impossible. It is made easier when we take the approach that every experience we have is one we can learn from. If people learn and grow from the experiences they have in this life, good and bad, then these occurrences have not been in vain. As recounted in Thomas 62, all of the author's experiences have led him to where he is now. Had the author not contemplated why these things were happening and what he could learn from them, he would have become like the man focused on his wealth, who dies the next morning. This is similar to the parable the Buddha presents, when he speaks of the pearl diver. The diver knows there is a price to pay for obtaining the pearl, which represents the road to enlightenment. The rocks and corals scratching the diver are the experiences of this existence. Through the lens of Thomas, these scars are invaluable lessons and remind us of the difference between the body and the soul.

Jesus' contemporaries made ritualistic sacrifices to gain favour with their god and to atone for the innate sinfulness they believed they inherited. This came from the notion that God is perfect and humanity is not. These actions were empty rituals, which became obligations, without any real meaning or connectedness. This is much like the many churchgoers of today who attend mass out of habit, or as a social event. These people are simply paying lip service with other motivations driving their actions. Being authentic in our desire to grow as spiritual beings is the key. The ritual practices of Yeshua's contemporaries were just another box to tick off. One might ask if priorities have changed at the start of the twenty-first century. In Thomas 63, we are asked to consider the *other*, before it is too late for us to aggregate the Father's Light and truly *live*.

64. Jesus said, "A person was receiving guests. When he had prepared the dinner, he sent his slave to invite the guests.

The slave went to the first and said to that one, 'My master invites you.' That one said, 'some merchants owe me money; they are coming to me tonight. I have to go and give them instructions. Please excuse me from dinner.'

The slave went to another and said to that one, 'My master has invited you.' That one said to the slave, 'I have bought a house, and I have been called away for a day. I shall have no time.'

The slave went to another and said to that one, 'My master invites you.' That one said to the slave, 'My friend is to be married, and I am to arrange the banquet. I shall not be able to come. Please excuse me from dinner.'

The slave went to another and said to that one, 'My master invites you.' That one said to the slave, 'I have bought an estate, and I am going to collect the rent. I shall not be able to come. Please excuse me.'

The slave returned and said to his master, 'Those whom you invited to dinner have asked to be excused.' The master said to his slave, 'Go out on the streets and bring back whomever you find to have dinner.'

Buyers and merchants [will] not enter the places of my Father."

Thomas 64 is linked to the events that occurred within the Temple grounds. In Mark: 11: 15-17, Yeshua knocked over the stalls of vendors trading goods within the sacred space. It should be understood, while Yeshua defended the ethical use of the Temple grounds, He did not see this as *the place God existed on Earth*. This is what Yeshua's contemporaries believed. Jesus saw the body as sacred only because it was *the Temple, which housed the seed of the Father* (the Source). Once the seedling has grown, the greenhouse (Temple) is no longer required; it would only hinder the spreading branches of the tree (Thomas 20 and 53). The greenhouse exists *for the sake of* the seedling within it, the seedling does not exist for the sake of the greenhouse surrounding it (Thomas 29).

Thomas 64 is also prophetic—the guests who decline the master's invitation are a metaphor for the church communities that established themselves after Jesus' death. The master is the Father (Source), where Yeshua and our soul came from. The *slave* is the Holy Spirit, working through Jesus. The instruction at the end, '*go out to the streets and bring back whomever you find to have dinner*', heralds the acceptance of gentile believers, before the disciples could see the possibility of it happening. In the twenty-first century (the three sevens), this request heralds the manifestation of *77ᵗʰ Pearl: The Perpetual Tree, which invites all souls* to its table of sacred wisdom.

In Thomas 64 Yeshua warns His contemporaries of how shallow and peripheral their lives had become. However, there is more to this saying. There is a reason for the scenarios given in this parable. The deviations from what truly mattered were evident in the faith of Yeshua's contemporaries. Furthermore, He could see that these weaknesses would transfer down through His disciples and ensuing generations. Within these first four invitations, we see the actions of the major religions of today; in particular, the Christian denominations, which have evolved over two millennia. The general statement referring to buyers and merchants also foresees the evangelical ministries, which use the Bible and Jesus' name to *sell their product*. This product is sold as a sense of security and belonging to a community, which represents a hope.

In the list of invited guests, first is the person awaiting payment from some merchants. In this scenario, the comparison is to church groups whose main focus is to build wealth. This also refers to those people who feel that giving money to their Church will buy them favour with their god—this certainly happened in Medieval Europe. In the second scenario, a person has purchased a house and has been called away because of it. In this situation we see religious groups who are focused on relics—supposed sacred objects—and the building of monuments such as temples and cathedrals. Their focus and reliance on *these physical objects removes them from what is important*. In the third situation we are presented with a person who seems to be doing an admirable thing in preparing a banquet for a friend's wedding. Interestingly, this action is not presented as admirable at all. Here, Yeshua speaks to us about churches focusing on the idea that the Saviour will return to earth, to judge the living and the dead. They are the ones in continuous preparation for the coming of the Father's Kingdom, one that will not come because *it is already here, but they do not see it*. This concept of a second coming, for the judgement of the living and dead, is derived from the Old Testament. In the fourth scenario, a person who has bought an estate needs to collect rent. Here, we see a church community who is focused on growing wealth through *holding the keys to a place for the purpose of building wealth* (Thomas 102 and 39).

When Yeshua says, '*Buyers and merchants will not enter the places of my Father*', He reveals a truth about these people and institutions. They do not know *the places* where God, the Source exists, because their actions and this realm blind them. They choose to decline a meal with another soul, due to concerns peripheral to the collective consciousness. Connecting to the Source through the activity of eating with others is a metaphor. The way the soul is nurtured by mindful *linking* to the all (Father/ Source), through prayer or meditation, is the action of the Holy Spirit (collective consciousness). The desires of leaders of these institutions become a veil to the truth. Material wealth and power are the means by which they attempt to ratify their position of authority. History has shown us how people in these lofty positions of power start to think they are outside moral and ethical behaviour. This is when we see physical and emotional abuse take place to those people subordinate to these leaders (Thomas 7).

Thomas 64 is also symbolic of a doorway. Not surprising, since *the Holy Spirit is the conduit (collective consciousness), the way into the realm of the Spirit.* The second last sentence sees the wealthy person asking the servant to '*bring back whomever [they] find to have dinner.*' This dispels the notion that Yeshua was here (exclusively) for the culture He was born into. He came to this world to lift-up anyone who wanted to listen. In this sense, when the Catholic Church forbids non-Catholics to have communion, they are going against Yeshua's wishes. His table is for everyone to come to—it is not exclusive, it is inclusive. Should it matter that Catholics see the bread and wine as the body and blood of Jesus, while other Christians do not? Consider what Yeshua would think of this, in light of Thomas 64.

65. He said, "A [...] person owned a vineyard and rented it to some farmers, so they could work it and he could collect its crop from them. He sent his slave so the farmers would give him the vineyard's crop. They grabbed him, beat him, and almost killed him, and the slave returned and told his master. His master said, 'Perhaps he didn't know them.' He sent another slave, and the farmers beat that one as well. Then the master sent his son and said, 'Perhaps they'll show my son some respect.' Because the farmers knew that he was the heir to the vineyard, they grabbed him and killed him. Anyone here with two ears had better listen!"

Thomas 65 and 66 are used in all three Synoptic Gospels—Matthew 21:33-46, Luke 20:9-19, and Mark 12:1-12. This also occurs with the parables of the sower and the mustard seed. In the synoptic narratives, the sayings in Thomas become part of Yeshua's intellectual conflict with the Pharisees. The Pharisees were trying to fault Yeshua so that they could discredit Him in the eyes of the community. The fact that Thomas 65 and 66 have been used in all three synoptic texts shows that these texts referenced the Gospel of Thomas; if not directly, then indirectly through Mark—the first of the synoptic texts written. Thomas 65 is presented in the synoptic texts as a direct attack on the Pharisees' hidden agenda. In the synoptic texts *the wicked tenants* represent the Pharisees, who killed the son (representing Yeshua). Yeshua is also the son in Thomas 65, but *the slaves* are symbolic of the spiritual leaders who preceded Him. This is not explained in the synoptic narratives, because these events were not understood at that time. We should note that the crop being collected is the grape, which would become wine. We learn through the Gospel of Thomas that the wine, which was given to Yeshua's disciples as His blood, is metaphoric of the unifying, nourishing conduit we know as the Holy Spirit (collective consciousness). The Holy Spirit established itself in this dimension through what Yeshua left us–His wisdom and knowledge. For this reason, the Pharisees, whose souls were influenced by malevolent entities (Thomas 24), wanted to stop Him. Thomas 65 is expanded upon in all three synoptic texts, which state that the Pharisees were instantly aware the parable was about them. They wanted to grab Jesus, but according to the narrative in the Synoptic Gospels they were afraid of the people, who saw Yeshua as a prophet. At this point, Thomas 66 is included in all three synoptic versions—Yeshua points out to the Pharisees that *the brick they have rejected would become the keystone.* We must recognise that Yeshua never intended on being the foundation stone of a kingdom on earth. The early Christians, who had an orthodox perspective of Jesus, devised this premise based on *traditions* from the Old Testament. We should recall Yeshua is our brother by virtue of the soul—what we are. The reference to 'the stone that the builders rejected' is therefore a way to give strength to those on the outside of society's expectations—the ones who do not fit in. This position is ultimately a privileged one. Marginalised people have *more potential* to see truth and become passersby (Thomas 42). This is also evident in Thomas 13.

The appropriation of Thomas 65 and 66, by the synoptic authors, illustrates that they had an unwavering faith in Jesus as the Christ, foretold in the Old Testament. This is what the Christian orthodoxy refers to as *the gospel*—a concept predating written texts. As it was not written down, nobody has evidence of this premise and it is therefore a matter of faith. *The gospel, in reality, is the Source (Father) reaching out to us,* the human species. The prophets have interpreted *Its* yearning for us through visions, clouded by the fog that is the material realm. They created stories of an ethereal being who would save His creation. This is a link to our evolution from a primitive creature, who sought protection and guidance in an alpha-male, patriarchal figure. For the same reason, the authors following the Abrahamic lineage were unable to see past *the concept of the Christ*. A significant number of the sayings in the Gospel of Thomas can be found in the canonical texts in some form. They are not the same due to their wording and the context in which they are placed—a persuasive narrative. A clear example of this is seen in Matthew 13 in which a succession of the sayings are appropriated. They are used in a narrative designed to frighten believers into being good Christians (discussed at length in the commentary for Thomas 9). Yeshua certainly positioned Himself as the 'Saviour' the prophets' spoke of (Thomas 52 and 88). However, His contemporaries did not understand *the position this actually entailed*. Yeshua was looked upon as the only Son of God, given to us as the perfect sacrifice for the atonement of humanity's sins; sins inherited from Adam and Eve in the Genesis myth. We see in the Gospel of Thomas that this premise was wrong. Yeshua tells us this when He asks that people do not place new wine (His teachings) into old wineskins (the Torah – Old Testament). The prophets did foresee the coming of Yeshua, but they did not understand who He was and where He came from—this is what Yeshua reveals in the Gospel of Thomas.

In appropriating Thomas 65 the synoptic authors ignore the inference that Jesus is killed. However, there is no reference to a resurrection in Thomas, which we consistently cite in the canonical texts. The reason for the absence of such a reference in Thomas is because the only *desirable resurrection* is the one involving the Spirit—when the flesh is removed (Thomas 53). It is the esoteric nature of the Gospel of Thomas that made it inaccessible to the early Christians. Therefore, the Gospel of Thomas was used in the only way these authors could cope with such concepts—through the Torah (Old Testament).

Jesus consistently used analogies His contemporaries *might have understood.* These are also metaphors relevant for today, derived from the mechanisms of our global culture. For instance, money can be made from a vineyard through the fruit from the vine. The fruits grow and are harvested, these represent the souls becoming enlightened Spirits. This is the *harvest* that is profitable to God, the Source.

In the first part of Thomas 65, Yeshua discloses a mystery about the Spirits who have crossed over from our realm to His. The vineyard is this world, which has been created *from the outer layer* of the Source (Father), *for the education of souls.* These are the souls that have evolved from the initial breath of life. The slaves are the enlightened spirits, *influenced by the other realm* to teach and assist souls in this realm. One of the most inspired soul leaders was the Buddha. He was *a slave* to the Source, in particular, its resonance of peace within the human. Buddha's teachings were about finding this peace. This was achieved through recognising life for what it is and accepting these truths (see commentary for Thomas 7). This teacher, like others, was presented with obstacles, because of the established beliefs within the community he was born into. These communities had indoctrinated customs and religions, created through observations of nature. This resulted in a wealth of myths, which stood as explanations for natural phenomena. John the Baptist was another spiritual leader who did not fit the parameters of this life. The difference in the teachings of the Buddha and John the Baptist, compared to their corresponding contemporaries, was that they were the vanguard of their time. They saw the disparity between this world's emptiness and the realm of the Spirit, respectively. To varying degrees, they both taught about either denying or withdrawing from this world. Yeshua did not advocate such a denial or withdrawal—*His yoke is gentle* (Thomas 90). It is presented to us as knowledge of the truth.

When we acknowledge our soul is inexorably a part of the whole, a part of God, we become passersby of this existence, the empty carcass.

When Jesus talks about the heir to the vineyard being killed, He speaks about Himself. Yeshua's Spirit was so strong that the transfer from His realm to the physical one did not impact Him. This is why His resolve was unwavering. As souls who have been cast out from the Father's expansion into the abyss (Thomas 97), most humans do not have the same *connection*— this is the journey they are on now. Yeshua represents the *perfect human* they should aspire to become, the kind that other spiritual leaders had to work hard to be a semblance of. The prophetic second last line describes how people who were the supposed bastions of their god in this realm (the farm tenants representing the Pharisees), had actually been corrupted by this world. They were concerned about their power and control being eroded, we see them hold onto the crop (human souls) at any cost. The lion we see in Thomas 7 had consumed them. Yeshua could see the way the Pharisees were thinking and the insecurities they projected through their questions. He could see the violence and injustice around Him. Yeshua knew that to open people's minds, to think freely, was as dangerous as any person fighting for democracy in a fascist state. The layered meanings in this saying demonstrate the depth and scope of wisdom this great man held through the collective consciousness. Yeshua's decision to allow these events to come to fruition stands as a powerful message. His life and death relate to the nature of human beings and how people must not become captivated by this life and existence.

66. Jesus said, "Show me the stone that the builders rejected: that is the keystone."

In the canonical texts, Yeshua uses this statement to reference the way the Pharisees were rejecting His authority. Using this saying in this context would seem a logical link, but it is a shallow and peripheral interpretation of a profound statement. Yeshua gives affirmation to those people who have been marginalised by the leaders of any narrow-minded society or culture. Humans place themselves into position within a community as mother, father, teacher, banker, or tradesperson etcetera—this becomes their identity. One can compare the song by Pink Floyd, 'Another Brick in the Wall' (Roger Waters), as an apt analogy. The song comments on the education system and its attempt to indoctrinate youth into an established system, one where thinking was not encouraged. Questioning follows thinking—this is a disease to well-established institutions and something the youth needed to be inoculated from. This faceless power, that makes young children believe they should aspire to certain positions or roles, drives behaviours focused on success within that society. This behaviour steals them away from contemplating who they really are. The focus becomes what they are in the eyes of their community—what they have and how successful they are. Humans begin to believe that to *live* they need to have a certain job, house, car, clothes, and so on. As we have seen previously, Jesus' definition of what it is to *live* concerns the essence of what we are, not the flesh and bone that clothes the human.

There is nothing new to the concept of withdrawing from the day-to-day experiences of life, for the purpose of reconnecting with the intangible. In parts of Asia, ascetics were practising extreme denial of the material world centuries before Yeshua appeared in this dimension. What is extraordinary is that He was the first to recognise the necessity to withdraw from a society—one that believed it was ordained by their god to be the way it was. When Yeshua asked His contemporaries to observe the Sabbath (Thomas 27), He was asking them to be authentic. He wanted them to use whatever time they had for rest and relaxation to contemplate *the other*—the self one cannot point to. Yeshua came to correct false assumptions and the empty rituals accompanying them. He compared Himself to the lamb, which was sacrificed in the Temple as an offering; this violent action represents this realm and has no connection to the *one* Yeshua represented (Thomas 30). He was the lamb that made the conscious decision to place Himself upon a cross. Yeshua did this for the sake of all—showing humanity the disparity between the flesh and the Spirit. Yeshua is not asking anyone to reject society and their position within it; He asks that people take the time to observe, and learn from this life.

The 'stone' society rejects represents the people who see the errors and injustices within the community, those who ask the uncomfortable questions. In doing so, they become *the keystone for the growth of the kingdom*. To be able to see outside the square is crucial, if one is to grow in Spirit. Up to the twenty-first century, significant examples of such souls are seen in Mother Teresa, Mahatma Gandhi, Martin Luther King Jr., and Nelson Mandela. While some of these may have had questionable pasts and faults along their path, they eventually claimed non-violent victories over the lion (Thomas 7). This demonstrates that the lamb is visible and strong in this realm, though much suffering is incurred for these successes to eventuate. This is the nature of the physical realm; this lesson is manifest in the *pacifist sacrifice* Jesus made for humans. People on the periphery of society can see its evils and be *observers* and *passersby* (Thomas 42). People should rejoice in being the stone that is rejected by society, for they become the keystone of the kingdom.

The Gospel of Thomas, which has been rejected by the Christian orthodoxy, is a part of this saying. This gospel is the very thing that allows for a new direction to be established. It dignifies each human as having a soul, which can potentially become a free Spirit. The Gospel of Thomas is free from social, cultural, and political motivation. It does not have aspirations of creating a global religion. *It speaks to the individual, as Yeshua intended.*

67. Jesus said, "Those who know all, but are lacking in themselves, are utterly lacking."

Thomas 67 refers to the difference between academic knowledge and wisdom. This saying warns that a person may accumulate a wealth of knowledge, which can be recited and recalled at ease, but this does not mean the individual is any closer to becoming an enlightened being. If one lacks the intuitive, logical, and critical response to the knowledge one accumulates, then that knowledge *has no life.* It does not benefit anyone.

When Jesus describes a person who knows all but is lacking in themselves, He refers to people like the orthodoxy and fundamentalists. They have closed their minds to the potential of a deeper meaning and they will not ask questions. They desire a simple, uncomplicated message, one that takes little thought. This is why a proportion of these secret sayings are presented in such a cryptic manner—they require *a desire to know*. People from the orthodoxy are often characterised by arrogance and *blind faith*, which denies them the connection with God, the Source—the one Yeshua calls Father. These sayings are not for people who are seeking the quick fix. The secret teachings of the living Jesus resonate in the soul and are only disclosed to those who are made worthy of the truth. These people have an ability to stand back and analyse this life (Thomas 62 and 42). Those who are worthy have *made themselves worthy* by knocking on the door with persistent determination (Thomas 94). This is not a simple, uncomplicated truth.

What is important to notice in Thomas 67 is the reference to *the self* through the words '...lacking in *themselves*.' We see here that it is primarily the journey and development of each individual person that is crucial. This is not something the faiths sharing the Abrahamic lineage provide or advocate. They see the kingdom of God as a pyramidal structure, like society within this realm—this is flawed. The focus for these groups is to build a community, based on common beliefs and practices, which preserves its growth through rites involving birth, marriage, and death. These rites and practices become rituals that become actions devoid of meaning. They do not connect the person with God, the Source. These rites and rituals may successfully build a community, but they do not aid the individual seeking a relationship with God, the Father. Only the person who is open to the intuitive and logical self can attain this goal (Thomas 19).

68. Jesus said, "Congratulations to you when you are hated and persecuted; and no place will be found, wherever you have been persecuted."

Becoming aware of the difference between you and those around you can be difficult and sometimes painful. People who see themselves as marginalised will naturally feel on the periphery of society and, at times, isolated from their peers. In Thomas 68, Yeshua tells us this is a good thing. It is good because we are in the position of the observer or passerby (Thomas 42). Often in these sayings, Yeshua asks us to come away from the day-to-day events in our lives, so that we can give time to the contemplation of the kingdom—the collective consciousness. If one feels persecuted in a place or situation, removing oneself from that situation allows for a fresh perspective, which enables a person to see things as they truly are. This allows for an objective look at the situation and for critical analysis to take place. In doing so, we learn a great deal about the nature of this world.

This saying is linked to Thomas 66, where Yeshua tells us that the stone which is rejected becomes the keystone. This is why Yeshua congratulates the marginalised—for our difference and our unique perspective. People should remember that Yeshua was persecuted and killed for being different. It was Yeshua's message that made Him *the stone the builders rejected*. His disciples, and the Pharisees, did not understand His teachings; Yeshua's message was so different to what they knew. Now, we benefit from that disparity

69. Jesus said, "Congratulations to those who have been persecuted in their hearts: they are the ones who have truly come to know the Father.

Congratulations to those who go hungry, so the stomach of the one in want may be filled."

In the New Testament we find statements similar to the sayings in the Gospel of Thomas. This is evidence of the re-contextualising of those sayings by the gospel authors. We can see an example of this by comparing Thomas 68 and 69 to Matthew 5. In this chapter we have what is referred to as *The Beatitudes*, spoken by Matthew's Jesus during the *Sermon on the Mount*. When we look at the differences between Thomas 68 and 69 compared to Matthew 5:10-12, we see that there were a series of particular intentions in the author's mind. Matthew's Jesus states:

'Blessed are those who are persecuted *in the cause of uprightness: the kingdom of Heaven is theirs*. Blessed are you when people abuse you and persecute you and speak all kinds of calumny against you falsely *on my account*. Rejoice and be glad, for *your reward will be great in heaven; this is how they persecuted the prophets before you*.'

The author's intent is revealed in the words that have been italicised. The author of Matthew wanted to make a strong and clear link to the Old Testament concept of Heaven and Christ. Therefore, we see the words, '*in the cause of uprightness:*

the kingdom of Heaven is theirs; on my account....' The difference we garner from the Gospel of Thomas is that Heaven is not a kingdom of its own *place*—it is not above, it is in humanity. Heaven is the collective, as we see in Thomas 3 and 51. Also, by stating the reason for the persecution as due to the adherent upholding the Law ('in the cause of uprightness'), the meaning is redirected towards the separation of Jewish believers and Gentile non-believers. This is not what Yeshua intended. The reference to, '*on my account*', also wrongly suggests that Yeshua wanted to be seen as God. Through these words, people are encouraged to believe in Yeshua as they would God and, in turn, potentially suffer for upholding what these authors were saying about Him. This is evidence of how *people have turned the messenger into the message.* Moreover, in the statement, '*this is how they persecuted the prophets before you*', we see how the author links the Old Testament to Yeshua. In comparing the followers of Jesus to the prophets of the past, the author attempts to rally people toward a cause—the creation of the Christian community. Through these verses, the followers are assured they are supporting what has been promised in the Old Testament prophecies. The people whom this addresses become the prophets of the Christian Church, based on the promises of a saviour in the Old Testament. This kind of culturally persuasive undercurrent is absent in the original language of the Gospel of Thomas. In this gospel the focus is just on the soul—the human *coming to life in Spirit.*

The observations relating to the New Testament authors, here and in other commentaries, are in no way a negative exposition of their character. They had good intentions and they served the purpose of the collective consciousness. Their rhetoric made Christianity a strong institution, which meant it could survive the ravages of time. If Yeshua were not thought of as the saviour Christ of the Old Testament, He, along with the Gospel of Thomas, would have disappeared into obscurity. The theological conflict between orthodox and gnostic believers ensured the survival of the Gospel of Thomas, because it was hidden away from the antagonistic leaders of the fledgling Christian institution. Through these events this gospel was protected from people who would have used those pearls to create dogma, or destroyed it entirely.

At the start of the twenty-first century, people have the capacity to understand what Yeshua wanted them to know. He wanted humans to stop looking at God as an entity outside of themselves. When people do this, they are able to use this external god for their own purposes, usually being power and control. We see the perfect example of this in the conflicts surrounding the Jerusalem Temple. In Yeshua's teachings, a person finds that God is among humanity, *It* is within humanity and *It* surrounds us. To orthodox believers (people who only adhere to the canonical texts), this is problematic. They see God as perfect and humans as flawed. This is true. Humans are not perfect, but the orthodox believers do not see the difference between the flesh and the soul. The shell, which surrounds the soul, is imperfect. However, this shell allows for the pearl within it to grow (Thomas 76). This is the way *God* (the dominion of the Spirit) has found to recover the sheep, which have gone astray (Thomas 107) onto the distant road (Thomas 97).

In Thomas 69, Yeshua gives us a clue as to the nature of God, the Source. He tells people that those who are persecuted in their hearts *are the ones who truly come to know the Father.* Intuitive responses and experiences are often said to be detached from the intellectual, analytical mind. They are also known as coming from, and affecting, the heart. Science may offer complex neurological explanations. However, the point of this observation is that we are considering the abstract concept of what it is to feel—enabling us to conceive of *what unconditional love is.* This kind of love is something humans are scarcely able to express, but it is what the collective consciousness (Holy Spirit) exemplifies. When people are persecuted, they feel the absence of unconditional love in their hearts. In this absence, they yearn to feel love. When a person is by themselves and meditates on the meaning of life and God, a deep connection is made, similar to the one they might feel for a spouse. Love is a *connection* and this is a linking with the Source, through the Holy Spirit. This process is entirely profitable to the soul. These two kinds of love are of course different, because one is directed toward a tangible entity (person) and the other is not. The latter is beneficial to the soul, because it is a whole and universal love.

In the mythical story of Genesis, God breathes life into Adam who is made from the earth. In reality, this was the first time primal man could *think in abstract terms*. When the first caveman contemplated the possibility of ethereal powers and souls within their own kind, a connection was made. This was the time Adam's hand reached out to touch the Father—the source of all things. What *Adam* did not know is that he *needed to search within himself* to truly make this connection. This is at the heart of the message Yeshua presents in the Gospel of Thomas. Unlike our primal ancestors, humans of the twenty-first century will be able to step away from what they experience in this world, seeing it for what it truly means.

We cannot ignore that through great suffering, we are changed; this is also a large part of Thomas 69. Through emotional upheavals we are made to contemplate the purpose and *meaning* behind suffering. Often, we cannot see the purpose in a terrible, personal experience, but after the experience has passed we can look at it as a lesson in life. When people analyse why these things hurt them, they come to see that these things were really not important. If these negative experiences are of a physical nature this is evidence of the feeble nature of the body. This is also a valuable lesson, demonstrating how tenuous and precarious our time on this planet is.

When Yeshua says, '*Congratulations to those who go hungry, so the stomach of the one in want may be filled*', He is speaking to those who have, or will, feel negativity and isolation. When humans experience persecution they feel the need to have it explained to them—why did this happen and what can I do about it? This is *the hunger* they feel. Yeshua tells people the answer is in the realisation of the collective consciousness (Holy Spirit). Humans must accept that what is important is to understand that they are all connected through the Source (Thomas 77). Those who persecute them do so because they are lost in fear, in darkness (Thomas 7). This is the knowledge that fills us; this is the food that stops our hunger. This is the pathway to the unconditional, ever-present love felt *through* the collective consciousness.

The last part of Thomas 69 flows in both directions, in the sense that God, the Source, is the one who also *hungers for us*. The Father hungers for reconnection with us (Thomas 107) and when people are forced to seek this out there is benefit for both. Since we share kinship with Yeshua, through the Source, it is reasonable to think that these feelings are connected, but for different reasons. The reasons reflect each other—one wants to know what will end the suffering, the other wants to end the suffering.

70. Jesus said, "If you bring forth what is within you, what you have will save you. If you do not have that within you, what you do not have within you [will] kill you."

This is a revealing metaphor about the true nature of what we are and of the way we *come to life*—the life that Yeshua defines, not the one defined by this outer, material layer. When we are asked to *bring forth what is within* us, we are asked to search for the thing we cannot point to. One cannot point to the self, since everything one might think of pointing to is *a spot on the body*. That spot, or part of the body, *is not you*. The soul is the thing we cannot point to. The body is a reflection, which changes as it decays. An enlightened Spirit does not decay—it grows. The thing animating the flesh, inside every cell of the body, grows in experience and wisdom—it is the soul. Yeshua would have spoken to His contemporaries with reference to their bodies, because this is what they believed to be their identity. When Yeshua said, 'bring forth what is within you', it was a challenge to Yeshua's contemporaries to consider something other than the body, as the self.

The second part of the saying refers to the processes humans go through when the soul is reabsorbed into the whole. Without the connection to the Source, through the collective con-sciousness (Holy Spirit), death leaves the soul lost, searching for a *place* to be. This energy, which was the soul, is reabsorbed into the material world, as that is all it knows. The thing that has *killed* the person, in this instance, is the lack of knowledge and acceptance of the true self. This results in the lack of connection to the Father/Source. These souls are perpetually new, the previous identity is scattered and lost, absorbed into the whole—the Source. This is why Yeshua states in previous sayings that those who are lacking *taste death*; those who are filled with Light *live*.

People who believe in reincarnation might find this premise difficult to accept. These people have to admit that there are very few examples of people who know of their past life with clarity and conviction. Their recollection is usually fragmented and clouded. This indicates that the *death of the self* is certain if the connection with the Source is not realised during physical existence. We might also consider, how is it that there are more humans on the planet Earth now than ever before—were they all reincarnated, or are they *fragments* of something else? It would seem there are countless souls, which are *sparks from the eternal source*, and each has the *potential* of self-realisation—to *live*. In countries like India there are numerous examples of children who remember a past life, to the point where they are able to identify where they lived and previous family members. This demonstrates how belief systems impact how a soul perceives existence. If a soul becomes convinced that a place on earth is its domain then it will be bound to it. Perhaps this *place* on earth offers these souls more potential for growth, perhaps they only know this place. Whatever the case may be, we recognise that every human soul has choice through knowledge and understanding.

Consider how clairvoyants who claim to speak with ghosts of the dead cannot have a conversation with a murder victim, leading to the capture of their murderer. Psychics are tapping into the Light of the Source, because they have a stronger awareness of their own soul's connection with this Light. They are receiving images and feelings from the living person, who desperately wants to communicate with their departed loved one. This is not to say that ghosts do not exist, but the identity of a soul fades away and is eventually reabsorbed. Psychics can also gather information from the environment around them, since they are connected to the Source and *this Light flows through all things*. This is reinforced when Yeshua tells us the thing that He is, is in all things (Thomas 77). This knowledge should bring us out of our complacent beliefs, which arise from books and movies depicting troubled ghosts resolving their issues and 'crossing over.' This becomes a rather romanticised presentation of what happens to souls—they are so disturbed by this life they need to resolve something. This is what Jesus means when He asks us to hate our father and mother in Thomas 55. If people are tied to this world and all its primal instincts and obligations, then they are veiled from seeing the truth and they cannot bring out what is within them. People cannot become the perfect human if they are attached to this life. They need to accept it for what it is and be passersby (Thomas 42).

71. Jesus said, "I will destroy [this] house, and no one will be able to build it [...]."

The time is coming when fundamentalists will have to change their beliefs; because they will see their god is not the omnipresent patriarch they had hoped he would be. Jesus started this process when He gave us the knowledge of the kingdom. It is here, but most people cannot and will not recognise it. It is within us, it is the Spirit existing in another realm/dimension. Yeshua is telling people He will destroy the institutionalised establishment of what He envisages for humanity. A vision derived from the realm of the Spirit, the collective conscious- ness. Men (not women) who felt the call of the Source, but were hampered by the thick fog that is this existence, created these institutions. Had women been involved, we may be in a very different situation.

The divide in Jerusalem between the Jewish Holy Temple and the Dome of the Rock, situated in the same area, illustrates the way God, the Source, calls people to understand the nature of what they really are. In this same place, Yeshua overturned the merchants' tables, accusing them of desecrating the sacred place. Thomas 71 is connected to this action. The lion in Thomas 7 has consumed the leaders of these two communi- ties, who have created so much violence and despair due to their desire for estate. Ironically, they claim the same lineage through the mythical character of Abraham. They cling to a piece of land, as the link to their god, when they do not see God in each other. This is what makes it so easy for them to kill one another. Their actions *make them invisible in the eyes of God, the Father.*

The 'house' is not a physical building. It is the relationship with God, the Father, the source of all things, through the collective consciousness (Holy Spirit). This is what they cannot rebuild while they breed hatred and conflict. It is a conflict based on parcels of land and a god that exists outside of who they are. Here the literal and figurative come together—neither will give in to the other, so neither will have sole ownership of those Temple grounds. They will also lack the security of an authentic relationship with God, *the Father* while they continue on that path. Without recognising the Soul within each other and respecting that Soul above all else, they are lost among the rubble of *their house.* These are the people who examine the face of heaven and earth but have not come to *know the one in front of them* (Thomas 91). Institutions that are based on a pyramidal power structure, with a god at the apex, are what Jesus destroys. Men make this kind of structure; it is the lion at work (Thomas 7). God is not one entity. It is a complex relationship among sentient beings. It is a consciousness beyond the current comprehension of humans. This is the mallet destroying that '*house*'.

72. A [person said] to him, "Tell my brothers to divide my father's possessions with me."

He said to the person, "Mister, who made me a divider?"

He turned to his disciples and said to them, "I'm not a divider, am I?"

The answer to the question in Thomas 72 is: yes! Jesus is a divider, but this has been taken the wrong way by orthodox Christians and fundamentalists. They have justified violence and war through their lack of understanding and lust for control (Thomas 7). Primal fear has driven their desire for control. The Gospel of Matthew 10:34-36 says:

'Do not suppose that I have come to bring peace to the earth: it is not peace I have come to bring, but a sword. For I have come to set son against father, daughter against mother, daughter-in-law against mother-in-law; a person's enemies will be the members of his own household.'

This is an adaptation of Thomas 16, where Jesus says:

'Perhaps people think that I have come to cast peace upon the world. They do not know that I have come to cast conflicts upon the earth: fire, sword and war. For there will be five in a house: there'll be three against two and two against three, father against son and son against father, and they will stand alone.'

As discussed in previous commentaries, there are other examples where the sayings in the Gospel of Thomas appear in the Synoptic Gospels. They are consistently placed within a narrative context, changing their intended meaning. We should note, Yeshua said He only discloses His mysteries to those who are worthy of them (Thomas 62). Yeshua would also test His disciples with cryptic and loaded questions, such as this one in Thomas 72. When people ask themselves which are the actual words Jesus spoke, they can start by comparing the context of similar sayings. Consider if those words are an attempt, by the Synoptic Gospel authors, to put the sayings into the framework of the Old Testament prophecies. Then consider how they look when they stand alone and unchanged, in the Gospel of Thomas. The appropriation of some of these sayings has been discussed at length in the commentaries of Thomas 9 and 65.

The key to understanding what Yeshua meant by these divisive sayings is in the last four words of Thomas 16—'they will stand alone'. Jesus knew that the lion would consume men, as we see in Thomas 7. They would use religious teachings to justify battles over land and control over earthly kingdoms. The conflict Jesus cast upon the earth is ideological. *It is the new way and the truth.* It *shows us what we really are* and the connection we share with God, the Source. This knowledge is the sword, which divides those who can comprehend such a connection, from those who will only ever look to a god outside of themselves. This is the god that can give them permission to hate, kill, and be killed.

In Thomas 98 Yeshua again uses the analogy of a sword. In that saying, people are given a definitive picture as to what *the sword* is about. *Jesus is the hand holding the sword*, which comes through the void separating these dimensions. The blade penetrating the void is symbolic of the prophets, heralding the coming of the Light, Yeshua. He is *the hand* wiping away fear and immature knowledge. In Thomas 72, when Yeshua asked His disciples if He was indeed 'a divider', He was testing them. He was looking for the correct comprehension of what He was and what He came to give to humanity. This is an ongoing test for all humans, to understand His cryptic teachings. Corresponding to the way Yeshua wants people to draw conclusions, we might look at how we cannot take our knowledge of God from the physical world—the two are not the same. The physical and metaphysical are completely different; therefore, our understanding of how they work must be different. Knowledge of the Spirit is linked to the collective consciousness; this is what lifts the Gospel of Thomas above all others. Canonical texts have been tainted by their author's desire to place them in the context of an earthly kingdom. Hence, in the New Testament, the emphasis is on encounters with demons. It becomes apparent that the Greek and Roman contemporaries of the gospel authors, and their myths involving malevolent deities, influenced these narratives. We see evidence of this in Paul's references to 'elemental spirits' and in how the character of Satan has changed over time (see commentary for Thomas 21). The emphasis in the Gospel of Thomas is finding the self, thereby reconnecting with God, the Father/Source. Enabling this lasting connection is the collective consciousness (Holy Spirit)—the active energy connecting all the beings of Light.

In the context of Thomas 72, it is appropriate to consider a *division* between religion and the world of politics and science. Throughout history, the overlay of religious beliefs onto political matters has caused conflict in the world. At the beginning of the twenty-first century, it still does. Yeshua tells us the journey to find the soul is a personal one. The soul is a part of and is connected to God, the Source. Although this Light is all around and through this dimension, It does not have a tangible presence. This is because physical material decays—the Source cannot. Religious beliefs are not supposed to determine political decisions—the physical and spiritual are separate. When religion is engaged with the day-to-day function of society we come across a problem—this world is in contradiction to the eternal nature of the kingdom within. As a result, the lion (Thomas 7) grabs hold. Those *consumed* fight for pieces of land in the name of a god they believe will grant them a renewed, earthly kingdom. In reality, we know deep within our psyche that this world is fleeting and impermanent. Some would argue separating religion from the mechanisms within society would erode it, but this is not the case. Mindful people know in their intuitive and logical self what is right and wrong. This comes from our connection to the Spirit, which seeks harmony, balance, and peace. Yeshua has indeed come to divide. He came to divide the physical from the spiritual. This is what was behind His acceptance of death at the hands of men consumed by the lion (Thomas 7). This was an *allegorical lesson*, which we must learn from, if the human species is to continue into a long-term future.

Post Industrial Revolution, new technologies have poisoned our environment and destroyed many lives, just as they have saved and improved many lives. This is the nature of the physical world—it is filled with good and bad. These good and bad things do not come from God, or a malevolent seraph. They come from the nature of the universe and everything in it. Science works with the material of the universe, and while the realm of the Spirit has its apparent influence through consciousness, it does not control this dimension. It was Rudolf

Steiner who made the statement: *'the body should eat food grown in healthy soil, if the Spirit is to free itself from the body.'* This is an apt analogy of the separation people need to make in their minds. Planet Earth needs to be treated well, so that human bodies (and all other creatures) do not suffer. When people suffer their focus is on the physical, rather than the eternal nature of *what* they are. Humans need to make appropriate decisions about where they live and what the population in a given area should be, so as to not overburden the environment and its limited resources. These are the concerns of science and new technologies. They must be supported by the political world, through dividing religion from the mechanics of this realm. Deluding uneducated souls that God will provide for them is harmful. For example, they are told that as long as they do not use contraceptives they are in God's favour. This is damaging to the Earth and to these communities, both physically and spiritually. People in charge must stop the collective psychosis. Humans must recognise that there is a divide between what it is to live in this dimension and what it is to live in the realm of the Spirit. This is what Yeshua brings to us. This news sets all people free from suffering. It should also stop people from attempting to fit a square peg (orthodox science) into a round hole (the dimension of the Spirit).

Yeshua also came to divide us from the limiting notion of a patriarchal, monotheistic belief system. Before the steadfast believers start gathering the stake and firewood, consider the teachings in the Gospel of Thomas. In here, Yeshua teaches us that we share an intimate relationship with *the one* He calls *Father*—remember that this is a symbolic reference and is unlike the patriarchal father *we know*. Jesus calls us His brothers and sisters, in preference to His blood relatives (Thomas 99). He also tells us that the nature of *what He is* can be found in everything (Thomas 77). Jesus describes the Father's Kingdom not as a place, but as a condition or action, in Thomas 20, 57, 96, 97, 98, 107, and 109. Thomas 3, 51, 91, and 113 tell us that the kingdom is here, but people do not see it. It is in each person. These teachings point to a very complex relationship and kinship with the Divine (Thomas 50). For the Christian orthodoxy, their understanding of what *God* was made them distant and fearful in that relationship. Yeshua is symbolically *cutting us free* from the idea of a separation between the Divine and us. In doing so, we are opened to a greater mystery, one that we are truly worthy of (Thomas 22). To believe in one God is monotheism, but this concept polarises a greater mystery; we are part of this god, as much as Yeshua is part of this god—He has told us this fact. It follows then that God is the collective consciousness, a kingdom of Spirits which are one and many, at the same time. They are *one who have become two—this is humanity*.

73. Jesus said, "The crop is huge but the workers are few, so beg the harvest boss to dispatch workers to the fields."

Yeshua's teachings were not one His contemporaries could easily fathom. Their beliefs were rooted in tradition, which clouded their vision of *the message*. The crop Yeshua was referring to is a symbolic one. The crop signifies the Kingdom of souls, which are, on this planet, human beings. Yeshua's contemporaries understood a kingdom to be made of majestic buildings and other such structures. *The kingdom* is not up in the sky, it is in people. The crop was and still is huge, because the Father's Light is immeasurable. To have a kingdom you must have a collective. The Light of God, the Father, seeking to reconnect with its progeny, remained in the darkness—falling back into this realm to *sprout* again (Thomas 57).

The wisdom of Yeshua is at odds with the notion of a patriarchal god. This god created humans *through his will* and punished them for their (apparently) sinful nature, as a human father might his children. This relationship is not harmonious and is the antithesis of what Yeshua describes in the Gospel of Thomas. In Thomas, we see our relationship as intimate, connected, and personal. There is no judgement from an external entity. People become aware, through Jesus' teachings, that their perceived sinfulness, or rather weakness, is symptomatic of the physical form. *The world, and the body it created, is the lion* (Thomas 7) which consumes the soul. While this soul presents as human, it is not the *perfect human*. Accepting the imperfections of the world and desires of the body, humans come to realise the soul is suffering. The soul cannot find peace in the context of the physical realm. Just as the Source is unlike this realm, so too is the soul unlike the body. Yet the soul can only come to life (become a living Spirit) within a body. This is why we must see the world and body as a carcass (Thomas 80 and 56). This dimension is incidental material, the discarded outer layer from the Source's expansion—the distant road in Thomas 97.

Some of the teachings in the Gospel of Thomas are not dissimilar to those of Gautama Buddha. However, the primary difference is that Jesus came to this realm *to confirm the existence of the Soul*—something the Buddha could not and would not do. The Buddha was a human prince who went on a quest to find a way *out of the cycle of suffering*. In this process, he became an enlightened Spirit (see commentary for Thomas 7). Yeshua, on the other hand, came *from* the realm of the Spirit to this dimension. In this sense, He was a Buddha who allowed His Spirit to be clothed in human form (Thomas 28). In allowing His human body to be destroyed, Yeshua pointed to the prime message behind His teachings. This was, and still is, *the power of the Soul, which is resurrected into the Spirit through the actions of the collective consciousness (Holy Spirit).* Through seeing all good things in this world as *reflections* of the realm of the Spirit, we open a doorway into the truth. This truth also exists in seeing the fractured nature of the things that harm people—they are the things made of the stars (physical matter). In the material universe, all elements come from the stars. Even the bodies we dwell in are composed of chemicals, which would not exist without stars. Those natural processes are the reflections of the other realm. Instead of simply existing in an endless void God, the Father has influenced the creation of places for Its Light to inhabit (Thomas 96). Through *this creation* the soul Light, within the human, may awaken from its sleep, bringing the progeny of the Source to *a new condition of being.* In the process, the soul comes to know what its relationship with all things truly means. The Father is a metaphor for *creative energy* and the connection we have to It.

How does one teach souls who are struggling for answers? This is at the heart of Thomas 73, and in Thomas 74 we see there were not many capable of delivering the knowledge. In this context, we might consider if all the apostles Yeshua selected were capable of His teaching. It seems they were not, as we have seen through Jesus' questioning and testing of them (Thomas 13). Consider also how in Mark 4:11-12, 'The Purpose of the Parables', we see a desire to exclude certain groups from understanding the *mystery of the kingdom of God,* which, in that text, had only been granted to Jesus' followers. However, if we look at the two verses, they give away the truth about the writer's intention. Mark 4:11 states: *'to those outside everything comes in parables, so that they may look and see but not perceive, and hear and listen but not understand, in order that they may not be converted and be forgiven.'* This sentiment stems from the first Jewish Christians, who were culturally exclusive, shunning the Gentiles. Then in Mark 4:13 Jesus questions the apostles' intellectual capacity when He asks: *'Do you not understand this parable? Then how will you understand any of the parables?'* Jesus then explains The Parable of the Sower to them (Mark 4:1-9). There are also parallels to the Gospel of Thomas sayings in Matthew 13, discussed in the commentary for Thomas 9. In Mark 4:11-12, we are told only the select few will understand. In the next verse, Yeshua confirms that the apostles themselves are the ones who do not understand. This contradiction points to a discrepancy between knowledge and understanding among the apostles. In Mark 4:11-12, the words revealing the fact that these are not the sentiments of Yeshua are: *'they may be converted and be forgiven.'* These are the words of an ambitious leader, wishing to build an *exclusive community.* The language also puts this text into a period after Jesus' crucifixion, since Christianity was not an established religion in His time.

In the Gospel of Thomas, people learn they can become worthy by seeking the truth. There is no exclusion when it comes to God, the Father, because the kingdom is the collective consciousness. People like Thomas were able to see further than what their culture had instilled in them—this made them worthy. Thomas 74 backs up this point—Thomas tells Yeshua that there is nothing in His contemporaries knowledge to quench the thirst for God, the Source.

74. He said, "Lord, there are many around the drinking trough, but there is nothing in the well."

Thomas 74 is an observation made by Thomas. Thomas was privy to information beyond the other apostles. In Thomas 13, when Thomas told Yeshua he was incapable of comparing Him to anything he knew, Yeshua recognised Thomas as different. As a result, he was given knowledge the others could not comprehend. What is most significant, is the way Thomas describes the other apostles' reaction to this information. In Thomas 13, Thomas tells the apostles that if he revealed the three sayings they would stone him, but *their stones* would turn against them. The conclusion we make is that what Thomas was told clashed with the other apostles' beliefs, which were rooted in the faith Jesus was born into. The apostles would have seen the sayings as heresy; the words would have attacked their faith. It is most likely that Thomas 2, 3, and 4 are the three sayings Thomas was referring to, as they are at the heart of this gospel.

The culture of Jesus' time was not ready for the knowledge He needed to impart to the world. One might wonder if anything has changed within the global community in over two thousand years? While there have been people wanting the truth, they have chosen an easy, comfortable, and uncomplicated truth. The ritual and dogma inherent in the major religions provide the easy path, one that only requires lip service and physical actions. Followers who could teach what Yeshua wanted people to know were rare; this is what Thomas

73 points to. Thomas 74 elaborates on this by making it clear the knowledge available was of no benefit, because it did not reflect *the truth*. The *watering hole* required digging in places where this knowledge could be extracted. *This spring would be found in people on the periphery of that society.* The ones who were less affected by their heritage; people who could think outside the square (Thomas 66). These people could evolve and grow. This was, and still is, crucial.

75. Jesus said, "There are many standing at the door, but those who are alone will enter the bridal suite."

In Thomas 75, Yeshua reveals that humans are joined to the truth when they are *metaphorically alone*. When people are free from preconceived notions of what *the relationship* with God, the Father is like, then they are open to the truth. Such notions are usually derived from a religion infiltrated with dogma and ritual, which override the essential truth. To enter 'the bridal suite', where the collective consciousness joins the human Spirit, a person needs to be stripped of all their baggage and misguided teachings. In Thomas 22, Yeshua asked people to become like newborn babies in order to enter the kingdom. This is the same metaphor presented to us here. The 'alone' is the essential us, the thing we cannot point to. Humans must strip away beliefs imposed through legacy, before they enter the place where the Source exists. Until they leave their misconceptions behind, people cannot understand the nature of God, the Mother (Thomas 101).

Most Christian religions base their faith within the structure of a community, as the word Church implies. Does Thomas 75 infer these communities are irrelevant? In the context in which these sayings were created, we know that the Jewish community was being led by corrupt Pharisees, whose lust for power and control motivated their actions (Thomas 7). Although this pattern has been repeated throughout history, in different religions, we must acknowledge that many good people have come out of these institutions. They have been the *individuals* who could work within an organisation and not lose themselves (Thomas 39). This is similar to the way Jesus asks people not to lose sight of their goal, by telling them to be passersby (Thomas 42). In Thomas 39, Jesus asks those who deliver His teachings to *be as sly as snakes and as simple as doves.* This statement recognises the potential dangers in preaching individual enlightenment, as opposed to a community religion built on dogma and ritual. Institutionalised faith has been a necessary evil. It has allowed for the identity we know as *Jesus* to survive into the twenty-first century. As mentioned previously, this also means that Yeshua's controversial and less understood teachings were preserved in the Gospel of Thomas.

Thomas 75 confirms we are alone in the experience of death, as we are in birth. Only the individual can experience these things. In knowing that the human soul is connected to all things through the Father/Source, people are released from suffering. Thomas 75 requires the human to strip away the romantic notions developed in this life, such as those about the never-ending love for a spouse, or family member (Thomas 55). These romantic ideals are an illusion based on what people have experienced in the physical world. Love is initially a series of chemical reactions, which diminish over time, to become familiarity and attachment. This limits the reality of what we are and where we come from. At times one may come across a person whom you have not met before, yet you feel very familiar with. This is a familiarity based in truth. We know certain souls because we have met this Light before. Their energy is familiar to us; it is this that we react to. In the Gospel of Thomas, we are asked to look at the big picture and where we fit in this narrative. Seeing attachments as an obstacle is necessary to achieve this goal. Sometimes this includes the knowledge people have become familiar and comfortable with. When they enter the bridal suite *alone*, they can be joined to Yeshua and the Source. In this state, a person has relinquished the preconceptions inflicted upon them, through this life. They have become one with the collective consciousness (Holy Spirit).

76. Jesus said, "The Father's kingdom is like a merchant who had a supply of merchandise and found a pearl. That merchant was prudent; he sold the merchandise and bought the single pearl for himself.

So also with you, seek his treasure that is unfailing, that is enduring, where no moth comes to eat and no worm destroys."

In Thomas 76, Yeshua tells us that we need to be discerning and value what is worthy of our heart and mind. One of these is the *Divine teaching* concerning the Soul and its relationship to the source of all things—the one Yeshua refers to as the Father. *The pearl* represents the precious and enduring truths given to us in the Gospel of Thomas. These teachings have not been altered or afflicted by moths or worms. The insects are metaphoric and represent people who have been overcome by their lust for power and control (Thomas 7).

Consider how the pearl is formed. It is a foreign object, which either accidently enters, or is purposefully placed inside the mollusc body. To protect itself, this *irritation* is covered in layers of substance, which forms the pearl. This is symbolic of what happens to the soul when it is wrapped in the flesh (Thomas 53). Moreover, *from the irritation and suffering has come something beautiful.* Just as the fig tree will fruit in rocky soil, or when its roots have been injured, so too, humans can take the negatives from this life and grow from them. In this way, we have treasured the thing that is unfailing—the Light of God, the Source. Through this process we become passersby (Thomas 42).

Often in the Gospel of Thomas, Yeshua describes the Father's Kingdom as an allegorical action, which reflects the pathway to the kingdom. Imagine being Jesus. You knew the truth; you had been thrust from the Spirit realm into this one, with this knowledge intact. In this privileged position, you could see how the things in this world distract souls, which struggle to *evolve beyond this transitory realm.* In this position, one would try to show people the cause of their suffering and how they could come to this realisation for themselves. In the Gospel of Thomas, we see Yeshua's desire to set people free from their suffering. The cryptic nature of these words reflects the time in which Yeshua entered this dimension. It was a time in which a cautious approach was required, to carefully disseminate contentious and volatile knowledge. A knowledge that makes people aware of the very personal and intimate relationship they share with Jesus, through the source of all things—the Father. This knowledge *is the pearl.* It is built from the suffering and the wisdom we acquire throughout our travels. Religious organisations would have us believe we cannot find this path ourselves, but Yeshua teaches us that this path is within us. The intuitive connection we share with God, the Source, through the collective consciousness (Holy Spirit), guides us to the truth.

77. Jesus said, "I am the light that is over all things. I am all: from me all came forth, and to me all attained.

Split a piece of wood; I am there.

Lift up the stone, and you will find me there."

It is difficult to put into words how profound this saying is. It describes the nature of *the Source of all things—the one Yeshua calls Father*. Jesus refers to Himself as this thing, because He is, as we all are, connected to this Source. Through Its very nature, It is everything, because It is in all things. In those beings that come to recognise this truth It aggregates and grows. It then becomes conscious—*It lives as a Spirit*. The soul is made of the Source and exists in all humans. It lives when It implants into a prudent human, becoming a Spirit through the action of the collective consciousness (Holy Spirit).

Science has proven the universe is expanding, as it is evident that galaxies are moving away from each other. It follows that the universe came out of a single point in the emptiness of space, when everything in existence was in a singularity. Then, suddenly and inexplicably, this Light expanded. This was the 'Big Bang', which created everything we have in the physical universe. This hypothesis is supported by scientific evidence, but it still leaves us with many questions. Where did that tiny spot, which contained everything we know in the physical universe, come from? What was around that singularity—was it nothing? What is nothing, what *is* the black emptiness of space? These questions create more questions, which signal a potential that is difficult to fathom. As scientists delve into the possibility of other dimensions, we come to realise that the language used in the Gospel of Thomas (by Yeshua), is not dissimilar to a scientist describing their hypothesis. The language in Thomas is different to what a contemporary scientist might use because the context in which Yeshua spoke these words was archaic. It required Yeshua to present cryptic symbols and metaphors, which could be relatable to the common man. At the same time, some of the sayings needed to have an esoteric quality to ensure their longevity, reaching humanity in the twenty-first century.

Light comes from a source of energy. When Yeshua talks about 'the light that is over all things', He is referring to the energy flowing over, around, and through everything. We could compare this to contemporary String Theory, or the Higgs boson, which explains how the smallest of particles obtained their mass. The difference in Thomas 77 is that there is a consciousness present—making a link between the Source and the Son (all sentient beings). This consciousness should not be confused with the popular belief known as *Intelligent Design*. This idea links biblical myths and evolution. Essentially, this belief suggests that God is the *designer* of evolution. The problem with this notion is that it does not recognise the physical world as separate from the realm of the Spirit. The laws governing each of these are entirely dissimilar. The fact that the Light Yeshua speaks of is through all things in the physical world does not mean this thing is *intentionally* responsible for its creation (Thomas 97). There are manifestations of this Light in the natural world, but these are mere reflections. We saw this previously, in the two elements that form water. When separate *they are one*, but when joined *they are two* and a source for life, as in Thomas 11.

Christian faith explains the imperfections and chaos inherent in this world as resulting from a *separation from God*, through the *action of the original sin*. Gnostic Christians put forward the premise of an imperfect demiurge, which has created a place for his own glorification. His imperfection is reflected in the suffering people experience and, as a result, he was perceived as jealous and vengeful in nature. In the Gospel of Thomas, people are invited to accept that this world is a distraction from our true nature, which is unlike anything in this universe. The soul is something humans cannot see, or experience with any of their senses. This is why humans must separate the physical from the spiritual. At the same time, they must recognise that to escape the physical they need to minimise their suffering. Religion should not steer their decisions, which should be based on common sense about our reality, such as population control and responsibility for the environment. Praying to a God to change what is outside the realm of the Spirit is senseless. This is not an argument against the possibility of miracles. It is the recognition of the reality of the soul and the reality of the physical as separate states of being. The mechanism of the physical universe is different to the realm of the Spirit. Recognising this liberates people from much of their suffering. Seeing the nature of this world as having its own phenomena, apart from the realm of the Spirit, brings peace—we know that the Spirit *flows through it*. The imperfections and chaos in this realm are symptomatic of the nature of physical materials, which have a finite life. Beauty in this realm does not last, because of its inclination to decay. These four dimensions are only a reflection of what exists in other stable dimensions. This is where Yeshua comes from and where enlightened Souls move into.

When Jesus tells us we can 'split a piece of wood' or 'lift up a stone' to find the *Source of all things*, He is liberating us. People from the Abrahamic lineage are released from centuries of isolation, stemming from a belief in an authoritarian father, who had imperfect, human emotions. *This is the god men created.* Jealousy is an emotion driven by primeval urges for power and control over others. These emotions are rooted in the want of the alpha-male to be the sole genetic father to the groups' young. A god who punishes by killing and causing suffering is a reflection of primal fear and anger. This god has nothing to do with the nature of God, the Father, which Yeshua speaks of. A vengeful god is in fact a creation *of men,* who have been influenced by the lion referred to in Thomas 7. Religious texts describing such a patriarchal god reflected the writers' insecurities and primal heritage, not the reality of the Spirit and its nature. This shows us how the prophets and disciples were looking through a thick fog—this realm, the 'powerful one' in Thomas 98.

Seeing what God, the Source is like is liberating and profound. If we break down all materials into the smallest of known particles, we find there are spaces between these components too. These spaces are the fabric of the Source. It brings peace and calm when we connect with it, because it is a constant—unlike the chaos of the physical realm. As mentioned in a previous commentary, people find solace and peace in rituals, as a pseudo connection to the Source. Rituals are calming due to their predictable nature. In times of great despair, religious rites and practices have great benefit, because people, momentarily, connect to this Source. Yeshua wants the connection to be *constant.* This is what He presents us with in the Gospel of Thomas—the steps toward the *perpetual link.* Through these words, we know Thomas 77 *is the pearl* the merchant has found in Thomas 76.

78. Jesus said, "Why have you come out to the countryside? To see a reed shaken by the wind? And to see a person dressed in soft clothes, [like your] rulers and your powerful ones? They are dressed in soft clothes, and they cannot understand truth."

A tone of frustration and anger is, again, evident in Thomas 78, as Yeshua attacks those who come to see Him preach. He attacks them because He knows they don't understand what He is saying. They are incapable of relating to the truth Jesus presents to them, because they expect knowledge to come presented in a certain way, from someone in a certain position. Yeshua sarcastically asks if they have come out into the countryside to see nature at play, while they listen to a rabbi speak to them. When they discover a man in ordinary, perhaps even soiled, clothes, they question His authority in their hearts. Jesus could sense this lack of faith and knew where it was coming from. He attacks the leaders of His contemporaries' faith, who dressed in the finest clothes and placed great importance on physical cleanliness. Yeshua points out that the clothes a person wears do not signify their capacity to comprehend the wisdom and knowledge He offered.

People must not accept the teachings they hear as truth, just because they come from a person, or place, that *appears* to have authority and knowledge. These people and institutions do not have the truth within them simply because they *look like they should*. In some of the oldest Christian Churches, there is a rather medieval fascination for materialistic things. The ceremonial robes some church leaders wear are of the finest cloth, inlaid with gold and even jewels. The immorality of wearing the finest garments, while people suffer in poverty and hunger, is shameful. The argument that they represent the divine and should therefore reflect this position is misleading to those who still rely on visual cues to relate to 'God'. However, there is a desire for change. The majority of followers see a great divide between the dated attitudes of the leadership, which steer the machine, and those at the coalface doing the work. Each individual must keep in mind that Yeshua asks us to be true to the self—the intuitive, logical self. If something does not sound right, or feel right, then people should question why. This is the first step toward searching for the truth. There is no cloth that can be as pure white as the Light that emanates from one who is truly connected to God, the Source, through the collective consciousness (Holy Spirit).

79. A woman in the crowd said to him, "Lucky are the womb that bore you and the breasts that fed you."

He said to [her], "Lucky are those who have heard the word of the Father and have truly kept it. For there will be days when you will say, 'Lucky are the womb that has not conceived and the breasts that have not given milk.'"

In Thomas 79, Yeshua corrects the notion that family members can claim some kind of spiritual privilege, simply by association to a prophet or enlightened being. This may bring into question the position of Mary, the mother of Jesus, who has had a contentious history among Christian denominations for some time. Marian Theology is a powerful force in the Catholic faith; arguably outweighing the importance of Yeshua, in the sense that people turn to Mary in times of need. The ethical dilemma of placing the mother of Jesus in such a high position, to the point of giving her the title of 'Queen of Heaven' in the Early Middle Ages, has its problems—particularly when we put her in the context of the Gospel of Thomas. The issues surrounding Mary would require a lengthy thesis in itself. However, for the purposes of this commentary, we can speak of Mary as someone who would have surely felt the pain Yeshua mentions in the last line of Thomas 79: '*Lucky are the womb that has not conceived and the breasts that have not given milk.*' Mary would have suffered greatly to see her son killed in such a brutal manner, but, for Yeshua, this saying is less personal than it is didactic. It speaks of times when all mothers, and indeed fathers, wish they had not had children, as they experience great torment and suffering *because of them*. When a child is sick, or has an accident, or rebels against the family, these events bring suffering and turmoil. This suffering extends to times of war and natural disasters. They are a result of the material world and its imperfections. These are the primal urges humans battle throughout this life (see commentary for Thomas 7).

At this point, we might consider the role of women. How were they perceived and what is their position in the eyes of the modern Catholic Church? In Yeshua's time, women were marginalised (Thomas 114) and would have had definitive roles in society—as would men of that period. The primary role of the woman would have been as a mother and a wife. This role would have been subordinate to the husband's role, in all aspects other than the *nurturing* of children. This aspect is one Mary, the mother of Jesus, has become venerated for, particularly in the Catholic Church. A difficulty arises when this role is combined with Mary's increased status, because observant

Catholics refer to her as 'ever-virgin'. Mary was married to Joseph; this is supported throughout the narratives in the Canonical Gospels. Joseph and Mary went on to have other children (Thomas 99) and this was not through divine intervention. The premise of this intervention is also a contentious one, since Mary was only in her early teens and naïve to the facts of life. Children of that time would have been protected from such carnal knowledge. This reality does not denigrate her position as *virgin*. This conundrum could cause grief to those Catholics who place Mary on the 'ever-virgin' pedestal, but it should not be seen as an obstacle. Reconciling the reality that is this realm, with Mary's veneration, depends upon the definition of *virgin*. The answer is found in the context of the Gospel of Thomas, through *77ᵗʰ Pearl: The Perpetual Tree*, which illuminates this pearl.

In Thomas 22, we see Yeshua point out that to enter the Father's Kingdom people need to break down their perceptions of what they are. In this sense, humans are not female or male, they are a soul, which is both of these at the same time. Venerating Mary for her position *based on being female* is incorrect, just as it is incorrect to think of the Father (the Source of all things) as we might our biological father (Thomas 83). So it follows, venerating Mary as 'ever virgin' is incorrect—*if people perceive this virginity as having to do with the act of sexual intercourse*. The way people are required to look at Mary is as someone who attained enlightenment, because she took up the path that her son created for *all* human beings. Mary can be considered *ever virgin*, because she became *untouched* by this realm, knowing her *soul to be separate from her body*. This is the *sacred mystery of Mary*, as revealed through *77ᵗʰ Pearl: The Perpetual Tree*—she was as Yeshua instructed, be 'passersby' (Thomas 42). She took up the task of having to be a mother to the greatest being that entered into this realm. On this difficult journey, Mary profited by recognising she was to be *untouched by this world*.

Even though she had other children and the same concerns and obstacles all mothers do, *she let all this pass her by and attained to the realm of the Spirit.* This is the greatest of lessons the *Virgin Mary* has given humanity. This is what we must learn at the beginning of the twenty-first century. Otherwise, humans injure the dignity of all women, because they think their sexuality is a barrier to attaining spiritual enlightenment. In truth, all humans can attain this level of inner peace—when they *become untouched* and passersby of this realm (Thomas 42). In Thomas 79, as in other sayings, Yeshua is concerned about the individual's potential to escape the distractions of this world. Filial love is certainly one of the most powerful of these distractions. In Thomas 55, Jesus asks that we hate our parents and siblings as He does. In doing so, people may free themselves from the suffering these connections carry with them. This is not a literal hate of the person, but a *disdain for the physical body* and the hormonal mechanisms that drive it. They are the desires to breed, to be loved, and to have pride in the other. All these things are transitory and fade away, but the Soul is constant. Humans are often veiled by the emotions love encompasses. As a result, the soul is pushed back into the darkness. When people see things for what they are, then they are *able to be passersby* (Thomas 42). What is crucial in Thomas 79 is that people recall what Yeshua affirms: '*Lucky are those who have heard the word of the Father and have truly kept it.*' When a person does this they have activated their inner ear, the ear of the heart (Thomas 33).

80. Jesus said, "Whoever has come to know the world has discovered the body, and whoever has discovered the body, of that one the world is not worthy."

The religion of Jesus' contemporaries saw the world as created by their god, Yahweh. This god created Earth and everything on it. Superior to all, he made *man*—in *his own image*. This concept is flawed. It comes to us from the limited observations available to humans in this dimension and not from the knowledge delivered by Yeshua.

Joseph Campbell (1904-1987), a mythologist, presents a thorough analysis of the myths humans have created in the television series and book 'The Power of Myth'. Presented as a question and answer series with journalist Bill Moyers, it poignantly describes creation myths (and others) and how they have comparative, parallel threads among different cultures. Campbell shows how unrelated cultures, from all over the globe, have created similar myths to explain the mysteries within this life and our existence in it. People experienced natural phenomena and linked these with stories involving ethereal beings or deities, which explained how or why the phenomena occurred. For example, when the Ancient Egyptians experienced the Nile Valley flood, bringing rich sediments to the valley basin, they did not realize hundreds of kilometers upriver the rainy season had started. The flooding of the Nile Valley became something magical, something that, in their limited understanding, must have been driven by divine beings. To ensure this flooding would occur on a seasonal basis, the Pharaoh was installed as intermediary, offering prayers and sacrifices to those gods. Through *77ᵗʰ Pearl: The Perpetual Tree*, we see that these similar narratives and beliefs across the globe, are the *Father's Light seeking out Its own* (Thomas 107).

Unlike any other person since the dawn of humanity, Yeshua was aware of *His connection* to God, the Source, from His youth to the end of His mortal life. He was an enlightened Spirit who came into this realm, lifting the veil of fog humans experience in this dimension. This is at the heart of Thomas 80. Yeshua's wisdom was not based on, or conceived from, observations in this world. His is a sacred knowledge, brought to humanity from a dimension most people cannot experience in the physical body.

The visual metaphor of the world as *the body* is a powerful analogy. In the faith of Yeshua's contemporaries, the world was a paradise waiting for God to reclaim it—post Adam and Eve's disobedience and subsequent punishment. Yeshua tells humanity this concept is wrong. The world is made of physical matter, which has its own laws. The soul comes from another dimension, which is unlike anything in the physical universe. A body is created through *physical actions* and a soul inhabits it—this is the Source. It is aggregating Its energy in a human body, to *come to life*. If the individual becomes aware and nurtures the truth, this energy draws in to itself, becoming the mechanism by which the *human Spirit is brought to life*. The awareness awakens the collective consciousness (Holy Spirit) to this soul, distinguishing it among all the sparks of Light in this dimension. This conduit then nourishes its growth. Through this process, people's eyes become opened to the disparity between the material universe and the Spirit. Humans then correctly see the world as a body, which perishes. This line of thinking enables the individual to understand the way the soul exists. Additionally, through this understanding, the world becomes a body, which may be inhabited—just as the flesh is inhabited. With this truth, humans also realise that just as the body dies, so too must the world. Science shows us that eventually the world will cease to be inhabitable. This is an inescapable fact.

When Yeshua states, '*whoever has discovered the body, of that one the world is not worthy*', He is commending those people who see themselves as a soul, as distinct from the physical body. In Thomas 56, Yeshua calls the world a carcass and congratulates those individuals who see it as such. They see the truth, which allows them to delve past the physical, into the realm of the Spirit. This is an extremely important and valuable attribute; too often the material world, and all its distractions, disconnects us from this potential. *These distractions steal us away from a fuller, holistic existence.* The trap for humans is their physical senses. They are so powerful they tend to override the Light within, which seeks to be recognised and be joined to the Source. In a sense, this place humans inhabit is a double-edged sword. While it allows for *the Light* to find a vehicle, within which it may become *realised*, the sensual body, and tactile world, can easily obscure it. This should not mean people reject these pleasures. Nor should they make for themselves a situation where they devalue the self; self-deprecation, of course, becomes an obstacle (Thomas 6 and 14). When poets and painters have romanticised and glorified nature, they have presented to humanity their weakness for this realm. People must realise the manifestations of beauty within this universe are simply *unstable reflections.* They are reflections of what exists in other, stable dimensions—ones that have existed since before time in this dimension began. After all, this realm is the outer shell of God, the Source.

81. Jesus said, "Let one who has become wealthy reign, and let one who has power renounce <it>."

Yeshua would see an individual who is aware of their spiritual nature as being wealthy. These are the people who *should* be leaders and be held in the highest regard within communities. In reality, humans know that this world is, more often than not, led by people consumed by the lion (Thomas 7). In Thomas 2, we see Yeshua point out that *one who finds* will become *disturbed* and when they become disturbed *they will marvel* and *then they will reign over all.* This privileged position is not one that holds any power in this world. It is a profound knowledge and understanding, which places us above those who are still searching. A person who has worldly power is infatuated with this realm and blinded by it. This is why Jesus asks those individuals *in power* to renounce that position—*for their own sake.* This also speaks to religious leaders, who are at risk of falling for the appeal of positions of power. The desire to work up the ranks within religious communities is a reflection of this danger. It distracts from the true purpose of *the Light* within, which seeks to be recognised. Among such communities, the aspiration to climb the ladder of influence is often driven by superficial desires. Their successes would secure favour with their God, leaving them a legacy which glorifies the individual and their achievements. This kind of motivation is what Jesus warns against, because the focus is not on the *Soul.*

The *denial of earthly power* is a large part of why Yeshua *chose* to fulfil the Old Testament prophecies, rather than becoming a leader within His community. This is linked to the reason Peter was angered by Jesus' proclamation that He would be killed and why Jesus rebuked him. Moreover, when Yeshua spent forty days and nights in the desert, Satan offered Him all the Earth's kingdoms and riches, but Yeshua chose to reject the offer. In this symbolic story, Yeshua is *denying the power that is in this world*. This is reflected in Thomas 81. The symbolic action of walking into the hands of death destroys the idea that *we are flesh*. The action of choosing to sacrifice the flesh *for many* also teaches us that we need to make decisions that *empower us, in Spirit*. After all, it is the Soul that is in the *likeness* of God, the Father. The collective consciousness (Holy Spirit) links the Source (father) and the Son (all beings throughout this universe and the other realms). None of the three have the need for power in this realm. *When people recognise the three facets for what they are, they become wealthy and then they 'reign over all'* (Thomas 2).

82. Jesus said, "Whoever is near me is near the fire, and whoever is far from me is far from the (Father's) Kingdom."

In Thomas 82, Yeshua uses an analogy people of His time might have been able to comprehend. A fire is something that has many life-sustaining functions in the material world. Fire would have provided light and warmth, and been used to extend food. These positive attributes of fire, essential in Yeshua's time, are symbolic of the importance of His teachings regarding the soul's journey. As we have seen in other sayings, this is a warning to those who assumed their knowledge was correct. Their lineage was from successive legendary and mythical figures in their history. To be close to Jesus was to be in the Light, where the truth is visible. To be close to Jesus is to be warmed, comforted, and nourished by the knowledge these truths offer.

This saying is a good example of words that could be taken up by those who are consumed by the lion (Thomas 7); making them into rhetoric for exclusion and injustices against non-be-lievers. This is why there must be a deeper understanding of what Yeshua means when He says, '*whoever is near me is near the fire*'. Physical proximity is not what Yeshua speaks of. It has been the orthodox faiths that have made this into a ritualistic initiation—so that it is physical. Previously, circumcision was a similar attempt to create a physical sign and bond (Thomas 53). *Whoever is near Jesus* is aware of the spiritual self. They can see beyond the physical existence humans suffer through, in this unstable, chaotic dimension. The closeness to Jesus is experienced when people recognise that the same thing that His Spirit is made of, is in us and in all things (Thomas 77).

The Buddha Dharma reflects much of what we see in Thomas. This system, in its purest form, has never caused suffering to others, nor does it advocate violence against any beings. If we look at the life of the one who became Buddha, born some 560 years before Yeshua, as Prince Siddhartha Gautama, we see one man's struggle to come to terms with the suffering experienced in this existence. To discuss this man's life journey would make a lengthy biography. For the purpose of this commentary, it is sufficient to think of what Prince Siddhartha accomplished, something akin to *building the first half of a bridge*. The Buddha (meaning one who is enlightened) extended the first part of a bridge *from this realm*. Yeshua completed the bridge by extending the other part, *from the realm of the Spirit* (Thomas 98).

Prince Siddhartha is known as the Buddha, because he was the first to discover a path to enlightenment. His eyes were opened to the truth of this realm, ending suffering and the cycle of birth and death (for him). This is the ultimate goal, for some followers. However, Siddhartha Gautama could not, and would not, answer the questions regarding the existence of, and connection with God, the Source. What Siddhartha did do is resolve how the link with the Source can be made, *through the removal of perceived obstacles*. They are created through fears and desires, which are rooted in the primal heritage. This path is a difficult one, which requires complete removal of physical needs, emotions, and desires. Yeshua's yoke is gentle (Thomas 90). It simply requires a deep understanding. Through Yeshua, people are given this knowledge and are able to cross the bridge connecting these realms. The human becomes aware of a relationship they have with God, the Father. *It* binds all things, in all the realms. In learning from what the Buddha discovered, to not be disturbed by this world and accept it for what it is, people cease their suffering. When they cease their suffering they become passersby (Thomas 42). The soul walks past this realm into the next – *this is the motion and rest* (Thomas 50). In the Gospel of Thomas, Yeshua tells us the Father's Kingdom is our heritage and legacy. It is here. Next to this fire we see and are comforted, knowing where we are and where we are going. Humans are the kingdom, found in each other.

83. Jesus said, "Images are visible to people, but the light within them is hidden in the image of the Father's light. He will be disclosed, but his image is hidden by his light."

In Thomas 83, we see a profound description of the soul, which is not unlike God, the Source and *its nature*. Yeshua uses the word *light* as a comparison between these two realms, because light *sustains life and allows us to see.* This *Light* is not light as we experience it in this world. This *thing* flows through all of us; It is in everything (Thomas 77). Humans cannot experience this energy, because they are limited by their senses and the *familiar phenomena* of the natural world. This is evident when Yeshua says the Light within people *is hidden in the image of the Father's Light.* This indicates the Source is something most people cannot experience. *The nature of the Father's Light hides It* from us, because this Light is not something tangible.

Yeshua goes on to say God, the Source 'will be disclosed, but his image is hidden by his Light'. This tells us the Source is revealed to people as they become awakened to the truth or after death (Thomas 11). The most significant words in this saying are the last seven: 'his image is hidden by his Light'. This dispels the idea of a God that is in one place and is one entity. It also ratifies our understanding regarding the Holy Trinity. In Matthew 28:19, we see a reference to the Father, Son, and Holy Ghost. In the orthodox doctrine, the Father, Son, and Holy Spirit are *three separate persons*, but not three separate gods—they are all God. This definition shows how people have tried to fit a square into a circle, without much success. It is another example of how Old Testament proclamations, together with misunderstood teachings attributed to Jesus, have led religious leaders to strange conclusions. It is not disputed that Yeshua spoke of the Father, Son, and Holy Spirit, as we have seen in Thomas 44. What is disputed is how Yeshua defined these three. In the Gospel of Thomas, the 'Trinity' are seen as characteristics, or facets, of the one thing—not three separate persons and one God. In Thomas 44 Yeshua emphasises the importance of the Holy Spirit above the concept of Father and Son. This tells us two things: as one is considered more important than the other two, they are not three separate persons, one God. That would be denigrating God, since the orthodox view would argue all three are equal. It also confirms, just as blood nourishes and sustains the body, the Holy Spirit sustains the link between Father and Son. It is the collective consciousness because to be conscious is to be aware, alive. This is the link between God, the Source and all beings in this universe (and other dimensions).

We have seen throughout the Gospel of Thomas that the Father is the Source of all things—*It* is in everything. The Son is Jesus. He *is symbolic of humanity* and the people who recognise the soul within the flesh. We are as He is (Thomas 99). The Holy Spirit is the thing awakening, connecting, and intertwining us in an intimate relationship with God, the Source. It is a profound connection because it is the collective consciousness. The Holy Spirit is the *active energy* linking the Source with *Its Light* in us, which humans call the soul. In Thomas 83 there is an emphasis on the *image we expect* to see. There is in fact no image of God, the Father/Source, since Its Light—the thing that constitutes what *It* is made of, is everywhere at the same time. *It* is hidden by the nature of what *It* is—It is ubiquitous. *It* has no physical comparison. *It* is between the fibres inside wood and under a rock at the same time (Thomas 77).

Why does Yeshua refer to God the Source as the *Father*? It is clear the heritage He was born into made it necessary for Yeshua to speak in metaphors His contemporaries could associate with. The place in time Yeshua entered into this realm was ordained by sequential celestial events, which enabled His Spirit to be thrust into this dimension. It was a time in human history the collective consciousness foresaw as the best opportunity for *this Spirit* to be recognised. Had these events not occurred in this way, *His name* would not have survived the ravages of time (Thomas 98). Jesus often used the term 'Father' when referring to god. This kind of language caused the Pharisees' insecurities to grow. The Pharisees knew their God as Yahweh. While this god is seen as the patriarch of the Jewish nation, individuals would have been cautious in claiming a direct personal relationship. However, the use of the word *Father* was necessary for Yeshua's ministry. This description ensured His contemporaries knew He was referencing the prophets. Unfortunately, their idea of a saviour was akin to a warrior king, not a teacher and guide for the Soul. The use of the title *Father* is layered; it goes beyond the practical link to the Old Testament prophecies. This title holds some surprises when we analyse what it actually means. The meaning, in the context of Yeshua's teaching, is a symbol relating to spiritual *inspiration*. If we consider what Thomas 83 discloses, it follows that the *Father* is not a single entity. Nor does *It* behave as *a father* in the way we might experience a biological father. Jesus has told us, in Thomas 22, that humans should not consider themselves male or female if they are to successfully enter the *Father's Kingdom*. Therefore, *the Spirit is above the parameters of male or female.* This clearly negates the idea of the *Father* as the patriarchal alpha male. This is the god most Christian churches revere. It is also the one they believe Jesus called His Father. The key to unlocking why Jesus chose '*Father*', as the reference to *the Source*, is in the *symbolic action of this Light.* The Father's Light enters a body so that this Light, or soul, may aggregate the substance of the Source, becoming an awakened Spirit. This is similar to the actions of a human father, one who traditionally offers *genetic material and lineage.* This was particularly true in Jesus' time, hence this metaphor. The sperm cell determines the sex of the child and only forms a body once it is *inside* the egg cell. The sperm cell is like the soul, which *reflects the action of the Father's Light.* The *egg is like the body and this planet.* In this way, these mechanisms *mirror* the actions of the spirit realm. The two become one, but upon death, humans become two (Thomas 11). They are joined with their true Father and Mother (Thomas 101). It is not unusual then, that some belief systems see the physical world, our planet Earth, as a mother goddess. The Earth *creates* the environment and provides a place for souls to inhabit, not unlike a womb. The important thing to consider, in the symbol of the *Father*, is that just as our physical father does not own us, nor does the Source. People are individual entities, which need to grow and make conscious decisions, awakening them from the sleep symptomatic of this realm. While we are individual entities, we are also a collective and a crucial part of God, the Father/Source. Through the action of the collective consciousness (Holy Spirit), the sustaining link is made—without this, the human soul tastes death. Our inheritance from the Source has enabled us to make intuitive decisions about what is right and wrong. As long as we do not harm others, our experiences in this life amount to lessons along the path to resurrection (the Soul coming to life as a Spirit).

For some faiths, the reason humans have been separated from God, the Father/Source is a matter of conjecture. The Gnostic

Christians created complex mythologies to explain this separation. However, it is evident that these ideas are reflections of
observable behaviours, common in humans. These stories vary,
depending on the reference, but they generally have a common
theme. The myth starts with a self-generated, invisible presence,
which created emanations—'Aeons' (lesser consecutive derivatives of the first, each one less perfect than its predecessor)—to
accompany it. One of these Aeons was *Sophia* (representing
wisdom). She created Yaldabaoth, without the consent or
union of the self-generated one. Gnostics believe that because
of Sophia's decision to create without the self-generated one,
Yaldabaoth is an imperfect demiurge, evident in his pride,
vengeance, and jealousy. To the Gnostic, he is also known as
Yahweh, from the Old Testament. For Sophia to correct her
errors, she imparts wisdom to human beings. She also played
on Yaldabaoth's pride, convincing him to give humanity the
breath of life, so that they could worship him—in *his own
image*. As humans become re-joined to the self-generated one,
Yaldabaoth diminishes and is eventually absorbed back into
the Light. This skims the surface of the Gnostic thesis, which
explains people's dilemma in this realm. It illustrates how the
early Christians, who tried to follow the secret teachings of
Yeshua, were limited by their understanding of the world and
human nature. They were reliant on *what they could observe
and experience in the natural world*. This is not dissimilar to the
way the Ancient Greeks and Romans attributed Gods to all
manner of daily life, such as drinking, fighting, and hunting. In
some portrayals of Yaldabaoth, he is depicted with the head of
a lion, which references Thomas 7. This demonstrates how the
early Christians *did not have a vocabulary* that could unpack
the metaphors.

In the Gospel of Thomas, the teachings regarding our situation
in this realm are clear. The words in Thomas are intimate,
describing a close connection with God, the Father/Source.
We are not pawns in a malevolent god's self-indulgent game,

like the Gnostics concluded. In reality, the truth is simple. When we consider the infinite potential within this universe and the other dimensions, there is no end to the possibilities. Therefore, since the Source is everywhere, *It* is also here in the material universe, as *It* is in the realm of the Spirit. This dimension, realm, or kingdom, where the *Father* exists, is not up in the sky (Thomas 3). It is what we are, a soul. *It* is *through* this realm—in the spaces between the fibres of wood and under a stone (Thomas 77). The Holy Spirit constitutes the spaces between thought and feeling – *It* is the collective consciousness. When these two are complete within us, our soul becomes a Spirit—awakened from the sleep, resurrected. The Source will be revealed to humans, but for now, *Its* image, like our soul, is hidden *by the nature of Its Light.*

84. Jesus said, "When you see your likeness, you are happy. But when you see your images that came into being before you and that neither die nor become visible, how much you will have to bear!"

Yeshua warns people that their present, physical form is not *what* they actually are. This concept flows on from Thomas 83. The image people see in the mirror is not the thing that they are—that thing (the soul) is invisible. The orthodox view of the self is considered to be the body, which was made from the earth and animated by God – this point of view is taken from the Genesis creation story. Humans generally identify themselves as either male, female or intersex, with particular features attributed to this form. Most humans who believe in an afterlife, see themselves coming back to life in the form they currently inhabit, so that their family and friends could recognise them. In this saying, Yeshua warns that this is a delusion. People are made of the same invisible, intangible matter that God, the Source is composed of. Humans are a soul, which is invisible to their physical senses. Humans are individuals and yet, they are one. When a person becomes a Spirit, their individual characteristics are not externally visible. The Spirit makes themselves recognisable by connecting with the perceptions of the one still in a material body. *The Spirit relates the Light, which has replaced the flesh, to what the living person might know or recognise.* This knowledge gives us an insight as to the actual experiences of the disciples after Jesus' death. What they *perceived* as being resurrected was, in their presence, very real. He was a Spirit constituted of *the Light,* not flesh.

In Mark 14:3-9, a woman uses very expensive oil to anoint Yeshua's head, in a loving and symbolic gesture. After this, He rebukes those people who said the oil could have been sold to help the poor. Yeshua reveals to us the truth of His death, stating: '*She has done what she could: she has anointed my body beforehand for its burial*'. This statement confirms that Yeshua understood His body was to be destroyed and disposed of. Allowing the woman to do this to His body was also Yeshua's way of thanking the human form which clothed Him. Yeshua needed to detach from His physical body, but He knew His followers could not do the same—Jesus' body would become a relic. For this reason, and to ratify the concept of a physical resurrection, Yeshua knew His remains should be hidden. This was a necessary action because Yeshua would have known His body would become a relic, if people knew of its location. Moreover, this would have seen His story fade into obscurity, since most people of that time (and arguably two thousand years after) were hopeful of a physical resurrection. They were not ready for the truth Yeshua delivered through Thomas. In

Mark 16:12, we see how Yeshua appeared to His disciples in Spirit: '*After this he showed himself under another form to two of them as they were on their way into the country*'. This supports the revelation in Thomas 84 of *an image that came into being before the flesh*. Yeshua would have trusted the people who were closest to Him, like Mary (His mother), James, Thomas, Mary Magdalene, and John, to ensure His body would be hidden. They would have been the ones who understood the necessity for such a duty to remain a secret.

The removal of Jesus' body is further supported when we see the author of Matthew add to the story of Yeshua's burial. Rumours must have filtered through about what really happened to His remains. The author of Matthew attempts to quell these with a scenario which adds to Mark's account (Mark being the first gospel written). Matthew 28:11-15:

'Now while they were on their way, some of the guards went off into the city to tell the chief priests all that had happened. These held a meeting with the elders and, after some discussion, handed a considerable sum of money to the soldiers with these instructions, 'This is what you must say, "His disciples came during the night and stole him away while we were asleep." And should the governor come to hear of this, we undertake to put things right with him ourselves and to see that you do not get into trouble.' So they took the money and carried out their instructions, and to this day that is the story among the Jews.'

In the Gospel of Mark, there are no soldiers at the gravesite, which suggests the fabrication of these events. Matthew's account attempts to explain why such rumors existed. This supports the claim that the author of Matthew was more interested in linking Jesus to the Old Testament prophecies, rather than writing an accurate biography.

When Yeshua says, *'your images that came into being before you and that neither die nor become visible'*, He is referring to the soul. This is an energy (Light) that is constant. It is the spark of Light from the Source, seeking to grow and become a Spirit (Thomas 96). In Thomas 84, Yeshua confirms that humans, and other beings where the Light has found a home, are energy, which has numerous iterations. They have been here before and have passed away. Many have faded back into the ubiquitous Father/Source. A common experience for these beings is to realise they are in a loop. In coming to this realisation, frustration and anger arise. In the physical form, they had become deceived by the notion of *self*—the ego we see in Thomas 7. This is the warning Jesus gives in Thomas 84.

85. Jesus said, "Adam came from great power and great wealth, but he was not worthy of you. For had he been worthy, [he would] not [have tasted] death."

Yeshua confirms the concept of the first man, purposefully and intentionally *created* by God, is an error. Moreover, we see in Genesis that the body was formed from the earth and it was called Adam. This suggests that the body preceded the soul, which is incorrect (Thomas 29). We now know human bodies have been formed to house God, the Source's Light. The inner realm has influenced the mechanism and likeness, but this has not been of its own volition (Thomas 97). The *great power and wealth* that created the myth of Adam and Eve was the Jewish nation—the heritage of Yeshua's contemporaries. The first line of Thomas 85 is also a confirmation of the *creative power* of people who instigated these myths. These stories are based on observations relative to this existence. In a sense, it is also a reference to the wealth and power of this realm (Thomas 98). The physical elements and body became the reason for the expulsion of humanity from paradise. In stating Adam *tasted death*, Yeshua tells us that the generations before Him had also tasted death. Their souls did not attain the level of the *perfect human*; they were absorbed back into the whole. The collective consciousness—the Source of all things, did not recognise these generations, as *they did not recognise It*. This is the absence of the Holy Spirit, the conduit. It is why *Adam was not worthy of us*. We are the generation that can recognise the kingdom, which is within humans. When Yeshua uses the second person, *you*, He speaks to *us*. We are the souls that seek the truth. This truth is in the logical, intuitive self and comes from the link to the collective consciousness (Holy Spirit). If people allow fear and erroneous teachings to mask them from the *Light*, they will taste death.

Science tells us that we evolved less than half a million years ago and that our universe came about approximately fourteen billion years ago. Physical laws cannot be ignored—they are the nature of this realm. When the first primate came down from the trees and was able to think in abstract terms (drawing, creating music and dance) *the breath of life came into them*. This was the doorway for the *Light* to become realised—the presence of a soul in these bodies (Thomas 96). In turn, this dim Light began to grow, aggregating toward an enlightened Spirit. The *wealth* of myths and legends that have accumulated in different cultures are a testament to *the Light* within the flesh. The Soul has been struggling to find truth and con-nection with God, the Source – this is both the hunger and quest (Thomas 69 and 107). *77th Pearl: The Perpetual Tree* is a revelation from the collective consciousness, which dispels the misunderstandings of the past and heralds the potential of all humans.

86. Jesus said, "[Foxes have] their dens and birds have their nests, but human beings have no place to lay down and rest."

The physical world is not designed for the *perfect human*—the risen Spirit. The Soul seeks to be joined to the source of all things, from where it came. It does not rest, because the physical world is at odds with the soul. The reason ceremony and ritual is attractive to people seeking their true nature is because these things reflect what *the Father* is like. Order, harmony, and unity are the nature of the *Source* and the kingdom within. Ceremony makes humans feel at peace. It takes them away from the chaos and uncertainty which surrounds their lives in this dimension.

A fox and a bird, once fed, are content; they dream of the everyday experiences they go through. Human dreams involve abstract emotions such as love, hate, and various life scenarios. This is the soul seeking to resolve the things that are not of its nature. These are the things that get in the way of a person awakening and seeing the truth of this realm. The Soul wants to be at peace and in harmony with all things. This state of being reflects the nature of God, the Source when it is two (Thomas 11). A peaceful meditative place enables the Soul to aggregate the Father's Light and, in time, connect with the collective consciousness, becoming a roused Spirit. Yeshua asks us to be *passersby* (Thomas 42), so that we do not become disturbed by the world. The journey through *this life is the motion; the realm of the Spirit is the place of rest*. We can see this through the thread linking Thomas 50, 86, and 90.

87. Jesus said, "How miserable is the body that depends on a body, and how miserable is the soul that depends on these two."

In Thomas 87 Yeshua warns that it is not healthy for a person to depend on another for physical and emotional support. This includes dependence for sexual gratification and reliance on companionship. Male insecurities are the reason why, in some cultures, women have been oppressed and treated as a possession for the husband's pleasure. At the early stage of the twenty-first century, in some cultures, women still are treated this way. This was the attitude of men in Yeshua's time. However, as we have seen in Thomas 22, Yeshua saw past the stereotypes associated with gender. Generally, this kind of unhealthy dependence on a relationship has changed since that time, but the pressure to fulfil *societal expectations*—of physical appeal, marriage, and procreation—is still relevant. These *dependencies are aspects of the body* and peoples primal heritage. They are rooted in the reliance of the hierarchy within the drove, *for survival.*

Yeshua tells people that the souls who place great importance on physical unions are *miserable.* In attacking such unions, He is, by association, chastising people who see these as an avenue for propagating *the glory of God.* Thus, communities whose faith encourages them to *multiply for their God* have been misled by their leaders. This attitude has caused much suffering and grief. In economically disadvantaged countries parents of large families cannot provide for their children. Lack of education, particu-

286 | 77th Pearl:

larly for women, has resulted in overpopulation. In Thomas 49, we see that we are on a lone journey toward awakening the soul within. To think marriage and children are a guarantee of an afterlife is miserable. Moreover, to believe a god would reward having children for self-glorification is presumptuous (Thomas 79). The soul cannot depend on physical actions for its growth and advancement. Religious leaders consumed by the lion (Thomas 7) have made the propagation of life, within marriage, a holy activity. Outside of marriage, procreation is imbued with sin, through the act of sex for pleasure. This propagation also ensures the growth and maintenance of their particular community. Therefore, it is profitable to maintain the premise of a god seeking physical unions. It is admirable for people to have children, because this sacrifice of their time and emotional stamina can inhibit the growth of their soul. If this is the path chosen by individuals, it must be in the knowledge that these beings are not their property—they are vehicles for souls to grow and become enlightened Spirits. Parents must be invested in their child's growth as a disciplined and caring individual. They should demonstrate these same positive attributes by providing developing minds with parameters to follow. Parents who do not teach social values, respect, and equality, are harming the child's capacity to grow as a complete human being. Through active parenting, the world becomes a more favourable place for producing enlightened Spirits. In this way, suffering is also decreased, through the nurturing of a world dominated by harmony and unity. This is the nature of God, the Source, *in union* with the collective consciousness (Holy Spirit) and all beings (the Son).

88. Jesus said, "The messengers and the prophets will come to you and give you what belongs to you. You, in turn, give them what you have, and say to yourselves, 'When will they come and take what belongs to them?'"

The messengers and the prophets give us hope and the desire to search for truth. This belongs to all human beings. We in turn should give these people support. This may be by meeting their physical needs and responding to their teachings with sceptical enthusiasm—*the ear of the heart*. This saying informs us that the prophets and messengers were lacking something essential—the understanding of the true nature of *self* and where the kingdom actually *exists*. The majority of messengers and prophets preceding Yeshua, and a number of those that followed Him, lacked this essential knowledge. People of past generations placed God outside of the self. In their eyes, there was a disconnection, a falling away. This made the individual feel unworthy to be in the presence of their god. Yeshua asks: '*When will they come and take what belongs to them?*' What belongs to them is the kingdom, the link to the collective consciousness. They were unaware of the invisible Light generated by the Source. They were unaware this Light was their soul, *what* they are.

Most religions have some degree of wisdom and truth within their teachings. They all stem from a desire to explain the dilemma we face in this material existence. The cycle of birth, intermittent joy, suffering, and death has, for most humans, incurred questions which are difficult to answer. The difference in Yeshua's teachings, particularly those found in the Gospel of Thomas, are the references to humanities dual nature. The nature of *what* we are, outside of the body we inhabit, is paramount. The focus in Thomas is not on persuading readers Jesus has a Divine lineage, or proving His authority over unclean entities. The focus is on how to navigate through this life, by realising what we really are. The way Yeshua, carefully and cryptically, discloses that messengers and prophets do not have the answers, reflects the time in which the words were spoken. His contemporaries would have seen a clear statement, questioning the authority of messengers and prophets, as sheer blasphemy. The prophets were, in Yeshua's time, seen as direct links to their god, who spoke *through* them. However, the reality was that these people were speaking through their link to the Source and the collective consciousness, albeit through a thick fog. This Source is the Light that was within all people, from the beginning, but they could not comprehend *It*. This is 'what belongs to them'; it is the *Light* they did not recognise. In not recognising this intimate connection with God, the Father, they were divided.

Just as prophets and messengers were thought to hear the voice of God, psychics are believed to be able to communicate with the dead. A soul that has not nurtured its connection to the Source eventually fades. It is absorbed into the whole, to re-enter the material universe in a new form. Psychics tap into the Source's presence, through the collective consciousness, because they are more receptive to this Light (Thomas 77). When they believe they are communicating with the dead, they are often picking up the thoughts and feelings of the living. They are also able to sense the events of the past and future. Time is an element of the Source, because *It* has no linear sequence—*It is the whole*. Understanding this is important because people have the tendency to place perceptive individuals in high regard. Having these skills does not mean a person has benevolent intentions. They may, unintentionally, contradict the wisdom of Yeshua (Thomas 4 and 11). A psychic's ability is a positive sign of the Source's Light in action, through the collective consciousness. However, their perceptions of what is actually happening can be damaging and misleading to impressionable minds.

Ratifying the existence of paranormal abilities in humans is the work done by Remote Viewers, employed by various government agencies around the world. These people are usually given a number or coordinates linked to a place, event or person. The Remote Viewer records information they perceive with words and drawings. There are well known cases of these people finding military devices of opposing countries. Some have also viewed the existence of extraterrestrial bases in various parts of the globe. This gives the knowledge we receive from the Gospel of Thomas gravitas, as we recognise that even military people know the collective consciousness is real. It is an *active agent* in this material realm.

89. Jesus said, "Why do you wash the outside of the cup? Don't you understand that the one who made the inside is also the one who made the outside?"

Beyond an attack on ritual cleansing, which was so important to Yeshua's contemporaries, this saying is a revelation of an important mystery. Thomas 89 is a definitive description of our lineage to God, the Father (Source). It also describes the origin of this realm—'*the one who made the inside [also] made the outside.*' Thomas 89 negates the Gnostic concept of a malevolent god who created this world for his self-glorification. Yeshua defines the Source of all things as *the Father*. From *this Source*, all things have (unintentionally) been issued forth into existence (Thomas 97). This realm, as imperfect as it is, was influenced by a logic reflecting the realm of the Spirit. They were a sequence of events people now call evolution. These events allowed for Its scattered Light to have a medium (planets and bodies) through which It would be found by Its progenitor (Thomas 107). Now, through Jesus (Yeshua), the Holy Spirit (collective consciousness) *is active* among humans. However, this dimension is the unstable outer layer of a stable centre. At the centre of everything is the Source, which exists in all things (Thomas 77). The nature of the outer layer is not like the inner. The invisible Light (Thomas 83) is not like the Light we experience in this realm—this is a concept that needs to be recognised to be experienced. The evidence of these layers is in *the world that is a body, which becomes a carcass* (Thomas 80 and 56). Souls are housed in temples (bodies) to become enlightened Spirits. Like all temples in this realm, they are ephemeral—time, as humans experience it, will destroy them.

Consider the cup as a symbol. A cup is made of a terrestrial material such as a metal or clay (the outer). It generally holds some kind of liquid (the inner). The liquid is primarily made up of two elements, which create water (the logic that *reflects* the Spirit realm). When the two elements become one, they are life giving and sustaining. This *symbolic action, seen in the natural world, is a reflection* of the soul's desire to join with the Source—*the one Yeshua calls Father*. This metaphoric action is evident in Yeshua's instruction (in Mark 14) to His disciples, which looks innocuous at first, but is loaded with meaning. Mark 14:13-14:

'So he sent two of his disciples, saying to them, "Go into the city and you will meet a man carrying a pitcher of water. Follow him, and say to the owner of the house which he enters, "The Master says: Where is the room for me to eat the Passover with my disciples?'

The *thread* of a container (the pitcher and cup), the water and wine within them, leading to a room where all the disciples gather in *communion* (with the whole), is not accidental. The water and wine (or blood) is symbolic of the soul—what humans are. The room is the realm in which the Spirit exists. This seemingly unimportant request by Yeshua is symbolic. It is the path He set down for us when He destroyed the flesh that clothed Him—shattering *the cup*, so that the Spirit may return to its origin. Interestingly, we can also see how the coming of the Age of Aquarius, in 2021, links to the shift in thinking and understanding garnered through *77ᵗʰ Pearl: The Perpetual Tree*.

The body, like the cup, is made of this realm. What it contains will eventually leave that vessel, just as steam leaves a cup.

The soul can no longer be *physically experienced* because its container has decomposed. If (hypothetically) the water were able to become conscious of itself, it would not separate into the elements from which it was formed and disappear. It, like the Soul, would be self-realised and not taste death. It would remain as water, the *one becoming two* (Thomas 11). This truth brings new meaning to the Passover Meal Jesus celebrated before His crucifixion—Mark 14:23-2:

> 'Then *he took a cup*, and when he had given thanks he handed it to them, and all drank from it, and he said to them, "This is my blood, the blood of the covenant, *poured out for many*" [emphasis added]'.

Yeshua states that *His blood would be poured out for many*. This is traditionally thought of as the process by which humanity's sins had been forgiven. In a sense, this is true. However, it is not that sins have been *forgiven*, but that they are understood as *faults within the cup* (body). With this knowledge, people are able to realise that *sin is a perception created from this realm*. It can no longer weaken them—they become passersby (Thomas 42). This understanding (wisdom) is what saves humanity. People come to the realisation that Yeshua's actions demonstrate the power of the Spirit over this realm. Yeshua's blood is symbolic of the Soul and the collective consciousness (Holy Spirit), being linked and nurtured. The Holy Spirit sustains and creates a link, thereby unifying God, the Source, and all beings throughout all dimensions. The blood is also a metaphor of the thing Yeshua is—that thing is Spirit. This is what we symbolically take part in, through our acceptance of Jesus' teachings. Through this acceptance, *the one becomes two* (Thomas 11); we are joined to the Father/Source. The collective consciousness (Holy Spirit) makes this action productive. The words He gave us through Thomas become the nourishment giving us life in the Spirit body.

It is significant that Yeshua celebrates His last meal with the disciples at the Jewish Passover. When Moses brought down plagues upon the Pharaoh's people, so that the Jewish slaves might be set free, the final plague was to bring about the death of the first-born child. In order for God to recognise the houses of his people, lambs' blood was placed above the doorway of those homes. This would ensure the hand of God would *pass over* their houses. In Yeshua's death, and the blood that *He poured out for many*, we see *a new sign of freedom and protection*. Willingly walking into the hands of those controlled by the lion (Thomas 7), Yeshua showed us that *He was the lamb whose blood is spilt*. This was done *for every human* who feels enslaved by this realm. Yeshua's blood (death) gave humanity the knowledge that the Soul is *what* people are. It overcomes and supersedes this realm. This is the new freedom He brought to humanity. Through Yeshua's actions, we become aware of our intimate relationship with God, the Father. In knowing this truth, *our god is within us*. We have no need of a sign above our doorway, identifying us as part of the Source's Light. Indeed, we now know that those who stand outside our doorway (the ones who would enslave us) are part of the same Source—but they do not see it. We also acknowledge that the one who made the inside also made the outside. In this vessel, souls are able to grow to rejoin with God, the Father, the Source.

90. Jesus said, "Come to me, for my yoke is comfortable and my lordship is gentle, and you will find rest for yourselves."

Yeshua tells us *His 'yoke is comfortable'*, meaning that if we embrace His teachings, and *place these around our neck*, we will not feel burdened by this world. Nor are we burdened by a faith which is pulling us back. In accepting His yoke, the notion of sin, which religious dogma has placed on humanity, is *lifted away*. Yeshua's leadership ('lordship') is gentle. It is not based on fear of a patriarchal, vengeful, and jealous god. When humans know they are joined to God the Father and Source they find rest for themselves. They also see that those things upsetting them, in this life, are not of any real importance. The human becomes a *passerby* (Thomas 42) and observer of this life. In doing so, people can be philosophical about the things they might have become disturbed over in the past. This is essential for their spiritual growth. This is also the most profitable healing any soul can be given.

91. They said to him, "Tell us who you are so that we may believe in you."

He said to them, "You examine the face of heaven and earth, but you have not come to know the one who is in your presence, and you do not know how to examine the present moment."

Humans generally want an easy answer to things. This is certainly true in spiritual matters. History shows us that people prefer a religion with definitive rules and accompanying rituals, which conveniently satisfies their needs. This is reflected in the first part of Thomas 91, where we see the disciples wanting Yeshua to define *who He is*, so that they could have their beliefs confirmed. Instead, Yeshua's response tells us much about the truth of this realm and the inadequacies of humans. It also confirms there was no *language* available for His contemporaries, so that they could *examine* and comprehend His teachings. This was to come over two millennia after His *passing*. It is here.

Since humans (evidently) came down from the trees and began to think in abstract terms, they have grappled with the cycle of life and what happens when it ends. This capacity, to think in abstract terms, is the time when *the breath of life* entered people. While the universe has been forming over fourteen billion years, the human species has only evolved in the last half a million years. At that point, the Source, through the collective consciousness, was able to aggregate in bodies, enabling Souls to become enlightened Spirits. To find the answers to these mysteries, humans in the past *examined the face of heaven and earth*. They created elaborate mythologies, based on observable phenomena seen in the stars and on this planet. Yeshua tells us that we have been looking in the wrong place. Humans had not come to know '*the one [in their] presence*', because the concept of the invisible Source, which flows through everything, was foreign and inconceivable. People still have no tangible evidence of this presence. The notion that God was in *the self* would have been seen as blasphemy. God, for them, was instead seen as a single, *separate* entity, which created the universe and everything in it. *Yeshua asks us to examine the Source, which is in our presence—It is in us and in all things* (Thomas 77).

In the last line of Thomas 91, Yeshua confirms that most of His contemporaries were unable to understand the concept of the Source's Light (Thomas 83). Their indoctrinated knowledge limited their scope of understanding. They did not know *how to examine the present moment*. Yeshua came into this realm to give humans knowledge of who they really are and of their link to the Source—the one Jesus refers to as His *Father. This creative spring of invisible Light flows through everything, It is what we are*. It is how we share a kinship with Jesus and all beings throughout the universe. This is a concept Yeshua's contemporaries could not fathom. It is something we are made aware of through the Gospel of Thomas. It is *the new language.*

92. Jesus said, "Seek and you will find.

In the past, however, I did not tell you the things about which you asked me then. Now I am willing to tell them, but you are not seeking them."

Yeshua reveals there was a time when people were willing to seek the mysteries of what it means *to live—in Spirit*. However, the *Source*, the one Jesus refers to as *Father*, did not deliver into this realm someone who had the knowledge of these mysteries '*then*'. Yeshua uses the first person, '*I* did not tell you the things about which you asked *me* then [emphasis added]', to conceal the fact that it is *the collective consciousness (Holy Spirit) speaking through Him*. In the last line, Yeshua repeats the first person reference, but this is, again, the collective consciousness—the conduit between the Source and all spiritual beings. In this last line, we see that the civilization where Yeshua entered into this realm, referred to as 'you', was unwilling to embrace the message He came to deliver. They had a faith that was in conflict with the essential truths of Yeshua's teachings—they were *not seeking* the answers to life's mysteries. Prior to this civilisation, people were more open to *concepts* which were not as rigid and prescriptive as the faith of Yeshua's contemporaries. However, for strategic reasons, the time was not right for Yeshua to enter into this realm until the Abrahamic lineage appeared. If He were not born into this lineage, and His life had not been woven into the tapestry of the Old Testament prophecies, then Yeshua (Jesus) would have disappeared into obscurity (Thomas 98). Again, in a strategic sense, it was necessary for the schism between the Gnostic and orthodox Christian groups to occur. This separation kept the actual purpose and teachings of Yeshua alive, through the Gospel of Thomas. These mysteries are now manifesting to the enlightened generation through *77ᵗʰ Pearl: The Perpetual Tree*.

93. "Don't give what is holy to dogs, for they might throw them upon the manure pile. Don't throw pearls [to] pigs, or they might ... it [...]."

This saying tells us the reason Yeshua chose to disclose these mysteries to one of His disciples, in a cryptic manner, so that they remained obscured until *77ᵗʰ Pearl: The Perpetual Tree*. The danger with religious texts is that they can be used in damaging ways to form and control communities. This is evident in those communities sharing the heritage of the legendary character of Abraham. These three communities still struggle for control over parts of Jerusalem, where they claim to have a sacred site associated with their god or prophet. It is the nature of the lion (Thomas 7) to want to form such communities. These types of communities run under a pyramidal structure of power. This is reflected in their belief system, where their god is at the apex of the pyramid. One of several problems with this structure is that the teaching becomes geared towards the family unit, which will ensure the continuation of that community. The individual is ignored, at times shunned, because they are seen as a dangerous element to the *pride of lions*. This was a significant reason why the Gospel of Thomas became unappealing to authorities, like Bishop Irenaeus of Lyon c.180, during the formation of the early Christian Church. The Gospel of Thomas focuses on the personal journey, because God is seen as within, not outside of, the human. For the same reason, people who are seen as different, or not conforming to *the pride*, are generally marginalised (Thomas 66 and 68).

At the start of Thomas 93, Yeshua uses the metaphor of excrement to emphasise the nature of the lion. In this reference, the dog is the lion from Thomas 7. Manure is the end product of food, which sustains life and has been used up, then disposed of, by the body. In a similar way, those people who have been consumed by the lion use only what will benefit them from within their religious text. The rest they discard—it *becomes their waste*. A wise person sees manure can be the catalyst for rich soil, which may *bring forth a new crop and abundant flowers and fruits*. This is what happened to the Gospel of Thomas. However, its casting aside was part of a strategic series of events. The Gospel of Thomas was discarded and now it has produced a tree of many branches, which has become the shelter for souls (Thomas 20). It has become, *77th Pearl: The Perpetual Tree*.

Pearls symbolise something precious, this is a logical link. In the time of Jesus, the oyster would have required quite some effort to be extracted from the ocean. Then the shell would be forced open to see if it may contain a pearl. *The Buddha* used the pearl as an analogy for the fruitful struggle to enlightenment. In the Buddha's parable about the pearl diver (representing those people seeking enlightenment), one may become scratched and damaged by the corals (representing the experiences in this life), but the journey is an intrinsic part of the destination. The struggle to obtain the pearl is also a way *to inspire a search* for a way out of that suffering, experienced in the cycle of Samsara (the cycle of birth and death). Yeshua compares the mysteries given to us in the Gospel of Thomas to pearls—*something precious and desirable*. When we try to force people to listen to, or appreciate, these teachings, we may be casting pearls to swine, because they do not see the value in these teachings. Nor would such people have *the desire* to understand these truths (Thomas 19). Swine are known for devouring food without savouring its flavour, hence the term, 'eating like a pig'. The Gospel of Thomas requires a discerning gastronomist, one that knows what is good, appreciating every bite.

People should not feel anger or resentment towards happily ignorant humans. They are on a journey that is part of the whole. While the Light within many of them may be reabsorbed into the whole, those ignorant people become lessons for others who seek understanding and wisdom. In these people, we see the truth of suffering when this realm is not recognised for what it truly is. To be 'passersby' (Thomas 42) is the key, because we become observers of the way this dimension manipulates bodies into thinking, and behaving, in certain ways. These behaviours are driven by various fears and illusions of power, love, and material possessions. To observe and learn from these is empowering for the soul, which is on the journey to becoming an enlightened Spirit. If a soul is open to spiritual growth, a kindred Spirit will recognise *them* and present them with *the pearls* in the Gospel of Thomas.

94. Jesus [said], "One who seeks will find, and for [one who knocks] it will be opened."

Consider how the most popular topic for a song is about love. It is worth pondering why so many songs speak about loving someone or the pain of losing someone who was loved. Why do these songs resonate (in most people) a feeling of empathy and connection to those lyrics? The first response might be that love is a common emotion experienced by many; it is a powerful feeling (Thomas 87). If we break down human love, for family and for a spouse, we see that these feelings are based on primal needs for partnership, reproduction, and community. They are driven by chemical reactions within the brain, based on physical desires and companionship. So why are love songs so prolific and popular? The answer is in the nature of the human soul. It yearns for union with the Source, from where it originated. The collective consciousness (Holy Spirit) is from where people feel a pull toward God, the Source. It is the strong emotion people feel when they hear a love song—thinking it is about physically motivated love. This feeling is actually coming from the soul, yearning for this *metaphysical union*. This is yet another example of how the physical realm mirrors the realm of the Spirit. These emotions are *reflections of God the Father's desire to find us*. Humans are the sheep that are yearned for, above all others (Thomas 107). They have gone astray, into the abyss. In the love of family and/or partner, humans partially experience the union with the Source, through the collective consciousness, *because the one becomes two*. However, in this realm, the experience is fleeting, corrupted by the body (Thomas 56 and 80). Love songs are the sounds of humans *knocking on this door.*

Following from Thomas 93, those people who are actively seeking the truth of the Spirit will eventually find what they are searching for. In all religions, there are aspects of the truth; this is something people perceive in the logical and intuitive self. This perception is the aspect of the Source (the Father) that is within humans, *speaking to them through the collective consciousness (Holy Spirit).* The majority of westernised Catholics, in the early twenty-first century, describe themselves as *selective*— they select what they want from their religion, leaving the rest behind. This is a healthy thing to do, because the alternative would be damaging to the soul seeking growth. The problem is that most people in this position have become tired and complacent, they stop seeking and questioning. For these people, the easy answer becomes a religion that is based around rituals—a box to tick. Yeshua warns that this complacency is perilous; we can see this in Thomas 36, 41, 43, 67, 70, 76, 84, 85, 88, 100, 101, and 103.

In Thomas 39 Yeshua explains the nature of religious leaders who become consumed by the lion (Thomas 7). They lose focus of the essential purpose in religion, which is to support the development of the Soul. The last line of Thomas 39 instructs people who are seeking truth to 'be as sly as snakes and as simple as doves', in order to manoeuvre around and through these obstructions. The fact that information has been kept hidden and obscured, through on-going dogma, has not helped people seeking spiritual wisdom from Jesus. *77th Pearl: The Perpetual Tree* has presented itself to assist these souls and make clear the reason for Yeshua's journey into this outer layer. He is the sower of the invisible *Light* in this dimension, so that humans may truly *live.* If the reader has doubts regarding the Gospel of Thomas, in relation to other Gospels, then they should ask—is the message speaking to *the soul* or is it speaking *from a human?* Is the teaching coming from an individual suffering from shame and guilt—could it also be a desire for the expansion of a community and control over those within it? (Thomas 7 and 81). In Thomas 40, Yeshua indicates that eventually the large organised religions will vanish, because they do not support what the soul requires: '*A grapevine has been planted apart from the Father. Since it is not strong, it will be pulled up by its roots and will perish.*' The reason some people fall into a fundamentalist, or orthodox, belief system is that they search so extensively they become tired. Consequently, they give in to a neat package of answers. These institutions will come to an end, because they cannot hide their influence by the lion (Thomas 7). This is the eventual fate of all religions, whose structures are influenced by primal desires for control and power. These traits are not of the Father; they are of men and of this realm, which created these bodies. They are '*planted apart*' from the Source and the collective consciousness.

77th Pearl: The Perpetual Tree creates an opening into the future, which consolidates the needs of the natural world and the Soul. It recognises the truth of this realm as having its own nature, which is unlike the realm of the Spirit. At the very centre of everything—between the atoms that make up everything—is the Source, the one Yeshua refers to as *Father*, as we see in Thomas 77. There are several layers, which consist of different dimensions. This one is the outer layer, hence its imperfections, instability, and finite nature (Thomas 56). In the adolescence of the twenty-first century, this world is on the threshold of being reconfigured, with either technology we cannot yet imagine, or through the possible destruction of the human species as it exists. The way governing bodies solve issues such as population control and sustainability of resources, may save humanity from impeding self-destruction.

Among many, it is *77ᵗʰ Pearl: The Perpetual Tree* that heralds this *new logic*. The way humans produce food will have to move toward a harmonious interaction with the environment, because sustainable, organic farming methods support the environment and the body. Humans will predominantly become vegetarian, with the propagation of high protein crops. This will, in part, result from people's awareness that livestock are damaging the environment through the gases they produce. The suffering animals incur is also damaging to humanity's link with the Source, because the collective consciousness (Holy Spirit) does not *intend* any creature to suffer. The realisation that people must recognise the rights of animals as sentient creatures, not unlike humans, opens the eyes to the *Source. It* is stronger in the creatures that have greater capacity to think and feel. This is why humans must treat animals with dignity and respect. Human beings are the hosts chosen by the collective consciousness for God, the Source, to express *Itself.* Humans have the ability to think in abstract terms, beyond any other conscious creature on Earth. The source of all things, the one Yeshua calls *Father*, wants people to join with *It*. This can only happen when the distractions in this realm are kept to a minimum. When the body is healthy, the mind is free to knock on the door—*then it will be opened.*

95. [Jesus said], "If you have money, don't lend it at interest. Rather, give [it] to someone from whom you won't get it back."

On a personal level, Yeshua asks that individuals stop thinking about building wealth, because it becomes an ongoing concern, stealing people away from what is important. If a person gives money to someone who cannot repay him or her, then they have given it to the person needing it the most. They are giving *without conditions*. When people give for the purposes of receiving something back, such as praise or interest on the money loaned, this is motivated by the nature of the lion (Thomas 6 and 7).

In a broader worldview, the capitalist system benefits a minority of countries and a small percentage of people, which is something politicians of economically advantaged countries will have to address. Such material imbalances are damaging to the souls of people who struggle to have clean water and daily food, while others in the world have excess. These imbalances are also damaging to those who are in more fortunate positions. This kind of suffering is made visible to the global community through popular media, such as the television and the internet. The accessibility to such information is a positive thing, but the impact it has on individuals, *who feel helpless to change these imbalances, is a negative*. Images of other individuals suffering in poverty hinder the potential for the Soul to connect with the Source, because humans are empathetic beings. The images may bring about feelings of shame, sadness, and guilt for being in a superior materialistic position. Through the knowledge people gain in the Gospel of Thomas, they come to realise humans are one and are all connected. If one group suffers, they all suffer. This is why humans are suitable places for *the Father's Light*. Empathy is the nature of the Spirit, it affects the conscience. The condition of *empathy is the nature of the collective consciousness (Holy Spirit)*. It is an aspect of the human being that *links* the Source and the Son (all beings, in all dimensions). When this empathy is engaged in negativity it damages this connection—if the individual feels there is no way to stop the suffering. *Compassion* is another aspect of the collective consciousness, because it is *a form of linkage that is sacred*. Sadly, there are religious organisations benefiting from people's compassion and empathy, using images of people starving to extract money from individuals wishing to help. They use this public display of charity to confirm their status as a compassionate institution that helps the less fortunate. They are benefiting from this display, as they receive reward for their efforts through patronage. They ignore what Yeshua states in the second part of Thomas 95: *'give it to someone from whom you won't get it back.'* Essentially, they are using the people in this unfortunate situation to gain favour with those who are members of religious groups. Using donations to supply food and water to these communities is not a sustainable, long-term answer—education is. This is another manifestation of *the coin forged by men* (see commentary for Thomas 32). While some of these religious based organisations do benefit the people in need, the problems causing the suffering are not dealt with. They treat the result, not the root cause. Family planning, resulting in population control, is essential. Each country has a limited amount of land that can be used for agriculture, assuming the soil is suitable and there is enough rainfall. Farming land also needs to be balanced with the needs of local flora and fauna, so that these are maintained for future biodiversity and the benefits of the broader biome. These factors cannot be denied, which means the question of population control must be a part of the education system in all schools. To continue as things are in the early part of the twenty-first century is not sustainable. The world's population is reaching critical mass and fresh water will become scarce. These are scientific facts. Yet, the people who run multinational businesses can only see growth in population equalling growth in productivity and wealth. This is not a long-term view to a functioning, balanced society. Similarly, the leaders of the major religious groups see a growing population as their commodity—they are the income maintaining the institution's preservation. Religious institutions also have a responsibility to encourage family planning, limiting reproduction to one or two children. Thomas 95 asks people to do something selfless, without any strings attached. This also applies to the leaders of corporations and religious institutions. If the human species is to survive into the next millennium, these groups must give back resources and education, allowing for an informed choice. The result of this approach will be a healthy environment and an even distribution of resources. These are the problems and the actions that need to be addressed. Achieving this will require people with new ways of thinking and the capacity to see *the big picture*.

The global community must accept the notion of *oneness*—this is humanity's predicament on Earth. This is the big picture. Ensuring that all communities have the essentials of life such as clean water, food, shelter, and education is of prime importance. Some of the more affluent countries, which have debtors who cannot repay their loans, will have to release these debts. As stated previously, at the heart of this problem is population control—this can be resolved when religious institutions stop impinging on logic. Nature is telling humans that it can no longer support the world's population, which is ever increasing. 'God' will not change nature to suit irrational concepts. The Source and collective consciousness (Holy Spirit) do not determine birth and death—this is a factor of nature and chance. If people do not take charge of what they can control, they will cause their own destruction. The lesson in Thomas 95 is the importance of altruism—*looking beyond the self*. *The dice have been cast* in the form of this planet and physical body. The rest is up to the human Soul.

96. Jesus [said], "The Father's kingdom is like [a] woman. She took a little leaven, [hid] it in dough, and made it into large loaves of bread. Anyone here with two ears had better listen!"

In Thomas 96 and 97 Yeshua uses the symbol of a female to compare to the Father's Kingdom. This is significant, because metaphorically the woman represents creation, through the cycles relating to the moon and menstruation. However, in this instance, Yeshua is explaining aspects of the Soul and this universe. These two aspects have to do with the creative energy of the Source, which is not unlike the female body. These two sayings are also linked through the symbols of leaven and meal, which are used in making bread. This is an apt analogy because bread was an important part of the diet in Yeshua's culture. Thomas 96 and 97 refer to the story of souls—how they inhabit bodies in this realm (the leaven in bread), and how the Source created this realm through *Its passive expansion* into the abyss (the distant road).

In Thomas 96, Yeshua explains how the source of all things (the one He refers to as *Father*) has placed in sentient bodies a thing that has the potential to develop, expand, and multiply, because of its *generational link to God, the Father/Source*. This is an *allegorical action*—it refers to the capacity of the Soul to *develop into an enlightened Spirit.* The Source has no beginning and no end. Therefore, the potential for a soul to *take form* in this realm, and evolve into a Spirit, is immeasurable. If we also think about bread and what eventuates as the leaven makes it rise and expand, we can easily relate this to our universe. Science has shown that this universe is ever expanding, with galaxies moving away from the point of the initial big bang. This event was the expansion of the Source, which then created physical matter. The *leaven* is symbolic of the Soul and its potential to grow. It is at the centre of all things.

Consider also, the woman, who has placed the leaven into the bread, is outside of the bread. The bread is on a table, in a room, inside a house that is in a place existing in another dimension. This is symbolic of the structure of God, the Source and Its many layers. This realm (layer), like bread, has a 'shelf life' and is slowly decaying (Thomas 56). *The difference in leaven is that it is potentially endless.* The sourdough method of leavening bread, which Yeshua references here, started with the Ancient Egyptians. This method allows for a *generational* starter to be set aside for each new batch of bread. Hence the starter *can be handed down within families.* This is how humans can say their soul is of the *same family* as Jesus, because it *started from* the Source. As this saying implies, the leaven (soul) that is hidden in the bread (body) grows large loaves, *which are warmed and sustained by the collective consciousness (Holy Spirit).* The larger loaves have become bigger, because the Soul has grown into a Spirit (in this metaphor). This is the goal, but that does not mean all souls attain this stature. Some portions of leaven are more *active* than others and this is dependent upon several things—one of these is an *environment conducive to growth* (see commentary for Thomas 95).

97. Jesus said, "The [Father's] kingdom is like a woman who was carrying a [jar] full of meal. While she was walking along [a] distant road, the handle of the jar broke and the meal spilled behind her [along] the road. She didn't know it; she hadn't noticed a problem. When she reached her house, she put the jar down and discovered that it was empty."

In Thomas 97, Yeshua explains the creation of this universe. Just as in Thomas 96, Yeshua uses the symbol of the woman to make a link to the creative aspect of God, *the Source*—the one Jesus calls *Father*. The *meal*, also used in making *bread*, which we see in Thomas 96, represents the material substance of the universe – all the galaxies, stars, and organisms within it. In this universe, the stars are like the grains creating the meal. The natural action of stars burning releases elements, which create life as we experience it in this realm. Human bodies are composed of these elements, also known as *stardust*. In this way, the processes we see in nature mirror the realm of the Spirit.

Thomas 97 explains *an action* that is symbolic of *the creation* of our universe and negates Intelligent Design. Christians who support the notion of Intelligent Design would argue that God had carefully planned out creation and its ongoing evolution. This is not to suggest there is no *influence* from the realm of the Spirit on the material universe. However, the truth we see in Thomas 97 is that this realm is incidental to the actions of the Source. The Father (Source) is an energy composed of Light. It has immeasurable creative potential (the woman carrying the jar of meal). As the possibilities of existence are countless, they have manifested in many varied forms. When the Source (Light) moved out into the abyss *(the distant road)* Its expansion released layers *(meal)* from *Itself.* This Light took the form of physical matter, which we see in our universe. This was a passive action, not an intentional, premeditated one ('she didn't know it'). When *the woman* returns home, she notices *the jar* is empty. This is the realisation from the Spirit realm that *an expansion had occurred* and a new layer had been created—this universe. Through this action the creation of the material universe occurred, but the Father's invisible Light is here too (Thomas 83 and 77). This Light constitutes the kingdom, *It* is all around us, but humans do not recognise *It* (Thomas 3). Through the actions described in Thomas 96, we see that the Father—the aspect of the Source of all things that issues forth Its Light (becoming visible in humans but *'is hidden by his Light'* [Thomas 83]), seizes the opportunity to place fragments of Itself within bodies. These are the souls that *may become* enlightened Spirits. The souls are the leaven the woman in Thomas 96 places within dough (sentient bodies capable of growing through creative thinking). Successful links between the Source and souls are made through the collective consciousness (Holy Spirit), which is the aspect of the Father *having intent.* It is the thing of creativity, empathy and compassion.

The influence of God, the Source can be cited through Rudolf Steiner's book, *'Cosmic Memory: prehistory of earth and man'*, which presents an explanation of how our world and all the creatures that live on it came into being. He does this using a spiritual text known as the *'Akasha Chronicle.'* From this ethereal text, Divine wisdom is revealed to the one who is able to delve into its recording of the past, present, and future. This *text* is what Steiner uses to explore how the Earth and man came about, beyond what science (of his time) was capable of doing. Essentially, he taps into an *intuitive wisdom* to explain the implanting of the soul into the body. One can detect influences from Hindu theology in the essays (chapters) through the references to *ether* or the *etheric* body, which is the consciousness that *influenced* creation and that may be experienced as the aura of the soul. Moreover, one can see a Gnostic influence in this text. This demonstrates Steiner's struggle to reconcile traditional Christian edicts with intuitive logic and his contractions regarding his integrity, as he felt pressure from traditional science. In the chapter, '*The Hyperborean and Polarean Epoch*' (Ibid p. 107-118) we see Steiner describe the formation of life in a way that has parallels to what scientists have concluded—that all life forms started from single cell organisms. Some twenty-five years after Steiner's death, Stanley Miller and Harold Urey showed that the 'primordial soup' theory could indeed create amino acids, which are the building blocks of life. Steiner presents *how and why* the cells formed in the primordial soup when he writes:

'The soul or astral ancestors of man were transported to the etheric earth. So to speak, *they sucked the refined substances into themselves like a sponge*, to speak coarsely. By thus becoming penetrated with substance, they developed etheric bodies. *These had an elongated elliptical form, in which the limbs and other organs which were purely physical-chemical*, but they were regulated and dominated by the soul. [Emphasis added]' (Ibid p.110).

As in most of Steiner's aforementioned text, this excerpt explains *how* physical life started, beyond the conventional, scientific hypothesis. Conventional science suggests accidental combinations of chemicals and environment caused life to spontaneously *happen*. As mentioned earlier in *77th Pearl: The Perpetual Tree*, it is an injustice to humanity that Steiner did not have access to the Gospel of Thomas, as it certainly would have added clarity to the grey areas in this form of *spiritual science* (Ibid p. 69). The information provided by Steiner gives us the confidence to know that we are indeed connected to God, the Father (the Source of all things). The knowledge of *how* the physical realm has been influenced by the spiritual realm is evidence of our link to this Source. This knowledge is supported in the Gospel of Thomas, through *77th Pearl: The Perpetual Tree.*

At this point, it is necessary to explore further the parallels we see in the natural world and how it *mirrors aspects of the inner realm.* Physical phenomena in this realm are not, of themselves, signs of what the Source is like. This premise is in error; it is why we have the problems derived from the Abrahamic religions. We have previously noted how water, symbolically, mirrors the soul, through the combination of two elements. The soul is seeking to connect with God, the Source, in order for the one to become two. In Thomas 96 and 97 we see the Father's Kingdom is like a woman who brings life (the soul), through the introduction of leaven and the accidental scattering of meal. Does this mean that women and men are different creations and serve different purposes? At first glance it would seem that this is the case, if we take what we observe in this life as our only point of reference. Through the Gospel of Thomas and *77th Pearl: The Perpetual Tree* we can move beyond this limited premise. In Thomas 22, we see that we cannot think in such simplistic terms. There is no difference in male or female when it comes to the Spirit. What we see in Thomas 96 and 97 is an explanation of one aspect of the same thing. The Father and the Mother are, in this sense, from the same point of origin, but these *aspects of the Source have different actions.*

Consider the way humans reproduce (without medical intervention). It requires the entry of the male (father) into the female (mother) for the seed (body) to be placed within the womb for gestation. Symbolically, these actions are like the female (*creative*) aspect of the Source seen in Thomas 96 and 97. The male (*father*) aspect *is the Light*, or energy, which we might think of as the Soul inside the body, like the foetus placed inside the womb (leaven inside the bread). The idea of a male and female aspect is not a new one. This can be seen within the Wicca tradition and Kabbalah, for example. In the context of the Gospel of Thomas, we now recognise that the Father/Source has not designed the male and female with intent. It has been a necessary evil, because this is the way this realm functions. These *biological organisms* (*patterns*) are not the end point. They are the reflections of different aspects of the Source, which are divided in this realm. Yeshua asks that we change our perception of these phenomena in Thomas 22. When they are two, they are in the realm of the Spirit (Thomas 11). When *they are one*, they are in their divided form, perceived as male and female. In Thomas 22, Yeshua asks that people see male and female as one (the genderless Soul)—*then humans are able to join with God, the Source, becoming two.*

Marginalised groups, such as homosexual, transgender, and intersex individuals, reveal to humanity a truth. Science has proven that genes determine sexuality. The reality that transgender and intersex people, whose brain is not the gender of their bodies, is fact. These traits are not choices. This kind of orientation and body dysmorphia happens among other creatures of this world. Sadly, a number of religions have used their narrow view of gender to convince others that their type-casting is something God has ordained. They make what is determined by nature into sin. In fact, it has nothing to do with sin. To attempt to force these marginalised individuals to fit such narrow stereotypes is damaging to the relationship they could have with God, the Father. They are representative of a kind of beauty, a kind of beauty that is cerebral, because they are *manifestations of truth*. It is a truth about this realm and how it *mirrors the inner realm*. Through Thomas, we see there is no male or female division of gender in the Father's Kingdom. These *reflections* become a rare and enigmatic truth seen in this fractured realm. Judgement of others is not what

Jesus wants of us (Thomas 6 and 14). When people release others, and themselves, from all notions of sin, they are free to grow. This is why it is important to see the reflections in this realm for what they truly are. *The human soul, along with the meal, has been scattered upon a distant road*, a universe of great diversity and wonder. The universe reflects the creative energy of the Father's Light. When humans accept all things for what they are, people will create a place of peace, where souls are united through the collective consciousness.

98. Jesus said, "The Father's kingdom is like a person who wanted to kill someone powerful. While still at home he drew his sword and thrust it into the wall to find out whether his hand would go in. Then he killed the powerful one."

In Thomas 98, we see Yeshua reveal a metaphoric action, where *a person* had the desire to *destroy something powerful*. This *person* is symbolic of the collective consciousness (Holy Spirit), because *it links* God, the Father/Source to the Son (all sentient beings). The collective consciousness is the invisible Light, it has intention, and it is the conduit between all dimensions. It is not the nature of the Holy Spirit and the Source to want to kill anything. This is an abhorrent and negative action, which is not the way of the Spirit realm. The material universe thrives on chaos. Violence and death are necessary mechanisms of its evolution. This can be seen throughout the animal kingdom and through people of dubious ambition, seeking control and power. These traits are an aspect of the lion, which Yeshua refers to in Thomas 7. The action of *killing*, we see in Thomas

98, is therefore a metaphoric one. It represents the *ending of a powerful hold* on those whom the Source seeks to join with—the ones most loved (Thomas 107).

In the second line of Thomas 98, the person *tests* the way the Light of the Father could be realised in this realm, a realm *unlike Its own nature*. The *thrust into the wall* was the Light of the Source searching for a place to aggregate in this physical realm (the powerful one). This became the breath of life within human beings. The breath of life is 'the sword' entering into this dimension, from the realm of the Spirit—the stable element, the inner layer, penetrating through into this unstable one. The purpose was to inspire particular souls to create a path to God, the Source. This was done *to find out whether his hand would go in—the 'hand' is Yeshua*. In the symbol of this sword, we see messengers and prophets as the part of the sword known as the 'edge'. The edge cuts through *the wall (the physical barriers found in this realm)*. This action has nothing to do with physical violence. It is an ideological and metaphoric battle, similar to what we see between the Christian orthodoxy and what we see here, in the Gospel of Thomas (see commentary for Thomas 16). In *77ᵗʰ Pearl: The Perpetual Tree* we see Yeshua release the sword and open His hand for humans to grasp onto.

The very tip of the sword, known as the 'point', represents the first evolving primates. When primates had the capacity to think *in abstract terms*, create tools, music, dance, and draw images, this was the soul forming within humans (the flesh). Closest to the handle we have the raised middle known as the 'fuller', giving the sword weight and strength as it meets the 'cross guard', which separates the handle grip from the blade. The fuller and cross guard are representative of Siddhartha Gautama Buddha, who sought to remove suffering in this life. Finally *the handle*, where *the hand* (Yeshua) grips the sword, was John the Baptist, who heralded the entry of Yeshua *into* this realm. Why did this 'thrust' into the wall take so long to complete? Under the mechanisms of evolution, which required time to create bodies capable of abstract concepts, *the sword* penetrated very slowly. Logical, since time in the Spirit realm is experienced as a whole, rather than a linear progression of physical light in this realm.

In the last line of Thomas 98, Yeshua tells us that the *action* of the collective consciousness (Holy Spirit) 'killed the powerful one.' The *action of* placing His hand (Yeshua) into this realm, had a significant result for humanity. *The powerful one* is something humans find very alluring. It is *this material world* and everything people experience in it, both good and bad (see commentary for Thomas 7). The gratifying experiences humans have in this life give momentary pleasures. Typically, it stops them from considering if there is anything better. This life often prevents people from comprehending what Yeshua means when He says to '*live*' or to '*taste death*'. The negative experiences humans have in this life make them begrudge their predicament. They may become envious of others who are in a better emotional, financial, or social position. This is another aspect of the lion in Thomas 7. When Yeshua (the hand of God, the Source) entered into this realm, He destroyed the notion that this is the first life we have, and the last. When Yeshua placed the flesh that clothed Him on the cross, He killed the powerful one with that weapon. This is what Yeshua came to do and this sword is the kind the lion fears most.

The Last Supper (described in the New Testament) carries a strong message, which relates to the story within Thomas 98. When Yeshua speaks about His *body and blood* being consumed by us, we suddenly realise what this symbolic action means. It is about sustaining the Soul, in order to *kill the powerful one*. His Body is the *knowledge* that carries us through this realm—to mature into an enlightened Spirit. After all, it is while we are in the physical body that we aggregate the Father's Light. Our physical movement through this realm involves learning and growth (Thomas 86). It is not an accident that we see Yeshua's body as *the bread*, which is linked to the establishment of this realm, in Thomas 96 and 97. These are symbolic analogies and threads. Through *consuming the wisdom* He brings us, we are sustained and we are made strong in Spirit. The knowledge of truth becomes our *metaphysical body*.

Yeshua's blood is symbolic of the Light that is over all things and flows through everything (Thomas 77). It is active through the Holy Spirit—the collective consciousness, linking all benevolent Spirits. Yeshua says His blood is the wine *we drink*—we see in Thomas 47 it is the *new wine*, which must not be spoiled by other, man-made, ideologies. Unlike bread, which is sustenance, ensuring life, wine is an added pleasure. It can emulate euphoria, akin to the feeling of being connected to the Source, through the collective consciousness. The sensation a glass of wine may also bring is similar to the calm and relaxed feeling people have when they are connected to the Source. There is a danger of becoming intoxicated—we see this in Thomas 28. This is the paradox and the fine line humans walk on in this world. It is an aspect of *the powerful one*, which represents the desire for quick and convenient solutions. This is characteristic of a person's physical existence. Through this analogy, we see that keeping the material and spiritual realms separate is necessary, otherwise we start to impose one on the other. This is when people *create sin for themselves*, through the mechanisms of ritual and dogma. The wine people have become drunk on is evident in the apostles' questions to Yeshua: '*Do you want us to fast? How should we pray? Should we give to charity? What diet should we observe?*' (Thomas 6). The new wine and bread is here, in Yeshua, through the Gospel of Thomas, carried in the *new wine skin*, which is *77ᵗʰ Pearl: The Perpetual Tree* (Thomas 47).

99. The disciples said to him, "Your brothers and your mother are standing outside."

He said to them, "Those here who do what my Father wants are my brothers and my mother. They are the ones who will enter my Father's kingdom."

One of the consistent threads within the Gospel of Thomas is summed up in Thomas 42, when Yeshua says, 'be passersby'. In Thomas 55, when Yeshua asks us to hate our parents and siblings, we see that it is necessary to separate ourselves from the notion of the *family* we are born into. This is also a call to recognise the illusion of these relationships, which are made by the physical world, also seen in Thomas 87. In Thomas 99, Jesus challenges the notion that the family unit is above all things, as would have been the attitude in His day. Yeshua presents to us a very different notion of what is important and whom we should actually consider as family. This is expanded upon in Thomas 101.

These cryptic sayings are lessons about our predicament in this realm and our ideal trajectory. It is not a directive on the way we should behave towards family. Families come in many varied forms and they are important for a person's development. However, they are not going to be with us for eternity. They serve an important function, which ultimately enables a soul to free itself from the flesh, through a healthy mind and body. People who have a negative experience of family may use this as impetus to search for reasons why humans behave in certain ways. This experience may lead to a discovery of *the lion* (Thomas 7) and its opposite in Jesus. In this sense, the experience becomes something positive. All experiences in this life can be vehicles for driving the human along a path to enlightenment. This is reliant upon how people perceive the experiences (Thomas 62).

In Thomas 99 Yeshua tells us that to be His family we are to see ourselves as the ones who come from God, the Source. This is what the *Father* wants of us—to reconnect, to aggregate Its Light in us. It is not an accident that the whole family is mentioned in Thomas 99, the mother, siblings, and father. This indicates the symbolic *unity and wholeness* of the collective consciousness (Holy Spirit). It is symbolic of how it is interconnected among all of us, when we open our eyes to this reality. In some cultures it is customary to bow when greeting anyone; this is an apt metaphor for the attitude we should have toward the Light within each other (Thomas 3). This attitude reflects what Yeshua desires of us when He says, '*do what my Father wants*'.

100. They showed Jesus a gold coin and said to him, "The Roman emperor's people demand taxes from us."

He said to them, "Give the emperor what belongs to the emperor, give God what belongs to God, and give me what is mine."

Thomas 100 refers to our perceptions about this world and its political reality, persisting into the start of a new age – the twenty first century. Yeshua instructs His followers to pay their obligations in taxes, including the other monetary expectations from within the community. This also extends to the laws within a community. While in the ideal world we would have no crimes or dictators, we know that, at the infancy of the twenty-first century, we are in a world ruled by those influenced by the lion (Thomas 7). They are the manifestations of this realm and its propensity to make individuals want control and power. They cause fear and segregation through this primal tendency. In Thomas 42, Jesus tells us we need to 'be passersby'. This relates to Thomas 100, where we are told that we should coexist in the places we go into and the places we live. However, at the same time, we should be observers of the way others struggle in this life. They are lessons for people about suffering and the nature of this realm. When we allow ourselves to stand on the outside and look in, we can see the place for the first time. This experience is the same as when we go through a significant event in our lives. This event may have felt terrible at the moment, but as time passes it becomes something to learn from.

The cryptic part of Thomas 100 is when Yeshua asks that they *give God what belongs to God* as being *separate from giving Yeshua what is His*. We have seen in the Gospel of Thomas a disparity between what Yeshua's contemporaries knew as God and what *Yeshua knew* as the Father—the Source of all things. This saying is linked with Thomas 39, where Yeshua tells His followers that the religious leaders of their community have hidden from them what is most necessary for their spiritual growth. They had become consumed by the lion we see in Thomas 7, as have numerous leaders of our contemporary religious communities. In being *as sly as snakes and simple as doves*, we are able to exist within these communities, learn from them what is of benefit and recognise their shortcomings. In this way, we give *their God what belongs to him*. At the same time we are fulfilling the last part of Yeshua's instruction—to *give to Him what is His*. What belongs to Yeshua is the kinship we share through the collective consciousness (Holy Spirit). Such a person is enlightened, alive in the Source, connected to all things. For this to occur, we give Yeshua our ears to listen and our open hearts and minds to process this wisdom.

101. "Whoever does not hate [father] and mother as I do cannot be my [disciple], and whoever does [not] love [father and] mother as I do cannot be my [disciple]. For my mother [...], but my true [mother] gave me life."

In Thomas 55 Yeshua asks us to reject the notion of family, as we understand it, by making the controversial request to *hate our parents and siblings*. This is a *symbolic rejection*, meant to make us see what our human birth and filial connections stop us from recognising—we are the *family of Spirit, we are one*. In Thomas 101, Yeshua expands on this to reveal the nature of His actual lineage. Here, Jesus only refers to the parents, which directs us to the understanding of where *He came from*.

There appears to be a contradiction in the first line of Thomas 101. Yeshua makes the statement that if one does not hate mother and father as He does, and love mother and father as He does, then that individual is not worthy of following Him. This is, essentially, the key to unlocking what has already been presented to us in Thomas 55. Yeshua asks that we recognise the disparity between the flesh and the Soul, which connects us to the Source through the heritage coming from *the Father* (Thomas 77). The parents Yeshua wants us to love are *the mother and father that are profound and whole. They are the Source—what we are connected to through consciousness.*

The feelings we experience for our human parents, particularly as children, are driven by primal instincts for survival—

protection, food, and a source of learning to navigate through this world. As we get older, becoming adults, these feelings generally change to respect and gratitude for the sacrifices made for our benefit. However, these things are *peripheral to the true self.* The sentimental attachments and feelings of obligation are part of the cycle intrinsic to this existence. It is a trap. This is why Yeshua makes such dramatic and seemingly unreasonable requests of us. The Spirit, the collective consciousness, does not know hate. Only while the Soul is in a body can people engage in such primal emotions. The love we have as humans needs to transcend the primal and become something profoundly linked to the Source. Thus, we are directed towards *the concept of the mother and father, which is of Divine origin, metaphysical.*

Humans must at all times remember that this realm is a mere reflection of the *inner realm.* The manifestations of male and female are simply reflections of the Source and *Its separate facets* in this realm. Imagine a person blowing a bubble of soap in front of a mirror. That person can only *experience* one side of that bubble when looking at the mirror, yet they know it is part of a whole three dimensional thing. Existing in this realm is like experiencing everything in *a reflection, because it does not allow us to experience the whole.* Consider also, the bubble the person has created will always become a perfect sphere. This reflects the *Divine wholeness* of God, the Source. All of Its *facets* are seamlessly joined, *It is one* at all times, everywhere at the same time (Thomas 77 and 83). In this realm, people can only experience a two dimensional *reflection* of the bubble (male and female). Intersex individuals are like glimpses of the three dimensional bubble. The outer layers of the Source are unstable and rely on physical materials, which are peripheral to the realm existing within. This is why we find a carcass if we discover the world as it truly is (Thomas 56). This *carcass,* with its enticing reflections, *is the powerful one* (Thomas 98), which *leads humans astray.* The world makes humans think in limited, four-dimensional forms. The reality is, when a person looks past the mirror—the reflections, there are more dimensions than humans are capable of experiencing. When they see what is in front of their face (Thomas 5)—the bubble in the room, the one within them, within all of us—then they will know all (Thomas 108).

The last line of Thomas 101 is a confronting revelation, Yeshua says: 'for my mother gave birth to me, but my true mother gave me life [missing words added]'. This refers to *one facet* of God, the Source—*it is both father and mother at the same time.* The *life* Yeshua refers to is not the *life* we experience in this realm—the physical birth and death of the flesh. The *life* Yeshua speaks of is the *Light within His body*, when He was wrapped in flesh. On His death it became pure Spirit, resurrected (Thomas 24 and 53). The creative energy of the Source is what brought forth His Spirit. *This creative energy is the facet referred to as the mother.* The collective consciousness (Holy Spirit) plays an integral part in this action—yet neither of these is male or female.

102. Jesus said, "Damn the Pharisees! They are like a dog sleeping in the cattle manger: the dog neither eats nor [lets] the cattle eat."

Thomas 102 shares a thread with Thomas 39. Therein, Yeshua tells us the leaders of the faith, in His time, had taken the keys of knowledge and hidden them. They did not enter into the place of this knowledge, nor would they allow others to do so. In a similar way, we see Yeshua compare these leaders to a dog sleeping in a barn. The fear and naivety of the religious leaders (the dog) prevents the parishioners (the cattle) from receiving knowledge of the truth (eating). The metaphor of eating relates to the partaking of knowledge, the nourishment for the Soul. This *knowledge* is something that is either soiled (Thomas 93) or hidden by those consumed by the lion we see in Thomas 7. The knowledge, and its resulting wisdom, is actioned by the collective consciousness (Holy Spirit) and speaks to us on an intuitive level. We find this knowledge in the Gospel of Thomas, because the words are unfettered by desires for power or control. That is why they have been presented as cryptic messages. Yeshua knew that souls who were consumed by the lion (Thomas 7) were unable to comprehend knowledge requiring an open heart and mind. These attributes are not of the lion; they are of the Holy Spirit, just as compassion and empathy are also manifestations of consciousness.

The nature of power is that it corrupts humans, particularly those who are not entirely in control of their desires and fears. The *primal body*, as we see in Thomas 7, drives these desires and fears. Religious leaders may have good intentions initially, but somewhere along their path they may become entranced by the position they hold. The materialistic security, power, and hubris such positions of power can bring also become an obstacle. This is why most organised religions are stagnant and are ruled by dogma. These elements inhibit the development of the Soul. The metaphor of the *sleeping dog*, which 'neither eats nor lets the cattle eat', relates to the human consumed by the lion (Thomas 7). The institutions such leaders have created are focused on establishing black and white rules (dogma). However, people need the shades of grey to make a complete, *realistic picture*. The leaders do not necessarily impose this dogma alone. They are often responding to the parishioners' desires and expectations—the ones who want a box to tick. This is the other side of the lion we see in Thomas 7. *The lion* likes to have a common set of rules the whole pride understands and can adhere to. If the rules do not exist, these people feel the structure of their society is weakened. Rules addressing every aspect of social morals create a safe place for these people—a safe place within *the pride*. The emphasis in the three major religions (sharing the Abrahamic lineage) is a faith within a community. Individual spiritual growth is not the focus in these groups. The connection to God is through the acceptance that *he* created them. They rely on *him* to be brought to life after death. The *Gospel of Thomas* is different. It is about the individual and the journey to spiritual enlightenment, which brings humans to *life in Spirit. This life joins us to the authentic community, the one worthy of us* (Thomas 85). It is a profound knowing and connectedness, which is beyond words. Words are what the Pharisees had, but *we have this.*

103. Jesus said, "Congratulations to those who know where the rebels are going to attack. [They] can get going, collect their imperial resources, and be prepared before the rebels arrive."

In the first part of Thomas 103, Yeshua congratulates people who are aware of *'where the rebels are going to attack'*. The rebels are the *distractions in this existence*. These distractions steal the human away from focusing on the growth of the Soul – *they* interfere with one's consciousness. The rebels come in many forms. They can be the importance we place on family, which we see in Thomas 55 and 101, or the emphasis we might place on being partnered with a significant other, as seen in Thomas 87. They can be as varied as the feelings of rejection in a broken friendship, the emotions stemming from being bullied, or not measuring up to other individuals' perceptions of intelligence or physical appearance, etcetera. In Thomas 42, Yeshua asks that we be *passersby of this life*. This is significant when we consider who the rebels are. It is when people engage in the problems within this life, allowing these to affect them, that they are no longer passersby. It is at this point that *the rebels* have people in their power. For this reason, the Spirit consciousness sent Siddhartha Gautama Buddha to humanity. The Buddha taught how craving comes from our senses engaging with the material world in an ignorant, childish manner. This disturbs the faculties and is the root cause of suffering. He called this cycle *Paticcasa-muppada* (*Dependent Origination*) and he taught how one can overcome this *domino effect* (see the commentary for Thomas

7). *Paticcasamuppada* defines the power of the rebels, so people may abate the rebel's influences. However, Yeshua's teachings added another layer to the Buddha's Dharma. Through a deep awareness of what one is, beyond the reflection in the mirror, one attains their *imperial resources*. The human then rises above the rebels' influence.

The second part of Thomas 103 reveals that we can move past the distractions which consume our everyday lives, by *collecting our imperial resources*. The imperial resources are the confidence and knowledge we have relating to what we are. It is the intimate connection we share with Yeshua in the Source, through the collective consciousness (Holy Spirit). This kinship gives us the confidence to move mountains. The mountains, in this case, are those things that have become the rebels. Interestingly, when Yeshua says to be prepared *before* the rebels arrive, we see an admission which points to the reality humans face in this realm. The implication is that the rebels will certainly arrive. However, having the knowledge of their *imperial resources*, a person can overcome these issues and be victorious.

In Thomas 103, Yeshua tells us to be vigilant in this existence, aware of the rebels that are its inherent components. People's physical pleasures, needs, and desires can become all consuming. Preoccupation with this life and the transitory pleasures it offers can make humans addicted to its promises. It can steal people away from understanding that this realm is a mirror of true beauty. The aesthetic is experienced at a higher level, in the inner realm of the Spirit. When a person has *their imperial resources* they see things for what they truly are—the rebels cannot infect them. When people come to this realisation, they are able to smile at the distractions. They can be free of their allure and, at times, their pain. In this way, the individual becomes a passerby (Thomas 42).

When Yeshua speaks of rebels, He speaks of a broad range of things that steal people away from the truth. We see in the New Testament Gospels a focus on Yeshua's authority over demons. This was the authors' attempt to highlight His Divine lineage and authority. Through *77th Pearl: The Perpetual Tree*, we have seen Jesus tell us, *humans are Satan* (see commentary for Thomas 21) and they are the ones who place obstacles in front of people who are looking towards the Light. This truth is revealed in the words of Mark 8:33, when Peter is rebuked by Jesus for not thinking as God would, but *as men do*. This does not mean that Peter was representative of Satan (the Devil), but that in a moment of weakness he gave in to thinking *as men do*, rather than in a spiritual sense, as Yeshua would have expected. This is an example of how humans can become weakened by the rebels. Often they are not demons; they can be the natural actions (human emotions) people encounter in this life.

Some people, who have been consumed by *the rebels*, have fallen into or have chosen a path that is in darkness. This darkness relates to the place where the truth does not *live* and where the *unifying Light* of the Holy Spirit is absent. These places are in disharmony and conflict, because these things are not of the Spirit, which is manifest from, and of, the Father's Light. They are of this realm, which we see in Thomas 7. These misguided souls work to keep *the Light* within us in this realm. They are generally not without a physical body, as we might imagine a typical demon. Consider how in several New Testament parables *people*, supposedly possessed of a demon, would recognise Yeshua. Yeshua would tell them to be silent, so as not to reveal His spiritual identity. Manifestations of the negative entities are many and varied. At all times, we must look to our intuitive and logical self, to reveal when these individuals seek to disturb us. They are more often than not wrapped in flesh and bone. They speak from the primordial fear within them, which knows no *Light*.

An orthodox interpretation of Thomas 103 would see the involvement of Satan and his minions. Placing a legion of demons under the control of an antagonistic 'prince of darkness' can become a trap in itself. We see this in texts that become focused on a battle between good and evil. The evil becomes the *antithesis* of God, the Creator. In constructing such a premise, these authors put themselves in a position of potential blasphemy against God, the *Father/Source*. They infer that these souls did not come from the Source. These souls' innate fear places them in darkness, which is a domain without knowledge of truth. Where there is fear there is evil. It is a fear we see in the animal world and is related to our primal heritage, before the breath of life entered humanity. *This primal fear is something we must excise for our species to move into the next phase of existence. This fear separates the human from the collective consciousness (Holy Spirit).* It is something we can only meet with compassion for the poor choices such entities make. Compassion for these lost souls is the way to disarm their antagonism, because they feed on anger and fear—an outcome of chaos. Consider Mark 5, the story of a man possessed of many demonic spirits, who calls himself 'Legion'. They beg Yeshua not to cast them *out of the land*, but into a drove of swine, which in His compassion Yeshua gratifies. The swine are startled by this action, resulting in the swine running into water and drowning. This story is symbolic of the lost souls' *lust for place* (existence in this realm). Their desire for a physical place resulted in them *tasting death*. This is why, in the Gospel of Thomas, Yeshua refers to those who either *taste death or live* (Thomas 1). *Legion* chose to be cast into another physical form, that could die, rather than choosing a new path, and so, they tasted death (again). If they do not change, this narrative will continuously repeat, until this realm ends. This is the lesson in Mark 5, revealed through the wisdom of the secret teachings in the Gospel of Thomas.

If these *lost souls* are also from God, the Father/Source, what of them? In Thomas 11 Yeshua reveals to us that this heaven, which is this universe, will cease to exist. This is something science has also concluded. The universe is expanding outwardly, presumably from the point of the 'big bang'. The hypothesis is that it will eventually either contract back to its previous condition, before this *expansion*, or extinguish as stars slowly dim. In Thomas 18, Yeshua tells us that if we are standing at the beginning, we will know where the end is. *This 'end' is the Father's Light* (Thomas 77). All things are resolved unto the Source and *become part of the whole*. The difference within humans who have the wisdom, found in Yeshua's teaching, is that they are connected to God, the Source, through the collective consciousness (Holy Spirit). This is when they *become two*, as we see in Thomas 11. These Spirits go on to dwell in the inner realm, which is not unstable and finite, like this one. The souls that have taken the path of darkness, without knowledge of truth, will be absorbed into the energy of the Source's Light with no knowledge of the self. They essentially become something else, because energy cannot be destroyed, it can only *change*. Human mythologies, which have seen the creation of concepts such as hellfire and purgatory, are reflective of intuitive knowledge. It is a *remnant* knowledge people have of catastrophic, natural events happening to them in other life forms. They are deep within the primal psyche. The reality of our planet dying from our own hand, or from the death of our sun, is certain. This has been repeated in other solar systems since the expansion of this outer layer. With our *imperial resources* we move beyond all of this and the rebels fail to deceive us.

104. They said to Jesus, "Come, let us pray today, and let us fast."

Jesus said, "What sin have I committed, or how have I been undone? Rather, when the groom leaves the bridal suite, then let people fast and pray."

Yeshua's Spirit was *thrust into* this realm, fully aware of the connection He had to God, the Father (Source), as evident in Thomas 98. It is a connection humans have lost through the inadvertent expansion of the Source. This event created the outer layers, which sentient bodies exist in (Thomas 97). Yeshua came to teach people about *the Light* which is over and through all things (Thomas 77). This is the *Father's* Light that humans aggregate, to become enlightened Spirits—the *one that becomes two* (Thomas 11). In Thomas 104, Yeshua tells His disciples that it is not necessary to pray and fast, if the reason is to eliminate the *damage of a perceived sin.* The *obstacle of sin, created in the human mind,* is the most damaging aspect of *supposed unworthiness* (Thomas 14). This is equivalent to the difference between the good and the barren soil (Thomas 9). The Christian, orthodox believers see themselves as unworthy of a direct, filial connection to God, the Father. They require an intermediary, which becomes the Church they belong to, with its hierarchy, dogma, and rituals. This is the essential difference we find between the Johannine and Thomasine understanding of Jesus. The author(s) of John saw Jesus as the only Son of God, who was sent to us to sacrifice Himself for the sins of humanity—this completed the narratives from the Old Testament, which Yeshua used to accumulate a following. He found it necessary to fulfill the prophecies so that His true purpose could live on. Thomas understood Yeshua as having a greater purpose, one of teaching, imparting crucial knowledge that led to Divine wisdom. This knowledge was to separate humans from the beast they evolved from. Homo sapiens sapiens needed to understand that they are more than the flesh. This is what Yeshua's death was meant to show us. We are a soul wrapped in flesh, evolving into a Spirit, like Yeshua. If people do not see *the wealth* that they are, then they continue to be the poverty (Thomas 3). Yeshua's connection to God, the Source, and the collective consciousness (Holy Spirit), allowed Him to see the error of His disciples' understanding. For this reason, He asks the rhetorical questions: '*What sin have I committed, or how have I been undone?*'

In the last sentence of Thomas 104, Yeshua tells people that when He has left this realm then there is cause to fast and pray. His wisdom would no longer be accessible to them. The *bridal suite* is this realm, where people join to Him through the collective consciousness (Holy Spirit). This happens through the teachings He left us in the Gospel of Thomas. They are *the flesh and blood we join with to become two*.

Thomas 104 reveals the frustration Yeshua felt with His contemporaries. They did not understand that their knowledge of God was not the same as the wisdom He came to reveal. Their desire to fast and pray was misguided. It came from teachings given to them by Pharisees, who were consumed by the lion (Thomas 7). The Pharisees created division through ritual scarring called circumcision (Thomas 53). They also instilled the notion of physical cleanliness, which they erroneously thought impacted on spiritual cleanliness (Thomas 89). Inadequacies were compounded through compliance and penance, established by dietary laws, ritual washing, animal and harvest sacrifices. Some of these practices continue to various degrees in the early part of the twenty-first century. These practices were, and to some degree still are, a barrier to understanding the truth of Yeshua's teachings. It was also necessary for Yeshua to become the replacement of the *sacrificial lamb* in the Temple, this is why His rhetoric had to be ambiguous. Without this prophetic link to the Old Testament, He would have passed into obscurity, being labeled an eccentric heretic.

The lamb and its blood are symbolically connected. Yeshua reveals this through the timing of the Last Supper, which occurred at Passover. In the legend of Passover, the Jewish people, who were enslaved in Egypt, painted *lambs' blood* above their doorways so that their God would not take the life of their first-born. This act ensured that only the first-born child of the Egyptian enslavers would be killed. In creating a new, symbolic, sacrifice for the Temple (Himself), Yeshua created a new pathway to God, the Father. At the Last Supper, Yeshua tells us that the wine has become His blood, which metaphorically represents the lamb's blood in the Passover. Yeshua's blood represents our spiritual union with Him, it is the collective consciousness in action, the Comforter. The bread Yeshua gave to His disciples is symbolic of His teachings—they are here, in the Gospel of Thomas, revealed through *77th Pearl: The Perpetual Tree.*

Like the cross that creates a symbolic crossroads at its juncture, humans can either travel across the horizon, or they can choose to look up. This is the direction where the endless depths of space *symbolically mirror* the Source's Light, which is over and through all things. When Yeshua tells people, *'when the groom leaves the bridal suite, then let people fast and pray'*, He is explaining that His teachings are revealed for their truth over two thousand years *after He is gone*. When Yeshua left this realm, people were to become observant of the teachings in this gospel. If fasting and prayer help these teachings come to life, for the individual, then these forms of meditation are appropriate. However, through the Gospel of Thomas revelations, the dark times of fasting have come to an end. *77ᵗʰ Pearl: The Perpetual Tree* heralds the epoch of the Light, which Yeshua sowed through His disciple, Thomas.

105. Jesus said, "Whoever knows the father and the mother will be called the child of a whore."

In the sayings Thomas 55 and 101, Yeshua makes reference to hating the father and the mother as a symbolic gesture, not a literal one. The gesture is an acknowledgement of *what the real father and mother are,* as we see in Thomas 101, when Yeshua refers to His ethereal mother giving Him *life.* Again, this is symbolic and is actually referring to the aspect of God the Source which *creates. It is both the father and mother,* because genders are ascribed to images in this realm, not the realm of the Spirit. We should recognise, in Thomas 105, that there is an intrinsic link within these sayings.

In Thomas 105, Yeshua warns people that if they are able to see their mortal mother and father for what they truly are—'whoever *knows* the father and mother'—then this person '*will be called the child of a whore*'. In Yeshua's time, for a woman to be considered a whore would have been the greatest of insults, bringing shame and dishonor to a family. The society of that time would have shunned a woman *labeled a whore.* Her offspring would also not have been treated with respect. When we consider what Yeshua meant by this language, we see that He would not have been insulting or judging anyone. What Yeshua was doing was creating a dialogue with us, in the twenty-first century, a time when we can look at the true meaning behind such a metaphor.

If Yeshua had spoken *openly* about His purpose and teachings, He would have been treated like the outcast He mentions in Thomas 105. Yeshua's contemporaries had narrow and judgmental opinions about those things outside of the acceptable norm. Their religious leaders determined those values cited here, for the purposes of control and power (Thomas 39 and 102). A woman who had been used for sex could not be married, because she was seen as damaged (in those men's eyes). This woman would have been marginalised within that society. Yeshua is telling us two things here. One is that He would have been treated like this, if He had not kept His *primary* teachings a secret. The other is that we can expect to be treated in the same way, by the majority whose beliefs come from an established institution. This indicates *organised religions are something most people desire*, because they give easy answers, with clearly defined parameters. Most people do not want to knock on a door for the answer (Thomas 94). They want the answer presented to them, in a neat package. This is the battle Yeshua was up against throughout His time in this realm. It is a battle people seeking the Light may also experience. For this reason, we are the children of the *whore*, who has been *damaged by men*. Through this rejection, and labeling, we should be proud, because we have come to know *what the mother and father* truly are.

106. Jesus said, "When you make the two into one, you will become children of Adam, and when you say, 'Mountain, move from here!' it will move."

In Thomas 11 and 22, Yeshua speaks of *the one becoming two or the two becoming one*. What we should recognise here is that these are references to different aspects of either our situation in this realm compared to the other, or the path to take in order to reconnect with God the Source, respectively. In Thomas 106, as in Thomas 22, Yeshua speaks about people's perceptions of the Soul being determined by the physical. Moreover, He points out that humans are not man or women, they are *a soul which existed before these genders*. Additionally, people are not Jewish, Christian, Muslim or Hindu, they are a soul. In Thomas 106, Yeshua reveals a truth about where humans actually came from. In Thomas 22, He demonstrates a pathway to mindfulness, by referring to the connectedness and 'oneness' of the Father's Kingdom. This is achieved by reconfiguring a person's perception of *this* realm. In Thomas 106, Yeshua proposes that if people can reconcile their physical existence as *incidental and transitory*, they can henceforth recognise the Soul. This is the true *identity*. If humans can see all matter as part of God the Source, then they can see *the two realms are one*. This becomes evident through *the Source being joined to the collective consciousness* – the Holy Spirit in action.

In Thomas 106, Yeshua says: '*when you make the two into one, you will become children of Adam*'. This is significant as it reveals a great truth. Unlike Thomas 22, here Yeshua directly speaks of where humanity came from. In the Genesis myth, we see that God made man from the earth and the first was Adam. Creation myths have comparative versions in different cultures, all over the world. Joseph Campbell explored this phenomenon in '*The Power of Myth*', showing how myths are derivatives of common experiences and observations made in this world. For going against God's command—to not eat from the tree of knowledge—Adam, and his partner Eve, were thrown out of paradise and made to suffer life as we know it. Through these simple words in Thomas 106—'you *will become* children of Adam [emphasis added]'—Yeshua cleverly reveals that, in fact, God did not create human bodies *before* the soul. People are sparks from the Source's Light, which *seeks to be rejoined, to be one*. This *spark* (soul) existed before the body.

Adam is symbolic of the perfect human—something all people should aspire to become. This symbolic, perfect human is neither male, nor female and yet *it* is both of these at the same time. *It is one* and perfect. When the human *(Adam)* evolved in this realm *it* (the body) became the separate parts of male and female. The Soul found its place to grow within this flesh. These sequence of events commenced after God the Source expanded into the abyss. It caused physical material to form, which eventually gave rise to human bodies, through the substance given off by stars. These truths are revealed through the Genesis myth, which community leaders have created through their intuitive knowledge of these events. However, their understanding of the true meaning behind this myth has been clouded by their observations of physical existence. The revelations in Thomas tell us that the body, and this realm, is a fractured and flawed mirror of the inner realm, which is stable and constant. When we *make the two into one*, we are ready to enter the realm of the Spirit, where the generation of the *symbolic* Adam dwells. This knowledge allows us to remove perceived obstacles from the path we take in this dimension.

In Gnostic mythology it was the third son of Adam and Eve, called Seth (Genesis 5:3), who was considered *the perfect human*. Seth, unlike his older brothers Cain and Abel, was without jealousy and the inclination towards violence. Seth was considered symbolic of the *enlightened generation*. He could see past the illusions of the Creator God, seen as malevolent by Gnostics. Interpreting Thomas 106 as it might first appear to the individual, one could see how the Gnostics' conclusions may have appeared to be correct. However, Yeshua would have known that His contemporaries considered themselves as *descendants* of the Adam appearing in the Genesis creation myth. In Thomas 106, Jesus tells them when they 'make the two into one, [they] *will become* children of Adam'. Jesus is stating that they are *yet to become the children of Adam*. Therefore, they are not the *intentional creation* of God (Thomas 97). In this way, Yeshua makes it clear their notion of Creation, linked to the *intentions* of God, is false. After all, in Thomas 29, Yeshua tells us the Soul came before the flesh.

If God the Source had purposefully created each individual body there might be cause for assuming an *inherent* link to the Divine. However, in Thomas we see, human bodies and this universe exist due to an incidental expansion of the Source's Light (Thomas 97). The reality that some people are born with disabilities also negates the notion of an intentional creation. Through the *mirror influence* of the inner realm lifeforms began to take shape and human bodies were formed. These are the first creatures that made tools and could think in abstract terms. They could draw symbols and create music and dance. Through these events, the *breath of life* entered the beings and souls became wrapped in ever-evolving flesh.

Through this 'motion and rest' they aggregate the Source's Light (Thomas 50). The evidence of this truth will become clearer when beings from other worlds and dimensions make their presence known to humanity. Some of these carry the same Light that is in us. They are our kin, in the Source's Light. We are connected to them through the collective consciousness (Holy Spirit).

This *evolution* has led humanity to the twenty-first century, where people are on the threshold of a new understanding of what they are and of their true nature—*as it will be*. The creation people find themselves in is not intentional, as we have seen in Thomas 97. However, the Source, through the collective consciousness (Holy Spirit), desires our growth. So that we may be in union with *Its* infinite manifestations, Yeshua came to this realm for the purpose of showing us *the truth, the way, and the Light*.

107. Jesus said, "The (Father's) Kingdom is like a shepherd who had a hundred sheep. One of them, the largest, went astray. He left the ninety-nine and looked for the one until he found it. After he had toiled, he said to the sheep, 'I love you more than the ninety-nine.'"

The use of the word *love* makes a link to the way humans *behave toward* someone they are drawn to, on a deeper level. The largest sheep is symbolic of *what we are*—souls on the journey to becoming enlightened Spirits. When humans become enlightened Spirits, they are *the largest sheep*, desired above all others. Yeshua tells us the *Father's Kingdom is like a shepherd* who seeks His most beloved sheep. This is a revelation about the way God the Source is *drawn to Its Light*, which has accumulated within humans to become *the largest sheep (a Spirit)*. The *toil* is a metaphor for the journey through this universe—from the time when the Source initially expanded outward, to the time when Yeshua's Spirit was thrust through the inner realm, into this one (Thomas 98). This is God the Father, the source of all things, working towards a reunion with the thing *It* had lost.

As with other sayings in the Gospel of Thomas, we see Thomas 107 presented in its original form. In The New Testament Gospels of Matthew 18:12-13 and Luke 15:4-6, we see the parable of Thomas 107 interpreted in a persuasive, hyperbolic manner, which denigrates the revelations within these words. The New Testament authors present this parable as a promise that God will come to *save the sinner* (the stray sheep), *bringing them back to the fold*. The implication is that humanity has gone astray, because they are no longer worthy of God. This stems from the Original Sin of disobedience, through the mythological story we see in Genesis. This lack of obedience was then redeemed through Abraham's willingness to sacrifice his only son Isaac, to Yahweh (God). This train of thought comes from the misguided understanding, within Christian denominations, that people are the design of a Creator God, from whom they have turned away. Even though they have done this, He will still love them *when they come back to Him*. In the Gospel of Thomas, we see that this parable actually talks about the *desire* God (the Source) has to join with human Spirits. This conclusion is logical when we read and meditate on all of these sayings collectively, thereby noticing the thread that has been laid down for us, by Yeshua. One of the most significant threads is the *Source's Light, which is over and through all things* (Thomas 77). We have not walked away from *It*; we have not gone astray through our own will (Thomas 97). We are the Light that can grow (Thomas 96) and become the siblings of Yeshua (Thomas 99). In the Gospel of John, this parable becomes a discourse by Jesus, about *the sheep* recognising Him. This author was passionately concerned with making people accept that Jesus was the Christ. He could willingly lay down His life, just as He could raise it up again. This is why we see the story of Lazarus appear in John. As discussed previously, it would seem that the author(s) of John had visions of refuting what existed in the Gospel of Thomas. They attempted to do this by casting aspersions upon Thomas's understanding and belief in Yeshua as *the risen Christ.* In the Gospel of Thomas, it is clear that Yeshua was human, flesh and bone. His body was destroyed, but His Soul was raised up, to become a Spirit, resurrected to the Source. His Spirit dwells in another realm/dimension, which humans cannot *experience* while in this existence.

A sheep is a creature that is inclined to go wherever its nose may lead it, or where the tail of another sheep might encourage it to follow. Having considered this trait, we can see that the sparks (souls) which emanated from the Source went onto *the distant road* (Thomas 97). The Light (*meal*) poured out of the jar, following the woman who represents the creative power of God the Source. Put simply, our souls are intrinsically connected to God the Father and we *followed its expansion into the abyss.* Through the nurturing of the collective consciousness (Holy Spirit), *we are found.* While consciousness is an intrinsic quality of humanity, it has taken eons for it to be fully recognised for its singularity. Yeshua delivered these secret teachings so that we may appreciate how we are all linked to the thing He came from. In becoming aware and meditating on this union, humans have found the Comforter, *the collective home.* In this galaxy, the human soul is desirable to God the Father, as are other beings that house the Light of the Source.

It is important that we recognise the condition of humanity. People have an inclination to deny the truth of what they really are because of their primal heritage. In the major faiths that claim Abraham as their lineage, we see obedience as a foremost point of concern. Indeed, the story of Abraham (Genesis 22:1-18) revolves around his willingness to sacrifice his only son to Yahweh (God). In this mythical character, we are supposed to see the ideal human, who is totally accepting of Yahweh's will, even if it means taking his son's life. Toward the end of this part of his story, Abraham is about to sacrifice his son Isaac. At this point, Yahweh's angel stops him and tells Abraham that he was being tested—because he followed *the will of God*, his lineage would prosper and grow. To replace Abraham's son on the sacrificial altar Abraham finds a ram stuck in bushes. It is not a coincidence that a sheep becomes the sacrifice. In the context of the Gospel of Thomas, we can see that the sheep represents the generations preceding John the Baptist and Yeshua. The sheep, that the Father *loves above all others*, was being destroyed at human hands. This attitude continued, to a lesser degree, after Yeshua. In this way, people's tendency to place God outside of themselves has actually *distanced them from the truth*. This tendency stems from peoples primal heritage, which saw them create mythologies based on their *literal observations* of the natural world, overlaid onto the spiritual realm.

The inherent fear humans had of the night and the chaos seen in natural disasters, gave people a picture of an authoritarian, alpha-male god. This god had an opposing other in a fallen angel, becoming known as Satan. If it was not God the father punishing his children, it was the jealous Satan creating obstacles for people, because humans were God's favored creation. (For an explanation of who *the satan* was see commentary for Thomas 21.) Such a patriarchal god is foreign to Jesus. The *Father* He speaks of is not one based on primitive four-dimensional observations. What then was Jesus casting out of those people supposedly possessed of demons? Demons are entities that have lost their way or rejected the Light. They fear the Light of the Source (Thomas 61), because their ego will not allow them to be one with the collective. They are the ones charmed and consumed by this realm (Thomas 7). All humans have demonic remnants and these characteristics stem from the creature people evolved from. Their beastly, antagonistic tendency is evidence of the primal man in battle with the collective consciousness (Holy Spirit). It is analogous to the chaotic transition that some humans experience as teenagers. The source of all things, the one Yeshua calls Father, extends past the fourth-dimension of time into all other dimensions. People can only experience this when they are liberated from the concept of self. *77th Pearl: The Perpetual Tree* is the catalyst for the realisation that *the sheep is no longer the sacrifice*. This wisdom opens the eyes of the human to the Father's Light—*the one* who seeks to embrace us, not destroy us.

Without looking at the Gospel of Thomas *as a whole*, and recognising the metaphors that have an *interconnecting thread*, it is easy to look for the obvious meaning. Yeshua knew this would be the case within His contemporaries. At the beginning of this gospel we see the author include a subtle warning. The reader is told that these are the *secret sayings the living Jesus spoke* and Didymos Judas Thomas recorded. For Yeshua's actual purpose and message to be revealed to the world it was necessary for Him to give these cryptic sayings to one of His disciples. It is also important to recognise that in the opening statement it says, it was the *living Jesus* that spoke these words. This is a subtle way to reinforce that these are the words Jesus (Yeshua) actually spoke—they are not edited or paraphrased comments. Their cryptic nature of more than half of these sayings made them inaccessible to the authors of the canonical texts. The Gospel of Thomas *is a symbolic representative of the shepherd in this realm.* These words have come to find us—the sheep desired above others.

108. Jesus said, "Whoever drinks from my mouth will become like me; I myself shall become that person, and the hidden things will be revealed to him."

Human history has shown us that very few people have *drunk from the mouth of Jesus.* Rather, they have chosen to listen with closed hearts and minds. They have not wanted to meditate on the secret teachings Yeshua gave us through Thomas, but have looked for the things that will suit their needs. The concern of the faiths sharing the Abrahamic heritage has been to focus on creating a community. These communities have particular rituals and underlying dogma, defining them apart from the others. This patriarchal trait is one that is driven by the lion we see in Thomas 7. To be fair, the general populace is not without blame, as they seek the easy, least cognitive option. The Spirit does not inspire this focus on ritual and dogma, which is exclusive, rather than inclusive. These things are born of the flesh and its weaknesses. They are a result of humanity's primal fears, which *men* have shared. They are a result of human evolution, which makes people *think like men do and not like God would.* They are the desires of men to control the way the community thinks and acts. This is the lion, manifest as human (Thomas 7).

At this point, it is necessary to address a contentious issue for most Christians—the Eucharist and what it means. Thomas 108 has links with the *concept of partaking* of Jesus (Yeshua), in *a physical way*—such as in the Eucharistic meal, (specifically) during the Catholic Mass. For most Christians, the Eucharist is not thought of as the *transformed* body and blood of Jesus Christ. However, the Catholics are taught that during the Mass the bread and wine are changed—in metaphysical substance, not appearance or actual material. This teaching comes from the Gospel of John, Chapter 6. We should consider, biblical scholars see the Gospel of John as being written, possibly, by three different authors, who added to the original, unfinished gospel. There are scholars who argue that it precedes all other Synoptic Gospels, because of its more accurate chronology of events and description of places. However, it's obvious aim to portray Yeshua (and Thomas) in a certain way brings into question its accuracy and intention. The language used and its content reveals an impassioned group of believers creating a persuasive text. The consensus among biblical scholars is that The Gospel of John was the last in the chronology of canonical texts. If one reads this gospel objectively, it becomes apparent that it is a subjective perspective and a rather romanticised one. It reflects the authors' passion for an ideology, which is Jesus Christ, as the *only Son of God*. As mentioned in other commentaries, the author(s) of John are antagonistic towards the Gospel of Thomas and portray Thomas as a simpleton. This was made possible by Thomas's response to Yeshua's question in Thomas 13, because Thomas did not have the language to say *what Yeshua was like*. Moreover, this distinction made Thomas *the new wineskin*, for the new wine, which was Yeshua's message disclosed to one disciple (Thomas 47). The other disciples looked to the knowledge that was rooted in myth and legend, found in the Old Testament (Torah). The author of John could not fathom the concept of *the Light*, which is in Yeshua, also being within all humans. Catholic apologists use the following sections of John Chapter 6 to argue their position on the Eucharist meal:

John 6:51: 'I am the living bread that came down from heaven; if anyone eats of this bread, he will live forever; and the bread which I shall give for the life of the world is my flesh'

John 6: 53-56, 'Truly, truly, I say to you, unless you eat the flesh of the Son of man and drink his blood, you have no life in you; he who eats my flesh and drinks my blood has eternal life, and I will raise him up at the last day. For my flesh is food indeed, and my blood is drink indeed. He who eats my flesh and drinks my blood abides in me, and I in him'

There is a strange irony in the attitude of the Catholic Church, as opposed to the Protestants and fundamentalists. The latter do not take these words literally, the Catholic Clergy do. A distinction is drawn here between the Clergy and parishioners, because a significant proportion of the laity either do not understand, or see the bread and wine transformation in a figurative, rather than literal sense. From the references in John 6, we see how the author introduces *the notion* of a ritual practice, which unifies believers with Jesus, in the only way they could imagine. This is because they did not understand the *Spiritual* Jesus, the one that is revealed to us in the Gospel of Thomas. They wanted to see Yeshua as the god-king, entirely different to mortal humans. In the sayings of Thomas, we see that we become a part of what Yeshua is— the kingdom, which is constituted of Spirits, unified through the collective consciousness (the Holy Spirit in action). The statements in John, attributed to Yeshua, are the passionate words of men. They were drunk with knowledge they accumulated from the Old Testament (Torah), and the notion of what Yeshua was (Thomas 28).

If we put Thomas 108 next to the last part of John 6:56, we begin to see how certain teachings of Yeshua had been taken out of context, or extrapolated to the point where they were distorted. Thomas 108 states: '*Whoever drinks from my mouth will become like me; I myself shall become that person, and the hidden things will be revealed to him.*' In John 6:56 we have: '*Whoever eats my flesh and drinks my blood lives in me and I live in that person.*' Notice, both are essentially saying the same thing. If we live in Yeshua and Yeshua in us (in John) the same is true when, in Thomas, we become like Yeshua and the hidden things are revealed to us. The human can only experience the hidden things when they are like Yeshua (Jesus). This link is fortified from the first part of Thomas 108, where we *become like Yeshua*, when we drink from His mouth. Again, the distinction between the two sayings is the inference, what it actually means to partake of Yeshua—is it from His knowledge (mouth) or is it literally His body and blood?

It is unlikely that the author of John was thinking of this in a literal way, but rather as an attempt to bring people closer to Yeshua. The author would have been encouraging Christians to see the Eucharist as Yeshua's presence with them, not in actual, *physical* terms. After all, if one could not fathom the teachings we see in Thomas, then how does one feel the connection to Yeshua and the Father? Take note of John 6:63: 'It is the spirit that gives life, the *flesh has nothing to offer. The words I have spoken to you are spirit and they are life.* [emphasis added]' Here we see the author of John being careful to affirm what we see in Thomas 108. *From Jesus' mouth we receive the words He has spoken. This is the bread of life*, which we should *take part in.* His blood is symbolic of the collective consciousness (Holy Spirit), which links all Souls seeking the Light. Again, in John 6:63: '*The words I have spoken to you are spirit and they are life.*' Remember, when Yeshua spoke of life, or to live, He was referring to the Soul coming to life, not the body.

What He aimed to show us is how to resurrect the Spirit in us—this is the only *circumcision* of value (Thomas 53).

Through the Gospel of Thomas, we see that the bread Yeshua speaks of is the knowledge He came to deliver. His blood was *poured out for us*, this represents the Holy Spirit—*the thing linking and sustaining every human seeking the Light*, it flows through all things with the Source (Thomas 77). This may sound contradictory, since we have established that God the Father (Source) flows through all things, but this, again, is where we meet with the concept of the Trinity. *The Trinity is an interrelationship* between the three elements, which cannot be separated. Where the Father is, so too is the Son and the Holy Spirit. In destroying the flesh, through the *pouring out of His blood*, Jesus showed us how the lamb defeats the lion. This knowledge is *food for our life*, the life in Spirit, not in the physical form. People must remember that this world, and the body we live in, is the carcass; it is the poverty Yeshua speaks of in Thomas 56 and 80. He would not advocate the thought of eating flesh and blood, because these are things from this realm, not the Spirit realm. As mentioned above, this is made clear in John 6:63: 'It is the spirit that gives life, the *flesh has nothing to offer*' [emphasis added]. In the Spirit realm these physical elements are, of course, different. They are mirrored here, in our universe, in tangible ways—*the words and actions of Yeshua*. In the realm of the Spirit, the bread is the substance of Spirit, *made active* by the collective consciousness. The life and the blood, is, as it is here—the collective consciousness (Holy Spirit), *It* unifies and nourishes these links. These are the *actions* of the woman, adding leaven to dough, in order to make large loaves of bread (Thomas 96). The leaven is what grows in us. It is the Soul. It grows into a Spirit—the large loaves. This is made possible by *ingesting what Yeshua came here to give us—the spring of life, the knowledge, and wisdom*. It is the knowledge of the hidden things. Declaring that the Eucharist becomes the actual body and blood of Jesus, and that people are ingesting this, is not a healthy position to take for the growth of the Soul. The maturation of the Soul and its successful and eternal link to God the Source was Yeshua's purpose in this realm.

The kind of ideology and practice we see in the Catholic Church also plays into *the function of the coin* discussed in the commentary for Thomas 32, in reference to exorcism. It is well known that some theistic Satanist sects have been involved in the stealing of the Catholic Eucharist. This is the coin at work. These people aim to do the opposite of what humans know is good, and right. They also wish to use *holy symbols* for their unholy and self-indulgent intentions—they are the *opposite side of this coin*. When a person wishing to inflict this kind of malice steals the Catholic Eucharist, it hurts those who believe it to be the actual body and blood of Jesus. In being given the tools by which to inflict this hurt, that individual or group succeeds in their intentions. This is how the coin functions in this situation, because, as mentioned previously, it has become a *symbiotic relationship*. It is a relationship mortal men have created. If the physicality of the Eucharist were not literal, as in the Catholic ideology, these people would not have this (perceived) power. This is another reason why people must separate the physical/material realm from the realm of the Spirit. This universe has been inspired by, and is influenced by, *the other*. It is not an intentional, perfect creation (Thomas 97). If it were intentional and holistic it would not be filled with suffering and chaos. Even the Jesus in the Gospel of John reminds us '*the flesh has nothing to offer*', so why make something sacred that is of no value?

If individuals seek to find truth, they will find it, because the path of the Spirit is true. There are many roads through the woods, the wood is *one* and the destination is the same. However, the question arises, what does the human soul become *when it joins* to that destination? (Thomas 11). In the human realising that the seed cannot exist without the tree, what then? The reality of *what we are* and *where we will go*, beyond this existence, is what humans need to come to terms with. Who do we join, to *become two*? It is only through the truth in Yeshua's words, recorded in the Gospel of Thomas and disclosed through *77ᵗʰ Pearl: The Perpetual Tree*, that humans will realise who they truly are. Humanity's profound connection to God the Source, the one Yeshua refers to as *Father*, is ratified in these secret teachings.

Thomas 108 is linked to Thomas 62, where Yeshua speaks about those who are *worthy of His mysteries*. We find, through this link, that people are made worthy by their desire to know the truth. In this way, they may drink from Jesus' mouth, because *He is as all sentient beings are*. When we look at the links, made throughout the Gospel of Thomas, we start to see there are strategic threads woven through these sayings. They reveal truths, but to find these threads one must actively seek them, as we see in Thomas 94. Through actively seeking truth people can see the threads. For example, it can be seen *woven through* Thomas 2, 5, 17, 19, 49, 62, 66, 68, 69, 70, 82, 85, 92, 94, 99, 101, 105, 107, and 111. These sayings make reference to the *individual journey* towards Divine wisdom. They reveal *the intimate link humans share with Yeshua, through the collective consciousness (Holy Spirit) and the Father's Light* (Thomas 77). In this way, these threads are also linked to Thomas 108.

The question of worthiness is very important. It is because of religious institutions, which have made people feel unworthy, that we must focus on the truth of what it actually means to be worthy. It is not the purging and denial of the flesh that makes one worthy of the truth (Thomas 6 and 14). One is worthy if one sees the world the way it truly is. It is made of physical material, which by its nature decays (Thomas 56). This extends to humans' mortal bodies, (Thomas 80) housing the immortal Soul. This realm makes humans inclined to violent and selfish actions, based on their primal evolution and heritage (Thomas 7). The struggle between the Spirit—seeking balance, harmony, and unity—and the flesh—manifest as the symbol of the fierce and proud lion (Thomas 7)—has created for us these institutions. They are somewhere between the *two opposing states of being*. In this facile place, between the two, the Soul cannot grow, because people are made to feel unworthy. The flesh becomes an obstacle—and it is a large obstacle, which has done much damage to the relationship humans should have with God the Father/Source. If people *drink from Yeshua's mouth* and become Him, what of this life and its obstacles? How do humans navigate these things with this new perspective? The answer is to look towards the logical and intuitive self. Reject the fear-based dogma generated by those consumed by the lion (Thomas 7). This then would become the dawn of the enlightened generations.

Consider how women in economically disadvantaged countries, having no access to education, do not have control over how many children they give birth to. The Christian orthodoxy removes this choice from them, because these women are led to believe that it is a sin to use birth control. Their body becomes the property of their god and not of themselves. This misguided attitude is the cause of much suffering. It is also leading to a point where the earth's resources will not be able to sustain future populations, as we struggled to do at the beginning of the twenty-first century. This is an issue on a global scale, but the concept of worthiness comes down to the individual plight. We see this when people who are not heterosexual are made to feel like their own creator shuns them. In the Gospel of Thomas the truth is revealed. The truth is that humans are not the flesh they are wrapped in. They must look at the things it does as mechanisms of its primal evolution, not as divinely ordained. The damage incurred is because of people's mythological vision of a Creator God, who has all things mapped out for them. This includes whom they should be partnered with, based on the notion that they should breed. This premise, rooted in primal needs for survival, must cease if this planet is to continue to be inhabitable by humans. If it does not stop, these bodies will perish and the Light within them will move to other sentient beings, which will evolve in the future. This has been *the pattern* in other galaxies and it will continue for a limited time in this universe (Thomas 111). This is why it is important that people see the truth and stop proliferating their own destruction. Those who are besotted by this life see benefit in making humans think they are unworthy. This keeps souls bound up in this dimension. It is entirely profitable for souls, captivated by this realm, to perpetuate suffering. What better way than religious dogma—a convincing mask. When people are free of suffering, then they can truly follow a path into the enlightened future. For this to occur they must nurture this world, so that suffering is minimised. When the body is healthy, the mind is free. Then the soul can evolve to its fullest potential.

In Thomas 108, we see something that turns most Christians' understanding of Jesus on its head. The language Yeshua uses in the Gospel of Thomas, and as re-contextualised by authors in the canonical gospels, has led most denominations to think of Yeshua as God, or the only Son of God. The Gospel of Thomas supports the idea that Yeshua was indeed *a Son of God*. Where Thomas differs is in the understanding that all beings seeking the Light are the Son of God. The definition of 'God' is not understood as an ethereal entity, which has created everything through a Divine Plan. It is the Source, defined as the 'Father', by Yeshua. Also evident in the Gospel of Thomas, His divinity is as a result from the intimate connection to this Source. The distinction between this gospel and the canonical gospels, is that humanity is very much a part of the same divinity. Yeshua is the one who opens humanities eyes to the hidden, invisible Light. When Yeshua says, 'whoever drinks from my mouth will become like me; I myself shall become that person', He describes a most wondrous event for us, which destroys all misconceptions of being unworthy or inherently sinful. This also tells us that we are intimately connected to Jesus, through the collective consciousness (Holy Spirit) and the Father/Source's Light (Thomas 77). When people drink from the knowledge and wisdom Jesus came to deliver, they are set free. They are also free from the narrow vision they may have had of Jesus. This is when they are able to become like Him. We are His kin. In this knowledge He becomes connected to us—then the hidden things are revealed.

109. Jesus said, "The (Father's) kingdom is like a person who had a treasure hidden in his field but did not know it. And [when] he died he left it to his [son]. The son [did] not know about it either. He took over the field and sold it. The buyer went plowing, [discovered] the treasure, and began to lend money at interest to whomever he wished."

As in other sayings in the Gospel of Thomas, we see the Father's Kingdom compared to a *situation rather than a place*, as some might typically envisage a kingdom. In Thomas 109, the Father's Kingdom is compared to a treasure. The treasure is hidden in a field and the owner of the land is unaware of its presence. When the land is sold off by a second generation, the new owner discovers the hidden treasure and proceeds to benefit from his find. This saying describes a process common to our human experience, as sentient beings. It describes the history of our spiritual progression. Yeshua had no concerns for financial gain, so it is clear that the wealth described here is from something spiritual. The interest that is gained is from the collective consciousness (Holy Spirit). This connection is priceless (Thomas 44).

The first time a primal ancestor was inspired to be creative, was the time *a glimmer of the treasure appeared in the soil of this field*. The field, in Thomas 109, is symbolic of this world and all the physical experiences humans encounter. The Soul (the treasure) is covered in flesh—people have to discover it, before they can *profit* from this estate. The flesh is symbolically related to the field; it is of this realm, which becomes the carcass (Thomas 56 and 80). The treasure in that field continued to grow as humans became increasingly aware of their situation, beyond the flesh and bone they experienced in this existence. The buyer in Thomas 109 is symbolic of the beings that were aware of a greater reality beyond this one. They were actively *searching* for the answers to humanity's predicament. This knowledge is related to *the treasure*. The first symbol of the *buyer* can be seen in the Buddha (Prince Siddhartha Gautama) and the next was John the Baptist. Yeshua was intimately connected to the treasure—the Father/Source—through the collective consciousness (Holy Spirit).

The Buddha was seeking a way out of the cycle of suffering, which he saw as inherent to this existence. He found freedom through the acceptance of the world as it is. In doing so, Buddha found a way to escape all desires, which he identified were at the center of human suffering. He described these, and how to escape them, within the *Four Noble Truths*. To see all experiences as clouds, which appear and disappear, was essential in this process. The acceptance of humanity's predicament brings people into a state of peace with all things.

It enables the human to become an observer and *passerby* (Thomas 42). Alternatively, the person may become a victim in this life. If they become a victim, they search for ways to clear themselves of a situation or negative experience. This brings them back to this life, in an endless loop (see commentary for Thomas 7 for more on the Buddha Dharma). Yeshua affirms what the Buddha discovered, through his struggles to attain enlightenment, when He tells us to *be passersby*. The Buddha unintentionally constructed for humanity one half of a bridge, which extended out *from this realm*—reaching toward the realm of the Spirit. Yeshua completed this bridge when He was sent to us *from the realm of the Spirit* (Thomas 98). In Thomas 98 we see Yeshua as *the hand* that holds the sword, which penetrated the separation between these realms. John the Baptist is the fulcrum between the Buddha and Jesus. John heralded a new beginning in people's relationship with God the Father/Source (Thomas 46). John could recognise the faults in the faiths that had Abraham as their patriarch. Those beliefs became filled with empty rituals and dogma. He indicated that the relationship humans were required to have with the Source was intimate and internalised, rather than a contractual one. This contractual relationship is all humans had as *mere creations of a Creator God*. John ratified this promise through baptism. It is not coincidental that we see water used in this process, as it is symbolic of the *two becoming one*. In this realm, all things attempt to imitate the perfect nature of the Spirit realm. However, just as the male and female are separate (Thomas 22), so too are the elements that join to become water. Despite John's profound desire to see a shift in the way people responded to God the Father, he was not aware of the true nature of this relationship (Thomas 46). John's attempt saw him use water to purify followers from their perceived sins, in the hope that they would feel worthy of God the Father (Source). This was problematic, since it did not recognise that God, *the Father, is not one anthropomorphised entity*. God the Father, the source of all things was, in reality, everywhere, at the same time (Thomas 77). Humans are Its offspring, by virtue of the Soul. In understanding and communicating about this relationship *Yeshua revealed the treasure that is in the field.* As a result, all people can now profit from this knowledge, immeasurably.

110. Jesus said, "Let one who has found the world, and has become wealthy, renounce the world."

Thomas 110 describes what the Buddha (Prince Siddhartha Gautama) discovered approximately six hundred years before Jesus. Prince Siddhartha was born into a royal family with great wealth and power. The young Prince's parents tried to shield him from the realities of the outside world. Eventually, he discovered that outside the palace walls his people were suffering. He set out to find a way to end the cycle of misery. The Hindu faith supports the notion of reincarnation—the society from which the Buddha came was of this faith. Prince Siddhartha became a disciple of various ascetic masters, to no avail, so he sought to find his own path to enlightenment. Ultimately, he discovered that we must not become disturbed by this life and that all desire is a path to suffering. If a person accepts things for what they are, they nullify the impact these material elements can have on the individual. This is the very same message Yeshua gives humanity in His simple statement, 'be passersby' (Thomas 42). Through this mantra, Mary, the mother of Yeshua, attained to the Spirit. Moreover, because of this statement, she could be considered *ever virgin.* Mary lived her life as a normal woman of her time, but was *untouched* by this world. In this way, she most certainly remained a *pure spirit* as she passed through this physical existence. Although Yeshua was not aware of the Buddha, the collective consciousness (Holy Spirit), which links all Spirit beings, made this knowledge available through the Source. God the Father (Source) has no linear time. It is the whole. It is therefore not a coincidence that this saying is here. Thomas 110 pays homage to the one that worked so hard to discover this truth.

In the European Middle Ages (c. 1000 – 1300 AD), people became focused on the next life; this was primarily a reflection of the power and influence of the Catholic Church. The Middle Ages saw the wealthy pay their way out of Divine punishment (called indulgences). This left the less fortunate to rely on devotion to the Church, in the hope of being saved from purgatory or hell. Those able to pay for indulgences believed they would bypass this retribution. They had, in effect, purchased favor from God. The God that had given the keys to the kingdom of Heaven to the, *presumed*, leader of the Christian Church in this realm. We see this evidence in Matthew 16:15-19. The author conveys how Jesus responds to Simon Peter's answer regarding *who* the disciples say Jesus is:

"'But you,' he said, 'who do you say I am?' Then Simon Peter spoke up and said, 'You are the Christ, the Son of the living God.' Jesus replied, 'Simon son of Jonah, you are a blessed man! Because it was no human agency that revealed this to you but my Father in heaven. So I now say to you: You are Peter and on this rock I will build my community. And the gates of the underworld can never overpower it. I will give you the keys of the kingdom of Heaven: whatever you bind on earth will be bound in heaven; whatever you loose on earth will be loosed in heaven.'"

We know that this is not an accurate account of what occurred, since this gospel was written after the Gospel of Mark, which was written approximately a century after Yeshua's death. The account in Thomas 13 confirms that it was Thomas who was worthy of the Divine truths. The other disciples were not able to fathom these teachings, nor would they have accepted them. This is evident in the last sentence of Thomas 13. In Thomas, 13 the question was: 'Compare me to something and tell me *what I am like*?' In Matthew's version the question is changed so that it becomes: '*who do you say I am*?' In this way, Matthew's question is less of a conundrum—it becomes a *leading question*, pointing to Yeshua's divinity, rather than a test. Through the test in Thomas 13, Yeshua saw that Thomas was the only disciple who *did not have the language to describe what Jesus was like*. In recognising this, Yeshua knew Thomas would be the one to record His mysteries, without the danger of editing or reinterpreting them. The language in Matthew 16:15-19 clearly shows an author's polemic intentions. This culturally motivated intention affirms previous commentaries, which present the notion of the Synoptic Gospel authors' desiring *a community (Church)*. These desires came from an underlying patriarchal belief system. In the last line of the excerpt from Matthew, the author adds a very damaging statement, one that gave the Catholic Church much power. This statement ultimately opened the church up to corruption by the lion, who presents as human (Thomas 7). The notion that one man could decide what is good for all souls, on earth and in heaven, is flawed when we consider the teachings of *the living Jesus, in the Gospel of Thomas*. This presumption demonstrates a complete lack of knowledge and understanding on behalf of the author of Matthew. Indeed, Yeshua was correct when He made the prophetic statement that He was to inadvertently bring suffering, not peace, into the world in Thomas 16. Yeshua saw that the lion (Thomas 7) ruled over men. He knew their need for power and control would see politically motivated individuals create institutions in His name. Institutions that yielded much destructive influence and power. While these individuals may have had good intentions initially, their lack of understanding saw them create texts which were open to dogma. Some dogma was based on Old Testament edicts and influenced by pagan beliefs, others generated from a need to create a community united in belief and practice. All of these are influences *from* this realm and not of the Spirit. The corruption of Yeshua's teachings peaked in the Middle Ages, when the crusades endeavored to claim back territories from the Muslims. Moreover, the social inequities in the Feudal System, supported by the Church, fulfilled Yeshua's lament in Thomas 16. These inequities within the community, and corruption within the Church, essentially led to the Reformation, which is also part of Yeshua's prophetic pronouncement in Thomas 16. In the Reformation, we see the splintering of the Catholic Church into Protestant Churches, which rejected the authority of the Pope and the dogma not already written into the Bible. The issues arising out of Matthew 16 give the instruction in Thomas 110 added weight. However, it is an instruction many did not comprehend—for it has hidden facets.

In Thomas 110, people could easily fall into the trap of thinking like the people of the Middle Ages—the physical life becomes unimportant. In the Gospel of Thomas, Yeshua asks us *to see the world as transitory and to be passersby* (Thomas 42). The focus becomes an awareness of the disparity between the flesh and the soul that inhabits it. This truth comes hand-in-hand with the fact that a soul has the opportunity to inhabit a body, so that they may aggregate the Source's Light. This is the key to Thomas 110. *Becoming wealthy* is a broad term for becoming *enriched in this realm.* A person engages with all its alluring physical and emotive pleasures for the purposes of learning from them. This experience is a double-edged sword. It is necessary for us to experience this life to come to the understanding that it is a mirror of the realm within. The trick is to find the world, *become wealthy in wisdom through experience*, and then let it go upon death. This is why Yeshua willingly gave up His body, so that humanity comes to know that all they have in this realm is fleeting and should not be *held onto*. In this way, Yeshua also died for people's sins, because He showed us that we have an intimate connection with God the Source—the one Jesus refers to as *Father*. In destroying the flesh, which people had been led to believe was a sacred and individual creation, they come to realise that the sins of the flesh are *created of the flesh*—that is, this realm's inadequacies. Sins of the flesh are *born of this realm* and they do not impede the Soul unless people allow them to control their lives (Thomas 6 and 14). All our experiences in this realm are lessons, which make us worthy to look at Jesus as our brother (Thomas 62).

Artists of the late Renaissance painted allegorical artworks that became a kind of genre and tradition known as Vanitas. These paintings implied the emptiness and pointless nature of pleasurable activities in everyday life. In these artworks, one might see a human skull that would represent the impermanence of life; an open book indicating the frivolity of excessive learning; decaying fruit, symbolic of aging and death; a peeled lemon that may look attractive, but is bitter to taste, just like life. This attitude is one we could easily derive from Thomas 110, but it would be incorrect to do so. In Thomas 29 we see Yeshua state: '*If the flesh came into being because of spirit, that is a marvel, but if spirit came into being because of the body, that is a marvel of marvels.*' This statement was covertly aimed at clarifying the true nature of our creation, which His contemporaries misunderstood. Indeed, this realm, and the flesh, was created from the *incidental expansion* of the Source's Light (Thomas 97). *Then sentient bodies evolved* to house Its Light (Thomas 96). The second part of Thomas 29 clearly shows us that to think the Spirit came into being because of the body would be a reversal of these events. Moreover, *the Father's Light is through all things (Thomas 77) and precedes all matter.* These events have played out just as scientists understand evolution. Humans are given the opportunity, through this world and these *bodies,* to come back to the Father, to re-join the Source as enlightened Spirits. This is *Its desire* (Thomas 107). The Vanitas allegories we can see in some late Renaissance paintings reflect *the attitude of a fallen people.* They believed their god had turned away from them, because they experienced this existence with a desire for knowledge and a passion for life. In the eyes of Church leaders, who mistakenly saw man as innately sinful, this reflected *sinful pride,* which was an affront to their god. To seek any truth beyond Church authority was seen as dangerous and assumed a position similar to Adam and Eve. They wanted the fruit from the tree of knowledge—*to be like their God.* In the Gospel of Thomas, we discover that *we already are like God the Father/Source,* if we choose to see it. If we do not, we become the poverty (Thomas 3).

Thomas 110 is liberating. It confirms that we as humans need to experience this life and all it has to offer. At the same time, we must not lose sight of what we are – a Soul growing in stature, becoming a living Spirit.

111. Jesus said, "The heavens and the earth will roll up in your presence, and whoever is living from the living one will not see death."

Does not Jesus say, "Those who have found themselves, of them the world is not worthy"?

Yeshua's wisdom, pertaining to the nature of this realm, is reflected in what scientists have learnt regarding the life and death of planets, stars, and galaxies. The evolution of this planet and all its life forms has been proven and accepted by the Catholic Church. Its eventual demise goes hand-in-hand with this evolution. The precise way it will end is difficult to know, since humans, consumed by the lion (Thomas 7), are a variable that may make this ending come sooner. The best-case scenario would be the death of planet Earth's sun, millions of years beyond the twenty-first century. The description of the *heavens and the earth rolling up in our presence* is apt when one considers the way the world may end, given the death of a star.

Thomas 111 has a strong thread linking it to Thomas 18, when Yeshua tells people that '*the end will be where the beginning is*'. This tells us we are an energy—best be described as Light. Light, in the physical realm, is a positive and creative thing. Metaphorically speaking, it reveals what is hidden—because of this it is void of fear and absent of evil (Thomas 61). At the time a person's physical body perishes, or when the planet Earth ceases to exist, the energy they become is the thing they really are—a soul. That thing existed at the beginning and it will be at the end. If a person does not make this realisation while they are in human form, when they die they will *look for the living one and they will not recognise It*. This is because humans do not see themselves as Its offspring (Thomas 59).

The first statement by Yeshua in Thomas 111, uses language that infers these events will occur to those He was speaking with, over two thousand years ago. The use of second person allows this statement to speak to us in the same way. This language device reveals a truth. The energy that is from the Father's Light is what we are—a soul. The Source seeks to join with the Soul (Thomas 107), by aggregating *Its Light* within the body. This happens through the knowledge and growing awareness of our intimate connection to the Source. This is *the time a person's consciousness links to the collective*, which is the Holy Spirit in action. Beings who see a physical body as their identity and image are in danger (Thomas 83). Souls that do not evolve into spirits are continually absorbed into the whole, remaining in this dimension. In this way, the event of the heavens and the earth rolling up is something unenlightened humans will experience, because *the Soul's Light is eternal*. The difference between *tasting death* and *coming to life* is being joined to God the Source. When the human is in this state of connection or union, their energy will not be reabsorbed into the whole, to become something else. The living Spirit will experience the phenomenon of the death of a star, just as one might in a movie theatre. After this experience they may leave the theatre and enter the foyer, to await the opening of a new experience. This is the human's soul in the state of *motion and rest* (Thomas 50).

Feeling familiar in an encounter with someone you have just met is a connection to the energy of that person. These energies (souls) have shared experiences in other lifetimes and forms. They will not look the same, but there is a familiarity, which is intuitive. This energy is also scattered and fractured, because it has been reabsorbed and has lost fragments of itself and accumulated others parts. This is what Yeshua alludes to when He states that a soul, who does not recognise their life as being *from the living one*, would *experience death*. They will eventually be reabsorbed into the whole for a final time. This is reflected in what happens to a decaying corpse as the earth reclaims all the elements that composed the body. In this sense, the souls Yeshua was speaking to in His time may still be experiencing this dimension. If they do not evolve, they continually *taste death*. In the last line of Thomas 111, we see the author (Thomas) reiterate this point by adding the rhetorical question: '*Does not Jesus say, "Those who have found themselves, of them the world is not worthy?"*' Meaning, people who recognise the Light within (the soul), nurture *It* through the collective consciousness, will live on as a Spirit.

112. Jesus said, "Damn the flesh that depends on the soul. Damn the soul that depends on the flesh."

In the first part of Thomas 112, Yeshua describes a state of faith that is in confusion. It is a common misconception. Those people who look outside of the self to find connection with the *living one* are referred to as *the flesh*. They are the people who see their physical body as their identity—this is the misconception. In Thomas 22, 50, 83, and 84 we see a thread appear relating to the *image* – what people think they are. In the Gospel of Thomas, Yeshua affirms that *humans are not the body they inhabit*—they are not of this dimension, which is *the carcass* we see in Thomas 56 and 80. To depend on something is to look to a thing that is *outside of the self.* The first part of Thomas 112 describes people whose faith sees a *dependence on an external entity.* This deity has no relationship to them, other than the body they believe this ethereal being created for them. To these people, they are merely creations of their god. They depend on their god to bring them to life after death. This is the flesh hinging on the concept that, as their god intentionally made their body and implanted the soul into it, then life after death is a given. These people are seeing the soul as assurance that it will live on. It will keep the same gender, appearance, and familial and personal relationships in that afterlife. We know this is untrue.

The fact that some people are born with disabilities negates the premise of a personalised body, as there is no justification why one soul inhabits an able body and another does not. There are eastern religions that believe this to be a karmic cause of a past life transgression. This is not logical as most people cannot not recall a past life. This reality and the illnesses humans encounter are evidence of the imperfect, chaotic, and unstable nature of this realm. This is the carcass represented in Thomas 56 and 80. It also confirms this *creation is not one that is planned*, but is as a result of the *incidental expansion of God the Source, into the void* (Thomas 97).

Yeshua makes a strong statement when He curses the flesh (human) that depends on the soul. This is a broad statement, which describes how humans have been prone to ignoring the duality of the body and soul. These people are inclined to believe that the flesh animates the spirit (Thomas 29 and 84). This attitude is evident in the way Synoptic Gospels have a strong focus on healing of the body. In the Gospel of Thomas, the soul and its maturation is paramount. In Thomas 14 we see the only reference to the healing of the sick. However, in the Synoptic Gospels healing of the sick is a common theme. The authors of these texts saw this as a way to highlight Yeshua's ethereal, Divine power and lineage. This inadvertently created a hierarchical divide between His followers and the now mystical Jesus, which He did not intend. Why then did Yeshua heal the sick? Yeshua healed those in need, but He did not want to become the focus of these *symbolic actions*. The initial cautiousness was primarily because these actions gave the Pharisees evidence against Yeshua, as an agitator and someone who may be aspiring to take their authority away (Thomas 7 and 78). What Yeshua wanted was for people to see that it was *their faith that cured them*—that is, *their own link to God the Source is what cured them*. Yeshua was the catalyst for this process and so we see the statement, *your faith has healed you*, which appears many times in the canonical gospels.

Yeshua is demonstrating two very important and *symbolic* lessons in this *action of healing*. The first lesson is that the Spirit, linked to the Source through the collective consciousness (Holy Spirit), can do anything—to the extent of removing some physical obstacles people encounter in this life (Thomas 48). The second lesson is that the flesh is not a perfect creation, it requires healing, and is therefore not of the spiritual dimension. This flesh is a manifestation from the external, material layer of the Father's Light (Thomas 77 and 97). This realm has formed through its tendency to mirror the internal realm. It forms human beings for souls to be involved in *this process of motion and rest* (Thomas 50). When Yeshua *damns the flesh that depends on the soul,* He rebukes the people who do not understand that *their faith* healed them. They should have recognised the Light of God the Source inside themselves (Thomas 70 and 111). Yeshua damns those who have made Him into *the only Son of God.* In doing this, these people deny the intimate connection they share with Jesus—as His brother and His mother (Thomas 99). They are the flesh that *depends on the soul.*

Thomas 112 has a link to the second part of Thomas 29 where Yeshua says: 'If the flesh came into being because of spirit, that is a marvel, but *if spirit came into being because of the body, that is a marvel of marvels.* [emphasis added]'. In *77ᵗʰ Pearl: The Perpetual Tree*, we have established that the first part of Thomas 29 is recognition of the fact that humans came into being so the soul (what humans are) may become an awakened Spirit. This truth is indeed a marvel. In the second part of Thomas 29, we see Yeshua use a sarcastic tone when He states that if the Spirit came into being *because of the body*, this would amount to a *marvel of marvels.* The reason for this is the order of things would have been reversed if that were true. When the woman (Thomas 97) went onto the distant road (the void) she left behind her the meal, which accidently spilled out of her jar. This was the expansion of God the Father/Source's Light, which unconsciously created all physical matter. Its Light flows through everything and creates all materiality in this realm. It becomes realised in humans. This invisible Light is the Source. It exists of Itself. The *Father created* all things—*It* is the Source in all things—but *this action was not a conscious decision*. It is the sarcastic statement in Thomas 29, which allows us to see why Yeshua damns the soul that depends on the flesh, for if the spirit came into being because of the body *that would be a 'marvel of marvels'*.

In the second part of Thomas 112, Yeshua speaks to those who are infatuated with the flesh and rely on their *physical relationships* for their identity, as we see in Thomas 87. This group of people would point to their family, spouse, children, and (or) reflection when asked who or what they are. In *reality*, it is not possible to point to something we cannot see (Thomas 83). This is something people need to realise, if they are to define themselves apart from this finite realm.

Thomas 112 is an example of spiritual rhetoric, which can be taken out of its context and used in a damaging way by those who have an agenda. When Yeshua states, '*damn the soul that depends on the flesh*,' this can be interpreted as a criticism of people who take care of their body by exercising and eating healthy foods or enjoying sexual contact. The fact that Yeshua saw the need to heal the bodies of His contemporaries, gives us an understanding that Yeshua recognised the importance of being free of physical suffering. The reason this was important was practical. If an individual is consumed by continual suffering, with an affliction or illness, then they cannot comfortably pursue the growth of the soul. This is also true of guilt. When humans are free of such physical and emotional obstacles, they are able to freely meditate on the connection with God the Father/Source, through the medium we know as the collective consciousness (Holy Spirit). However, this may become an issue when the focus on health shifts to a focus on vanity. In cases where people become obsessed with diet and exercise, because of the way they believe they should look, this may become an obstacle toward spiritual growth. The answer is moderation. The priority is a healthy body—all other benefits flow on from this. People who obsess about appearance have become victims of the lion—the primitive aspect of the sentient body (Thomas 7).

The second part of Thomas 112 may also be seen as making reference to people who desire and take pleasure in sexual contact. Unfortunately, Church dogma has involved itself with the questions of sex. This is more a reflection of the weaknesses and guilt of the clergy, which created this dogma, rather than the teachings of Jesus. Thomas 112 is not judgemental of people who enjoy and desire sex, because these activities are ones influenced by the body, its hormones and physical needs. Sexual desires are a manifestation of primal urges. They can be positive, physical experiences with the self or shared with another. If sexual coupling can be seen as making *a connection with another soul*, then this kind of sex has become profitable, beyond the physical satisfaction or release it may bring. It is not beneficial for religious organisations to create rules about sexual behaviour. This will ultimately *cause individuals to feel bad about the self, because of the body*. If the sexual activity is between consenting adults then it harms no one and should not be cause for *guilt* (Thomas 6). Sexual contact reflects the way the Soul desires to link with the thing it came from. This form of linking is yet another example of the material realm mirroring the spiritual dimension.

Allowing the body to become an obstacle to spiritual growth is placing the body above the Soul. If people are to *become passersby* (Thomas 42) then they cannot allow sexual activity to be a thing that blocks them from progression. If we look at the body as a vessel and tool by which we experience this life then we can move beyond such obstacles. For some individuals, things that are made taboo become more appealing, because of the implied danger that comes with engaging in these activities. If they are no longer taboo, they become less of a thrill. There is a vicious cycle some people may fall into. They may constantly desire the thrill which comes from doing something dangerous. Naturally, this is not healthy for the body and the soul. In such a situation, the individual must look to the self and ask why they are seeking to fill a void in their life. The replacement for this void ultimately leaves them empty, wanting something *more*. Looking to the self to find the appropriate questions, the answers will also come. This internal dialogue opens a window that lets light in—allowing the individual to see for the first time.

Engaging in sexual activity can be a multifaceted lesson. Individuals can learn about themselves and about others. They can experience how we all suffer in similar ways, because of the very human insecurities that come with a sentient body. This is not to suggest that all sexual experiences are less than pleasant or loaded with such psychological and layered results. Even humans experiencing how their physical bodies bring them momentary pleasures and relief from the realities of life can benefit through these observations. In this way, sexual activity can be a path of beneficial knowledge. If people who enjoy and desire sex allow it to affect their spiritual growth then they *damn the soul by allowing it to be dependent on the actions of the flesh* (saying altered for effect).

113. His disciples said to him, "When will the kingdom come?"

"It will not come by watching for it. It will not be said, 'Look, here!' or 'Look, there!' Rather, the Father's kingdom is spread out upon the earth, and people don't see it."

In Thomas 3 and 51, we see a thread which links with Thomas 113. In Thomas 113, Yeshua tells people that '*the Father's kingdom is spread out upon the earth*'. This tells us the nature of the kingdom and where it is. It is not a place anyone can point to, or give directions to. It is '*spread out upon the earth*', because *humanity is spread out on the Earth*. We are the sentient beings, in this solar system, which *carry the kingdom within us*. The author (Thomas) has created a poignant metaphor by having two similar sayings at the beginning and end of this gospel. We see this here, in Thomas 113, and at the beginning of the text, in Thomas 3. They stand as bookends, supporting the profound truths we discover within the Gospel of Thomas. When we look at the very different content and voice found in Thomas 114, the reason Thomas 113 is 'the end' of the mysteries becomes clear.

In Thomas 3, Yeshua tells us the notion of a kingdom above us is a misguided concept. When people think of *the Father's Kingdom*, their entire concept of a kingdom has to be reconfigured. In the past, this definition came out of observations from human society. A kingdom was seen as a strong community, built around a fortified city. The Father's Kingdom, as defined by Yeshua, is seen as *actions, rather than a place*. These actions occur in locations we cannot see, because they are hidden by the Source's Light (Thomas 83). *They live in the human.* That is why, in Thomas 50, Yeshua tells people to respond to the question, '*What is the evidence of your Father in you?*', by declaring it is '*motion and rest*'. It is the Soul's movement through these bodies, and this dimension, which enables people to amass the Father's Light within them. In this way, humans need to be in constant motion in this existence—experiencing, learning, and growing in wisdom. This is apparent in Thomas 86: '*…human beings have no place to lay down and rest.*' A soul only comes to rest when physical life ends. It either comes to life as a spirit, or becomes part of the whole, to be absorbed into a new body.

In Thomas 113, Yeshua reveals that those who are waiting for the day when He comes back to Earth, to judge the living and the dead, will not see such a day (Thomas 18, 38). This notion goes hand in hand with the kingdom arriving on earth, from heaven, with Yeshua as its king. In Thomas 113 we learn that it is already here. Since the kingdom is already here, there can be no rapture in the form of the 'second coming', nor can we expect to hear, or see, Yeshua in this realm again. There is a thread we can find within the Gospel of Thomas, which shows us that Yeshua was human—flesh and bone. At the same time, He was the *Son of God*, just as all beings of the Light are the progeny of God the Father/Source (Thomas 15, 28, and 65). Therefore, there is a definitive separation between the flesh and the Spirit, just as there is a separation between this realm and the holistic realm of the Source. To look for the kingdom with the eye of the flesh is flawed. Rather, people should look for the kingdom with *the eye of the heart*—the thing that is linked to God the Source. This is the collective consciousness (Holy Spirit) in action (Thomas 44).

In Thomas 10 contains a statement that could easily be taken out of context by those people who believe in a 'second coming'. Jesus says: 'I have cast fire upon the world, and look, I'm guarding it until it blazes.' One could take this statement as an implied second coming. Until the thing He brought to this realm is ablaze, He would not reappear. Thomas 10 is not about a literal second coming. It is a statement about the connection people accomplish with Yeshua, *through the collective consciousness (Holy Spirit), with the Source of all things—the one Yeshua refers to as Father.* When Yeshua's teachings cause a *blaze within the individual,* He re-enters this realm (Thomas 82). Through this connection there is a second coming. When Yeshua says He is *guarding what He has cast upon the Earth,* He speaks about His teachings. They are the words in the Gospel of Thomas, illuminated in *77ᵗʰ Pearl: The Perpetual Tree.* In a sense, this text *is the second coming* observant humans have been anticipating (Thomas 94). Through these words, Yeshua's secret sayings have been elucidated for the generations requiring this Light. Moreover, unlike previous generations, people of the twenty-first century will be able to comprehend these teachings. When the human soul attains this wisdom it is lit up with *life.* This is when the kingdom is realised—within the person, through the heart and mind, the conduit that is the Holy Spirit.

Several of the sayings in the Gospel of Thomas reveal a thread. They show us that Yeshua was a Spirit within a body, just as humans find themselves to be a soul within a body. Through examples in the Synoptic Gospels, we have seen that the apostles' experiences of Jesus after His death were metaphysical, not physical. In Thomas 28, we see Yeshua tell His contemporaries He entered into this world, appearing to them *in flesh*. It is clear then, the body Yeshua inhabited was not who He was, it was simply a vehicle for His Spirit. Thomas 22 further supports the notion of the duality of body and soul. The metaphysical aspect of *the self* is also supported in Thomas 24, when the apostles ask Yeshua to *show them the place where He is, so that they may seek it out*. His response is a reference to *light, which shines on the whole world*. This links to Thomas 77, where we find that the *Light* is not what we experience in this world. It is a source of energy and creativity, which is unlike anything in this realm. It exists in, and flows through, everything. Its anatomy is the collective consciousness, what we know as the Advocate and Comforter, the Holy Spirit.

In Thomas 65 Yeshua tells people *the heir to the vineyard would be grabbed and killed*. This indicated that He knew what the Pharisees were planning. It would eventually *lead to His death*, at the hands of the Romans. Yeshua turned this violent act, driven by insecurity, into the greatest sacrifice and *emblematic action* throughout His teaching. Yeshua demonstrated the discrepancy between the flesh and the Spirit. His sacrifice also demonstrated the way the lion (Thomas 7) is inclined to devour the lamb. The lion represents the material realm and the lamb represents the soul, which grows into the sheep—that is, a spirit (Thomas 107). In Thomas 37, Yeshua responds to the question of *when He will appear again*, with a metaphoric statement—*when humans strip off their clothes without being ashamed, 'like little children'*. This means that when a person is stripped of the body, which may create emotive obstacles, they are able to be in the same realm as Yeshua. Spiritual beings become connected to Him through the collective consciousness (Holy Spirit). Until such a time, people cannot see Yeshua. This is reinforced in Thomas 38, when Yeshua says: '*There will be days when you will seek me and you will not find me.*' People can find *Yeshua's Light*, which is throughout the world, because *It is the Source* we see in Thomas 77. When people contemplate the teachings that He poured out onto the earth, like a cup of fire (Thomas 16), they are awakened to the truth. If people are near Yeshua, and all spiritual beings through the collective consciousness, then they are joined to God the Source. When a person experiences this union, the kingdom is realised in them.

[Saying probably added to the original collection at a later date:]

114. Simon Peter said to them, "Make Mary leave us, for females don't deserve life."

Jesus said, "Look, I will guide her to make her male, so that she too may become a living spirit resembling you males. For every female who makes herself male will enter the kingdom of Heaven."

Jesus was an intelligent and wise being, far beyond His contemporaries. In Thomas 39, Yeshua tells His disciples to '*be as sly as snakes and as simple as doves*' when they are confronted with obstinate people or communities. In Thomas 114, Yeshua practices what He preached when He diplomatically appeases Simon Peter. Yeshua shows us His frustration with Simon Peter's complete lack of understanding. In Thomas 22, Yeshua teaches His disciples that to enter the Father's

Kingdom they are required to '*make male and female into a single one, so that the male will not be male nor the female be female*'. From this, we gather that Simon Peter's request is in complete error. It demonstrated his lack of understanding, regarding the nature of the Spirit being without gender. Had Peter truly listened and comprehended Yeshua's teaching, he would not have suggested that Mary leave their presence, stating females do not deserve the knowledge which *brings the soul to life*. In response to Simon Peter's request, the frustrated Yeshua relents with the statement: '*Look, I will guide her to make her male, so that she too may become a living spirit resembling you males*.' This part of the statement is very telling, when we keep in mind Thomas 22. In this context, Yeshua's words appear out of place and contradictory. However, what the statement shows us is the way He understood whom He was dealing with, in that time. These were predominantly narrow-minded misogynists. This statement recognises that most of Jesus' disciples would not be capable of separating the flesh from the Spirit. Their understanding of the realm of the Spirit would remain rooted in primitive observations, based on the material world. Their primal desire to assert their gender-based dominance is another aspect of the lion we see in Thomas 7.

Knowing that most of Yeshua's disciples would not be able to separate themselves from their sexist and chauvinist backgrounds, He re-contextualises what was said to them in Thomas 22; stating in Thomas 114: 'For every female *who makes herself male* will enter the kingdom of Heaven.' [emphasis added]. This is a subtle and clever restating of Thomas 22 when Jesus states: '…make male and female into a single one, so that the male will not be male nor the female be female.' If females were to '*make themselves male*' and visa-versa, then these individuals would be genderless. This androgynous state is the nature of the Spirit. It was of course a physical impossibility to change sex in the time of Yeshua.

This fact supports the esoteric subtext, which is intended in Thomas 114. It is a subtext that was incomprehensible to most of Jesus' contemporaries.

It is an appropriate metaphor to have this saying at the end of the Gospel of Thomas. It describes the obstacles Jesus encountered in His time, which continued for many centuries after His death. Indeed, much has been written by scholars regarding how the Christian faith might have looked if the attitude we see in Thomas 114 was not the prevalent one. Perhaps the Christian orthodoxy would have been a progressive and inclusive group of institutions, which nurtured the growth of the individual soul—this is something we will never know. What we do know is that the subject matter and tone of Thomas 114 is unlike all the other sayings in the Gospel of Thomas, so it is easy to think it may not actually be a part of the original text. When we consider the strategic position it holds in this gospel, we can look at it as a prophetic marker. It was, and to a large extent, in the embryonic twenty-first century, still is, an indication of the narrow-minded view *men* hold onto. It was this narrow point of view Yeshua had to contend with throughout His life and His ministry in this realm. Having this particular saying at the end of the Gospel of Thomas should remind the reader of the reasons why this gospel was delivered in such a cryptic manner. Through the puzzling language and obscure symbols in the Gospel of Thomas these teachings were protected. They were protected from those who could be consumed by the lion, the thing that represents the nature of this realm and the people who were, or are ignorant (Thomas 7).

77th Pearl: The Perpetual Tree
Where The River Meets the Sea

Let us step back and look at the big picture—this is a mantra we need to consider in our everyday lives and it has been the premise for the commentaries in *77ᵗʰ Pearl: The Perpetual Tree*. Prior to this text, people have had their noses right up against the painting we call our existence. Here, humans have been able to step back. Now, they see the whole painting and the wall it hangs on too. Now, the fog has lifted.

The male inclination to dominate and control has created various religious institutions. They have done much to damage the link the human soul desires with the Source, from where it came. The creature from which people evolved was reliant on a hierarchical community for survival. In this community, there was a structured order of leadership, necessary for the survival of the group. We can presume, from archaeological evidence, it was the males of the ancestral group that provided protection and the main source of food necessary for survival. Although different communities of the human ancestor developed in various ways, these basic structures were necessary. Women would have been burdened with childbirth and nurturing their young, while males built shelter and hunted animals. As time passed, humans began to search for reasons why things happened the way they did. This curiosity is an aspect of *the breath of life*. It is the pull of God the Father/Source's Light, wanting to be joined to humans through a conduit, which links all beings of compassion, creativity, and empathy. We now know this conduit as the *Holy Spirit. It is identified as the action of the collective consciousness.* When primal humans began to create drawings and perform rituals, with dance and music, the (metaphoric) voice of the Father/Source became louder, until that voice became energy unto itself. It then found a place in human flesh—the heart and mind. We now know it as the Soul. This is the same Light that is between the fibers of wood, under a stone, and between atoms, protons, and neutrons. It functions within the quantum field. This is the *77ᵗʰ Pearl*. Since this prehistoric time, there has been a battle raging between the different natures of these two life forms. The dimension of the material universe and the realm of the Spirit have been, and still are, at odds. These realms can both be defined as *life*, but are very different in their essential nature and structure, yet they are linked in ways humans are beginning to recognise.

How does the Gospel of Thomas (discovered in 1945 at a place called Nag Hammadi, in Upper Egypt) reconcile the erroneous concept that the universe was created, and then God put humans on this planet? The nature of the Gospel of Thomas is that it was conceived for the twenty-first century—when the sevens have resolved themselves. The necessity for figurative discernment is evident in the gospel author's opening statement. These are *secret sayings*; anyone who discovers their true meaning will not taste death. This means the Soul (what humans are) will not be absorbed into the whole—the ubiquitous Father/Source's Light. In the Gospel of Thomas, Jesus (Yeshua) tells us that it would be a marvel of marvels if the soul came into being for the sake of the flesh. In this knowledge, we know *the thing that constitutes a 'soul' existed since before time began in this universe.* Yeshua also tells us that we are *meal, scattered upon a 'distant road'* and that this happened unintentionally. This symbolic story explains how God the Source expanded into the abyss, the void. This was not a conscious decision. It was one realm creating another, as a byproduct of its expansion/ movement (this was the 'Big Bang'). Since *the woman* (the creative aspect of the Source) *returned home*, we know that the aspect of the Source, which is whole and in *Its* original state, has contracted back to *Its* place of origin. Humans refer to this place as *heaven*. It is not up in the sky, it is a layer, or dimension humans cannot experience with their limited senses. However, remnants of the Source's Light remain here, in this dimension. In our realm, the collective consciousness (Holy Spirit) performs the function of a linking mechanism, *which connects* the Source and the Son (all souls seeking the Light). The material constituting this universe, created from God the Father's dimension, has two distinct properties. The first is that it is not permanent and is inclined to perish. The second property is that it still has, *through it*, the substance (Light) from the Source's realm. Yeshua confirms this when He tells people that the Light, which constitutes His Spirit, is everywhere. It is in-between the fibers in wood and under a rock. This is the most precious pearl, the lost pearl, we have found here.

The Gospel of Thomas solves the age-old questions, which have plagued primal man for millennia. It also releases people from the premise of a patriarchal god, which is jealous and vengeful. God is not a single entity we must ultimately answer to, as a child might have to answer to a parent. Such ideas are derived from a primal understanding of relationships in this world, overlaid onto relationships within the Spirit realm. Recognising that this realm is unlike the realm of the Spirit dissolves this harmful premise. It allows people to see what they are, for the first time. In the Gospel of Thomas, we discover that humans are like Jesus. They are all made of God the *Father, which is the Source of everything*. When people become wise, aware of this link, then they become an enlightened, connected Spirit. The results of this link come through the conduit we know as the Holy Spirit. It lives in the heart and mind of conscious beings, capable of compassion and empathy. These traits are the anatomy of the Holy Spirit, because they are about connection and linking with the other. This is what UFO/ UAP researchers have noticed about people who have come in contact with this phenomena and the beings that pilot these craft. Communication is usually non-verbal, rather, it is telepathic. The quantum field, where the Light of the Source flows as one continuous stream, is where the Holy Spirit functions, linking minds at an instant. This is the collective consciousness.

If one is a Christian, why should the Gospel of Thomas be given credence? There is an innate problem with the Bible. The Old and New Testament have been linked through the proclamation that the prophecies of a Savior had been fulfilled in Jesus (Yeshua). Although Yeshua did little to prevent these assumptions through His actions and His words, in the Gospel of Thomas, His purpose was more personal than the one presented *through* the Old Testament. The problem occurs when we realise that Yeshua's teachings were not about fulfilling prophecies, which limited what He set out to do. Yeshua tells us that He is the new wine and to place His teachings *into old wineskins* would spoil them. When Yeshua spoke to His followers He would refer to His 'Father'. People assumed He was referring to 'Yahweh', the God of the Jewish community. The mysteries in the Gospel of Thomas have revealed threads of knowledge, which demonstrate that Yeshua was instead speaking about a great mystery. This knowledge came from a Divine heritage. In Thomas, the Father's Kingdom is described as actions, which tell us It is the Source of all things. These actions are metaphorically described as either a male or female, which become *representations* of what the Source has done or what *It* is like. When we link these threads in the Gospel of Thomas, we are given definitive answers. In the New Testament, the authors have tried to create a biographical narrative, which turns Jesus into *the Christ*. It is primarily the Christian orthodoxy that holds onto the premise Yeshua will come back to Jerusalem, forming a renewed kingdom on Earth—at this time, all the dead shall rise again. These are myths absorbed from the Torah, which became the Old Testament. They do not constitute what Yeshua's teachings were about. They are tantamount to peoples' fear of death and their feeble attempts at explaining an end-point, without understanding the beginning and middle.

We see a truth appear when we cast our minds back over human history, considering how most communities have given a living human being the characteristics of a god-king. People desired a leader who had superhuman qualities, qualities that surpassed the limitations of this material world. This is a reflection of the human psyche, which is connected to the whole. This psyche knows there is something more than humans can experience in this physical universe, because we are linked to this quantum field. This desirable, super-human quality reflected the need to connect to something imperceptible. It is how the New Testament authors could link the pagan myths with the Jesus miracles. Buddhist teachings are quite clear when it comes to the concept of worshipping a deity. The Buddha never presented himself as a deity, yet, a significant proportion of followers will worship and pray at the feet of a Buddha statue. This is the same message Yeshua gave to His disciples. It is reflected in the humble actions we see in the New Testament and in the statements we see in Thomas. However, most Christian faiths call Jesus *the only Son of God* and, at the same time, God. Catholics venerate statues of Jesus and Mary, as well as the preserved remains of saints—perhaps because these are *more tangible*. These people miss the point and want to make a man, like Jesus or the Buddha, into a god. It would seem as though it is easier to do this, rather than to try and comprehend their teachings. This is why people, seeking to establish a religious institution, have marginalised the Gospel of Thomas. A part of its content falls into the category of the *too hard basket*. However, Yeshua wanted it this way, for a very good reason. He knew that giving *pearls* to these people would allow them to be destroyed, because of their inclination to create an institution. Institutions, by their nature, have a pyramidal power structure. In most religions, we have at the apex of the pyramid a god, then the clergy of various ranks, and the people at the base. The Gospel of Thomas does not fit this pyramidal structure; it can only fit into a perfect circle. In a perfect circle there is no apex or bottom. It is whole, it is one. In this circle, there is no space for a super-human godhead, because everything in that space is connected and whole.

The first of the Synoptic Gospels written was the Gospel of Mark, approximately seventy to ninety years after Yeshua's death. The other gospels followed and were derivatives of Mark. Scholars assume there is one other reference that was used. It has become apparent that this other source was the Gospel of Thomas. It is the purest link to the *living Jesus*, because the sayings are presented as quotes and not as part of a narrative. The Gospel of Thomas is a contentious document, both in its nature and in terms of its point of origin. Some scholars argue it predates the Gospel of Mark; others argue it came after. However, the nature of these sayings, as direct quotes, gives them authenticity and gravitas. They are not written into a narrative form, by an author who was influenced by their Jewish or Greek heritage. If we consider the very nature of the Gospel of Thomas, we notice how it is an authentic representation. The Gospel of Thomas is ambiguous in its references. It was meant to be difficult to comprehend. If we accept that previous religious texts were documents meant to give clear instruction on the way to believe and avoid purgatory or hell, we realise the Gospel of Thomas is very different. *Its cryptic nature is evidence of a greater purpose*, a purpose that overturns past notions of God and the origin of the soul. This gospel was not aimed at creating a community, based on a common faith, built on rituals and dogma. The Gospel of Thomas is a document about the nature of what we really are and how we might come to this realisation. It is about the intimate connection we have with God the Father—the Source of all things. It is the way we come to understand that we are Jesus' kin. In this sense, the Gospel of Thomas is unlike any other Christian text which claims to be derived from Yeshua's teachings.

To illustrate the political and polemic undertone of most of what we see in the New Testament, one only need look at how the author of the Gospel of Luke vilifies the Jewish people, as the instrument of Satan. Through this, we see that there was tension between Jewish and non-Jewish Christians. The author of Luke was a gentile. The marginalisation he would have felt, from the Jewish Christians, influenced his views of that community and their role in Yeshua's execution. The Jewish Christians had already cemented Yeshua's role as the Messiah, based on what they knew from the Torah (Old Testament) prophecies. This was before anyone could establish a faith like the one Yeshua would have envisaged. Yeshua tested His disciples often. He could see that there was an innate problem with the contemporary culture He was born into—they were sexist, misogynist, and narrow-minded. This, coupled with their inaccurate knowledge of what God was and their community centred on a patriarchal religion, made it necessary for Yeshua to leave His teachings with one who would not be affected by all of these obstacles. Thomas's reply to Yeshua's question, regarding *what He was like*, allowed Yeshua to see that Thomas was different. Thomas replied to Yeshua by saying: *'my mouth is utterly unable to say what you are like.'* While the other disciples chose predictable comparisons for Him, derived from their contemporary faith, Thomas's reply saw that a *new language was required—a language he (in that time) did not have*. This made Thomas the one who could receive the secret teachings. The other disciples would have seen these sayings as problematic, if not heretical. Not understanding the mysteries Yeshua spoke of, they would have been left aside, for ones that made sense to them, ones they could use. We see a plethora of appropriated sayings from the Gospel of Thomas in Matthew 13, placed in a context that denigrates their broader and enlightened meaning. Such an impassioned use of Thomas is the end point, which we see in much of the New Testament. However, other followers of Yeshua, in the early Christian communities, recognised the importance of the secret sayings. As a result, we see the Gnostic Christians appear alongside the early orthodox believers (those who only accepted the canonical texts).

The word 'Gnostic' comes from the Greek word meaning 'knowledge'. The premise for their faith was based on the search for knowledge. This is proof of the fact that the *Gospel of Thomas is not a Gnostic text*. It is the catalyst which started *the Gnostic approach*. The first part of the Gospel of Thomas invites people to find the meaning in the secret sayings. This is what the Gnostics attempted to achieve. Their practices were influenced by the declarations we see in the first two sayings in Thomas. Gnostics believed that by gaining hidden knowledge, they would attain the life Yeshua spoke of in the Gospel of Thomas. The aim was to gain this secret knowledge, which gave them keys to unlock the various gates preceding Heaven. The Gnostics could see that the rejected Gospel of Thomas had very important wisdom within it. They attempted to decipher the cryptic sayings through various meditative processes. It should be noted that the Gospel of Thomas is absent of Gnostic mysticism. However, it does have unconventional concepts within it. *This unconventional knowledge was the purpose for Yeshua coming to this world.* The Gnostics did not have the language to understand what the 'secret sayings' meant. As a result, we obtain from them complex mythologies, which evolved through a process of scriptural meditation (an intense meditative internalisation of the text, to gain its wisdom). These mythologies prove to be derivative of this realm and the traits of men and women, which is unlike the realm of the Spirit and therefore inaccurate. This is not dissimilar to the way the ancient Greeks and Romans gave every aspect of life such as love, hunting, or drinking the position of a god. We see this similarity through the Gnostic explanation of creation, where Sophia, representing wisdom, creates a demiurge called Yaldabaoth. This creator god turns out to be imperfect, because Sophia did not consult with the self-generated one before producing the demiurge. Gnostics claimed that this was in fact Yahweh, from the Old Testament. The myth explained his tendency to be jealous and violent. These human traits and behaviours, played out in this creation myth, s*ignalled the absence of a language that could disclose the mysteries in the Gospel of Thomas.* It is a language people have access to now, in the infancy of the twenty-first century. *77th Pearl: The Perpetual Tree* is this new language, applied to ancient wisdom delivered by the multi-dimensional being, Yeshua.

In 2017, a hypothesis about human existence became popular among many reputable people in the global community. The concept suggests this universe is a computer simulation. This is an interesting notion, but a rather egocentric one. It is comparative to the way the Gnostics explained this life as being created by a malevolent deity. This new hypothesis would explain this creation as, 'the dice that have been cast, now let us see what happens.' It explains the negatives people encounter as tests in the simulation. If we take a moment to indulge this idea, using what we have learnt from the Gospel of Thomas, we see this hypothesis in a slightly plausible context. A computer capable of such a simulation would be something humans could barely be able to comprehend. The material, from which such a computer's component parts would be made of, would be a type of light. The circuits would be composed of, and function with, this light. It is not a machine, like people might envisage. It is a thing that has always existed. In this respect, the hypothesis of a type of computer, or entity, which has the capacity to elicit existence in various forms, is feasible. To test the aspect of the hypothesis that states this is a simulation, we would need to ask the question: why? The word *simulation* suggests something that is designed as a prototype of the final intention. Through the problems or errors that occur, improvements can be made. This notion comes from a human weakness, pride. Humans cannot imagine that they are just one of a myriad of life forms in this universe. This train of thought supposes that, surely, all this must be for humanity's benefit. If it fails, or the human species perishes, the computer will run a new, improved simulation. The fact is, a computer, device, or entity capable of this kind of creation, would make it perfect in the first place. Its consciousness would be so evolved it would see all the possible problems, designing the creation accordingly. Through the Gospel of Thomas, we have seen that perhaps we could see God the Father/Source as this consciousness, made of Light. However, this existence is not an *intentional* simulation. This is human narcissism speaking. This universe was created from a place that (unintentionally) expanded into the void. In the process it created physical matter. With it came the Light. It is still here. It is finding its way back to the dimension it came from. It is in all the beings whose soul emanates empathy and compassion for the other. The collective consciousness (Holy Spirit) is the anatomy of the Source. It is found in the minute spaces between a breath and a thought.

In *77ᵗʰ Pearl: The Perpetual Tree* we have seen extraordinary revelations. The unearthing of what the Father, Son, and Holy Spirit actually mean has been a powerful discovery. It reveals the *dynamism of The Trinity*. Catholic theologians explain the Trinity as *three persons, yet they are one God*. Through *77ᵗʰ Pearl: The Perpetual Tree* we have learnt that this definition, for the most part, is inaccurate. The Father is the one who is everywhere at the same time. It influences the creation of all matter as a mechanism by which *Its Light* may be realised. *It* is the Source. The Son is representative of the Soul, as it is the Father's Light, brought into an instance of motion, through the flesh. In this way, the Son (the soul) is like Yeshua. People who are on a journey to become an enlightened Spirit become His kin. The collective consciousness (Holy Spirit) makes the process of unification possible. It is *the Advocate and Comforter* for humanity. The Holy Spirit is above all else, because it binds and connects the Trinity. In this sense, *we are one entity through the action of the collective consciousness* (Holy Spirit).

This realm is like an oyster. The Soul has entered, but because it is foreign to this finite realm, it becomes wrapped in flesh and experiences both suffering and beauty. From within this oyster, souls grow in stature, to become two with the Source, through the action of the collective consciousness. Likewise, the three Abrahamic religions of Judaism, Christianity, and Islam have formed a glistening pearl, which have enabled the Light of Yeshua's wisdom to shine through *77ᵗʰ Pearl: The Perpetual Tree*.

References

Armstrong, Karen. *On the Bible : books that shocked the world*. Crows Nest, NSW: Allen & Unwin, 2007.

Batchelor, Stephen, interview by ABC Radio National. Batchelor, *The Secular Dharma*

—. *Buddhism without Beliefs*. G.P. Putnam's and Son's, 1997.

Berg, P.S. Rav. T*he Essential Zohar : the source of Kabbalistic Wisdom*. New York: Bell Tower, 2002.

Bhikkhu, Buddhadasa. *Paticcasamuppada: Practical Dependent Origination*. Vuddhidhamma Fund, Distributed by Thammasapa, 1992.

Catholic Bibles Publishers. *Holy Bible*. Wichita: Catholic Bible Publishers, 1970.

The Virus of Faith. TV ABC. Directed by Richard Dawkins. 2007.

Finkelstein, Israel, and Neil Silberman. *The Bible Unearthed: Archaeology's New Vision of Ancient Israel and the Origin of Its Sacred Texts*. New York: Free Press, 2011.

Gyatso, Geshe Kelsang. *Heart of Wisdom*. England: Tharpa Publications, 2001.

Kasser, Rodulphe, Marvin Meyer, and Gregor Wurst. *The Gospel of Judas*. Washington D.C.: National Geographic Society, 2006.

Pagels, Elaine. *The Gnostic Gosples.* London: Penguine Books, 1979.

—. *The Origin of Satan.* New York : First Vintage Books, 1995.

Pagels, Elaine, and King L. Karen. Reading Judas, *The Gospel of Judas and the shaping of Christianity.* London: Allen Lane Penguine Group, 2007.

Sacred Texts. *The Koran.* Translated by E.H. Palmer. London: Watkins Publishing, 2007.

stargazers.com. *stargazers.com/jesus.html.* 1996 йил October. www. stargazers.com/index.html (accessed 2011 йил 18-March).

Steiner, Rodulf. *Cosmic Memory: prehistory of earth and man.* Translated by Karl E Zimmer. Great Barrington, MA: SteinerBooks.

The Buddha. 2011.

The Qur'an. TV ABC2. Directed by Antony Thomas. 2010.

Printed in Australia
AUHW022332030422
361782AU00001B/1